Secrets of
Swiss Banking

An Owner's Manual to
Quietly Building a Fortune

Hoyt Barber

John Wiley & Sons, Inc.

Published by John Wiley & Sons, Inc., Hoboken, New Jersey.
Published simultaneously in Canada.

For general information on our other products and services or for technical support, please
contact our Customer Care Department within the United States at (800) 762-2974,
outside the United States at (317) 572-3993 or fax (317) 572-4002.

Wiley also publishes its books in a variety of electronic formats. Some content that appears
in print may not be available in electronic formats. For more information about Wiley
products, visit our Web site at www.wiley.com.

Library of Congress Cataloging-in-Publication Data:

Barber, Hoyt L.
        Secrets of Swiss banking : an owner's manual to quietly building a fortune / Hoyt Barber.
        p.   cm.
     Includes index.
     ISBN 978-0-470-13671-3 (cloth)
        1. Banks and banking—Switzerland.   2. Tax havens—Switzerland.   I. Title.
     HG3204.B355   2008
     332.67'31—dc22

                                                                   2007033364

Printed in the United States of America

10 9 8 7 6 5 4 3 2 1

To the individual quest for personal sovereignty and freedom

One good investment is worth a lifetime of toil.
—Investing for Profits by
H. L. (Herbert Lee) Barber, 1917

Special thanks to Christian H. Kalin and associates at Henley & Partners AG

and Hillary Lee Barber

Contents

Preface

Switzerland.

The word itself conjures up a multitude of images, nearly all quite positive and most virtually in the realm of the magical, mythical, and too-good-to-be-true. And, really, *is* there any other single place on this increasingly sordid planet whose reality is so close to fantasy, and maybe even perfect? Switzerland is a breathtaking wonderland of majestic Alps vaulting to the sky, charming villages nestled down deep in the valleys, pristine lakes of profound clarity, and cities of such cleanliness, beauty, and order that it seems like some deity designed and built them. And then, well, there's all that money! And what about all the fantastic things that such money can buy resting beautifully behind rows and rows of elegant shop windows . . . just amazing.

And banks! How can there *be* so many banks? And is it true that these banks, located in this beautiful fairy tale of a country, actually contain and control almost 40 percent of the world's private wealth? Yes? Wow. Well, *how come?*

Switzerland and the subject of Swiss banking have evolved over the past few decades, but the fabled ability of the Swiss banks to attract such incredible sums of money from all over the world has only increased over time, strengthening this little country's position in the world. Why? Although Switzerland *does* sometimes seem almost perfect, and in many ways, it really *is,* this small nation, like most other countries, is a part of the real world, and like them, it is faced with its own set of challenges. But the fact remains that Switzerland has groomed itself to grow stronger and to remain independent in the face of global geopolitics, including pressures from the international bodies like European Union (EU) to join them and the negative efforts of the Organization for Economic Co-Operative Development (OECD), which tries to coerce Switzerland's compliance and future to suit its specific agenda.

Of course, the United States government would *love* to see Switzerland abolish its Bank Secrecy Act, or at least compromise it just a little so that officials could gain access to the activities and affairs in Switzerland of "U.S. persons." But, alas, the government has been foiled at attempts to break Swiss secrecy for decades. And the EU has plenty of economically unstable nations crammed under the same umbrella with the richer economic engines of Germany and France. It would suit the EU well to have Switzerland thrown into the mix. Then it would stand a chance to force its will on Switzerland, and therefore the world in general, in a variety of ways. In fact, the mere act of joining the EU would homogenize Switzerland into a larger single economy, transforming its well-known individuality until the day there wouldn't be any. Threatened for certain would be the famous bank secrecy, and the general discretion in related matters that have contributed over time to Switzerland's profound economic success. The country would be blended into that massive economic block known as the EU and would serve to strengthen all the other members at its expense—first, effectively zapping Swiss independence and sovereignty, and second, dissolving the strong Swiss franc in favor of the euro.

And when the EU finally does pass a proposed constitution—which could be as early as 2009—all those nations, along with Switzerland, should it join, would be one big happy family. That sounds attractive, doesn't it? Well, maybe not, on closer inspection.

And, if that's not enough, the OECD, made up of a bunch of former tax collectors from various industrial nations, has its own plans. It has empowered itself to expand its global membership, which now comprises 30 democracies that, in its own words, "work together to address the economic, social, and governance challenges of globalization, as well as to exploit opportunities." Exactly what opportunities does the OECD plan to exploit? It isn't stopping with the EU either; there's a global push by the OECD to muscle its way in with sovereign powers to achieve globalization. And what is that? Globalization is a way to increase commerce in countries to get them to be more productive, tax the productive countries to pay for this expansion, close tax loopholes to increase the revenue flow, and impose universal tax laws worldwide. Sound like it may be leading to a one-world government?

The OECD calls for "fairness" among nations. The effect will be an expanded global economy so that the taxing bodies of the world can collect more and continue on their mission to increase tax revenues and inflate the economy, both of which result in the involuntary transfer of wealth. That's a form of robbery. At this point they would likely be very effective and essentially produce what would amount to a global populace of economic slaves. Does that sound "fair"?

Sound economics originate from sound fiscal policies and practices by nations desirous of preserving and fostering their sovereign interests. That, together with similarly minded countries operating in concert, can give rise to a prosperous global economy. Globalization is not economic salvation. Rather, it is a compromise, by nations and their people, of national and individual sovereignty at the hands of the few; a soon-to-be even more powerful elite.

Historically, the global economy prospered through sound economic policies and practices from around 1865 to 1914, even in the face of rising tariffs by competing countries. In 1879, the United States had re-pegged the dollar to gold, taxes were nearly non-existent, and the United States, with its newly stabilized dollar, experienced one of its greatest periods of growth in history. We need to revert back to the sound economic principles that have had a history of success, not a glossy sales job on how to relinquish our national and individual sovereignties, in part because we're too lazy to investigate the truth, and hold our elected officials accountable to "We the people."

How did Germany and Japan emerge from World War II after their defeats and ravaged economies? Both, directly and indirectly, backed their overinflated, worthless currencies with a gold standard. Germany did so by pegging their mark to the gold-backed dollar, and Japan backed the yen with gold, then lifted price regulations and drastically cut taxes. As we know from history, Germany and Japan went on to become post-war economic powerhouses that spanned decades and eventually gave the United States a run for its money.

A single country can tax and inflate for just so long—as the United States and other countries have been doing for years. Eventually the ravages of inflation catch up with them. There comes a point when they go too far and hyperinflation can kick in. It may sound ridiculous now, but the way the United States is fiscally and politically mismanaged these days, the prospects are very good that we are facing real trouble, and it promises to get worse in the not-so-distant future. The telltale signs have been cropping up, along with general indications that we are heading in the wrong direction.

But if seeing is believing, then be sure to stick around for the excitement. From the many responses I receive daily from readers of my book *Tax Havens Today,* Americans and Canadians particularly, have genuine and immediate concerns about the state of their countries and their own futures.

The rise to fascism begins in just this way: A government in power debases the currency, thereby undermining the economy, which ultimately leads to the collapse of the government. This action paves the way for a replacement regime, usually in an authoritarian form with a new leader who makes a lot of promises, imposes his death grip on society, then proceeds to exploit the country and its people six ways from Sunday, starting the cycle all over again—only worse.

In 1933, that leader was Adolf Hitler. Many of the clamps that were put into place after he took power can also occur in the United States, Canada, and elsewhere, as I outline in this book. As examples, consider any number of restrictions on your freedoms, including possibly the ability to travel or to move your money or other assets out of your country. Whenever there are signs—and today in the United States, there are plenty—of moves in these directions, your personal sovereignty and freedom are potentially threatened and your future stands a good chance of being severely compromised.

The *Chambers Dictionary* defines fascism as "the authoritarian form of government in Italy from 1922–43, characterized by extreme nationalism, militarism, anti-communism and restrictions on individual freedom." This is an interesting definition.

Sound at all familiar? Are we being led down the primrose path?

This book is not only about Switzerland and Swiss banking; it also describes the bigger picture of where Switzerland stands in the context of world events and the backdrop just described, where Switzerland is placed in the offshore world, and how you can use this unique and lovely country for your benefit.

Switzerland has long been a haven for frightened money. Maybe that's why it holds an impressive third-place standing among the major financial centers right up there with London and New York City. Your interest in Switzerland and potential participation in its offerings is a vote for what Switzerland stands for and in opposition to the forces that would like to see that change. In the process of stripping Switzerland of its national sovereignty, the "architects of change" would also, once again, be eroding our own personal sovereignty, as, for one thing, there will be fewer places to achieve financial privacy.

From all appearances, it looks as if Switzerland intends to remain free from such insanity and to hold its own in the face of outside pressures. Switzerland has developed as a successful international financial center based on its central belief in individual rights and national sovereignty. The Swiss pay high regard to financial, and general privacy, individual freedom, safety from the world's tyrants, stability in a volatile world, and the value of productivity and productive investment.

In my last book, *Tax Havens Today: The Benefits and Pitfalls of Banking and Investing Offshore* (2006), I covered some of my favorite topics: tax havens, offshore banking, asset protection, international investing, offshore and international business, and finally, near and dear to my heart, personal sovereignty and freedom. Knowledge that it would reach people who share these concerns and views brought me great pleasure.

Tax Havens Today allowed me to continue spreading some little-known ideas and opportunities, as I did in 1992, when I first wrote about them in *Tax Havens: How to Bank, Invest and Do Business—Offshore and Tax Free*. The themes of both of my tax haven books have included the methods used by the rich since the 1920s—*good for them*. Interestingly, in the past couple of decades, an increasing number of upper-middle and even middle-class Americans, Canadians, and others from the far reaches of the globe have discovered the many benefits of going offshore.

Today, the concept is also being embraced by people with various political and religious points of view but who are of a similar opinion about their government and their fading stature as individuals. These beliefs and feelings are stirred by the growing incidence that government oppression is mounting and could possibly envelop every aspect of their lives all too soon.

At some point, the ones who are paying attention will acknowledge the apparent fact that things are not going to get better and that continued faith in government will inevitably lead to personal loss and possible suffering. But the con is on, and government players will continue as long as they can on their self-destructive path, exerting their powers for as long as they are allowed, until it all comes to a thunderous head.

Gradually, when the poor citizens awaken to the stark reality of their plight, they naturally try to take action. Around that time, more and more people are trying to do the same thing—to gain back some personal control over their lives. When the moment of enlightenment occurs, individuals begin to place more value on their own self-worth. Maybe, just maybe, they might conclude that they possess more power and control over their own destiny than even they believed. Unfortunately, unless individuals recognize this dilemma early and can take the necessary evasive actions without delay, they may be too late. The window of opportunity will close at some point, and people will very likely find out that they cannot get their money, assets, cash flow, or even family out of the danger zone. Many millions of the tragic people of Hitler's Germany and Stalin's Russia would have shared their sad stories as a warning to others, but their voices were stilled too soon.

About 250,000 Americans each year are physically moving to other countries and this figure is expected to increase in just another year or so to 350,000. In fact, they are expatriating in record numbers! Why? Could it be that they know something you may not know, or perhaps that you *do* know and want to know more about, or something you feel in your bones? Maybe this is partly why you bought this book. I thank you! Those expatriates—"expats"—recognized sooner, rather than later, the necessity of getting out and securing their financial futures—and their physical well-being.

Before they left, however, they needed to lay the groundwork, moving their money offshore to places like Switzerland, Belize, and Panama.

There are still a handful of excellent tax havens today that Americans and Canadians will find attractive. An even greater number of folks are doing this with their finances every year, and because it's legal, they still can. I, for one, believe they must—*and very soon*—or pay the consequence for their indifference.

It's an exercise, if nothing else, in your right to personal sovereignty—to be the master of your destiny is within your very powers. Each of us is an individual sovereign. Our powers are bestowed on us from three prime laws: one God, one world, and one mankind. And in the theory of the Founding Fathers of the United States, all governments must derive their authority and power from the *individual*, who *is* a natural sovereign, born with basic human rights. And, contrary to what we may be led to believe, these are not rights acquired from government or the United Nations; precisely the opposite is true. Thus, it is *your* responsibility to recognize, exercise, and enforce these rights to preserve them for yourself, your family, and other sovereign individuals. Only then can you have true happiness, security, and freedom. Offshore is merely a conduit to that end.

I enjoy hearing the many stories from readers of their successes in going offshore and their perspectives on the state of the world, which have an all-too-familiar ring. They have expressed their thanks to me for writing the books and have related how they gained new peace of mind from having "gone offshore." Some relate the sense of security they feel for having expatriated and for rediscovering the concept of personal sovereignty. I even had one gentleman share with me that until he read my last tax haven book, he didn't know he *had* personal sovereignty! *After you read this book, you, too, will be doing the fandango.*

Once upon a time, on April 15, tax filing day in the United States, an IRS agent called my tax accountant to tell him how much *they* didn't like my first tax haven book. That was after it had been on the market for 10 years. The next attack on your rights and personal sovereignty may be to quiet the press, and one day it may be illegal to write, publish—*or read*—books like this. Sound outlandish? Actually, freedom of speech is being attacked in America right now.

Secrets of Swiss Banking is an effort to provide the reader with the crème de la crème of the offshore world. That being said, Switzerland is, despite appearances, not perfect. There's always the potential that it, like anything sweet and good, could go sour. Change is constant! It would be foolish to think that things will remain the same forever. So I write this book keeping that thought in mind, and even go so far as to present alternatives for further evaluation. Most likely, Switzerland or the alternatives, or a combination, will suit each person who considers these strategies. And, most likely, Switzerland will have much to offer for a long time to come. Let's hope so. More important, and much more urgent, is that it may be a *real* solution to increasing your wealth, protecting your assets, and planning for your family's future—today.

Switzerland has a long, successful history with other people's money, and the trend continues—even in opposition to growing pressures from foreign governments, international organizations, powerful interests in the European Union, and the monetary fiscal recklessness of other countries. In fact, Switzerland stands for financial security, preservation of personal sovereignty, and optimism for the future in the face of heightened global threats.

You will discover here all you need to know to capitalize on Swiss banking, the heart of the Swiss financial community—regardless of where you live. Switzerland is *the* premier money manager with, as mentioned before, as much as 40 percent of the world's private assets managed from this quaint alpine oasis. But this book is more than just about banking. It's about your financial security. This book reveals the ultimate investment plan; it is the best asset protection structure in the world, and the finest way to quietly build your fortune, starting right now, at your own pace, and even during bad times.

You can build your nest egg safely, quietly, and out of the reach of your own government, partners, creditors, nasty bosses, vindictive spouses, and maybe worse. Your estate, your banking, and your investments—the core of your new financial being—can be shielded by innovative Swiss structures and other strategies, that will insure that *you* and *your family* do not come up losers in the current global power game. What's at stake? YOU! *No time to lollygag*—let's take a look.

Chapter 1

Challenges and Threats

The Chinese character for "crisis" is a combination of two characters: "danger" and "opportunity." For me, this interpretation by the Chinese is a very interesting cultural, philosophical, and linguistic phenomenon—one that also contains a very nice lesson for living. But I also feel that it is a picture of a crossroads that applies to our current world. Today we are quite likely at the brink of a global economic crisis—and that sounds bad, right? It's critical that we prepare for the danger inherent in crisis, but also stay alert for the opportunities during much of what is ahead for us. More than anything, this book is about this concept.

You have chosen to read this book; clearly that puts you among those who are aware that daily we are sensing crisis in our lives—possibly even impending doom. It means you have taken the hardest, first step to making things right for yourself and your family: awareness. But those feelings of doom and gloom can be harnessed, like parade horses, to march to your advantage. Your survival instincts tell you something bad could be on the horizon. Good! Keep your eye on that ball, take charge of your own destiny, and realize that no matter what they say or we might hear, the powers that be most likely really don't care about what happens to *you*. But that's okay, because it's within *your* power to care and to *act* to do something about it.

A good place to begin is to take a close look at yourself—to take inventory, make a few hard decisions for the good of yourself, your family, and your future, because no one else will worry about your situation, now or any time soon.

Likely you already sense that sometimes you need to think philosophically, adapt new ideas, change your thought processes, open your mind, and think outside the box, the envelope, the cage. Sounds like a lot of clichés—but therein resides the core of what we need to do to find our own reality. Perhaps the place to start can be found in this quote by Epicurus: "Wealth consists not of having great possessions but in having few wants."

Personally, I'm tired of being taxed, even on my few wants. But isn't that the job of Madison Avenue, anyway—to create demand for things we really don't need and didn't know we wanted in the first place? And, thereby, to fuel American consumerism and ultimately fund sources of cheap imported goods like China. Isn't your personal debt inflated enough? Red China, for one, is the real beneficiary these days. It has become the fourth largest economy in the world, in part, thanks to the support of American buyers for their exports. We helped; and we may be creating a monster, as China is still a communist nation and a real threat to the United States. International trade is wonderful, but we might want to think twice about financing our enemies in any form. We can use those same dollars to invest in *our* future.

Herein you will learn about the state of Switzerland today, how it has changed, and what it has to offer you. Fortunately, there is plenty to talk about. All the information you need to pursue your interest in banking and/or investing in Switzerland is covered, including how to begin, and where to go. Swiss banks can handle every form of investing, either directed by you or managed by an expert. Certain investments and economic subjects are covered at length, such as the importance of precious metals and strong currencies in your portfolio, and what causes inflation, and how you can actually profit from it, instead of letting it erode your wealth. I reveal an ultimate plan, showing you how, if your situation fits the parameters, you can avoid U.S. reporting requirements *and* defer taxes on investment earnings. You can accomplish this automatically while getting the world's best asset protection and estate planning known anywhere. Incredibly, you even can bank in secret through this creative and legal shield. I also explain how to establish a perfectly legal and totally secret bank account that can be your last resort in an extreme emergency. Your own private monetary policy is more than just a personal financial survival plan, as it will show you how to right your course before it's too late, toward future profits and personal freedom, as you will discover in Chapter 4. You can preserve your individual sovereignty without relying on the government and the destructive monetary practices of the Federal Reserve. Consider this your owner's manual to quietly building a fortune even in the midst of looming crisis. What better way to profit from economic and political change?

The Economic Front

Why discuss challenges and threats when perhaps you bought this book just to learn about Swiss banking? Well, the two are intricately tied. Aside from the fact that Switzerland is the third largest financial center next to London and New York and manages up to 40 percent of the world's private assets, it has also been the premier haven for frightened money for decades. *That* has been the driving force underlying Switzerland's profound development and growth for decades. Many threats in history drove the more fortunate to use Swiss banking when they had the need and opportunity.

Some choice examples are presented throughout this book, but right now, as you are reading these words, headlines are being made reminding us of what a crazy world we live in. History is on the verge of repeating itself in many ways, including via government oppression, war, and more war, economic chaos, and worse. We should learn from the past and from the lessons others have paid a high price to discover. But we need to be aware of not only these developments that we hear about in the news, but also the ones that are taking place behind the scenes. If the present-day scenario in America seems bad, with its threats from local crime, terrorists, and rogue states, try to imagine these things as just a prelude to bigger, more drastic developments in the world. Do you believe the hands of time can be turned back to a simpler, less threatening existence? As a nation, we may have already crossed the point of no return. But, as sovereign individuals, there is still a window of opportunity.

Today we ought to focus on underlying economic concerns and how they can impact us personally. It's easy to be distracted by politics and the endless noise of war and terrorism. However, the United States is sitting on a ticking economic time bomb and a number of problems that could cause a major meltdown.

National and Private Debt

While the rest of the world appears to be doing well overall, the U.S. economy is running out of steam. Often, the United States has been the engine of the world economy. What happens when the engine stops running? Although, according to the talking heads on television, in the last five years we have experienced the largest economic expansion in U.S. history, this expansion has also been unsuccessful at paying down the deficit. In theory, the growth should have created a greater economic base on which to tax and collect revenues that normally would decrease the national debt. But, unfortunately, the war on terrorism, the war in Iraq, and the war in Afghanistan have cost a lot money. As I finish this book in September 2007, the United States is spending $10 billion a month in Iraq alone. And there is no end in sight to our "war on terror." Bush is seeking $110 billion from Congress to fund the war through 2008. David Walser, head of the U.S. Government Accountability office says the U.S. economy suffers from "fiscal cancer, and that the Iraq war will have cost the U.S. over $1 trillion before it's over." Next we'll have to deal with Iran and Pakistan.

According to George W. Bush, the national debt has been reduced from about $400 billion to $298 billion. If the deficit has come down at all, it's because the "healthy" economy produced revenues to offset the growing national debt by some degree over and above government spending. But at some point the deficit figure will increase again as the economy slumps.

Remember, at the end of Bill Clinton's eight-year reign, the nation was in the black and had a significant surplus. That surplus vanished quickly after Bush gained control, and we haven't seen daylight since, not even after a "long" economic expansion. In the near future, the national debt could really balloon as revenues decline from slow economic growth. Hence, politicians want to close what they think of as tax loopholes while at the same time increasing taxes.

But wait just one minute! Bush recently gave us those figures regarding the national debt. Unfortunately we've been listening to the wrong man all along, so how can we believe those figures? Let's examine the national debt a little closer. Bush is using cash-basis accounting as if he were balancing his personal checkbook. However, he's running a government, not his household finances, and that requires better disclosure to the taxpaying public. Businesses use accrual accounting, and by law, public corporations have to use this method because it provides greater disclosure and a truer picture of a company's financial health. Once again, we are not getting the entire truth. Bush is conveniently using cash-basis accounting that only reveals the current indebtedness of this country, not our total indebtedness. Estimates reflecting the true federal deficit run as high as $65 trillion.

This astronomical figure includes not only Bush's $298 billion, but all the money due to holders of government notes, bonds, and bills from the past. These instruments alone exceed $8 trillion, and they come due regularly. Let's not forget Social Security, which pays out public retirement benefits and government employee pensions and health care benefits to Medicare recipients. These additional debts are real obligations of the government, and they disclose important financial information needed to fully understand the country's financial position. Illegal immigration also contributes to the increase of these figures. Government should be required to report economic figures the same way they require businesses to report so that stockholders don't get conned by management and creditors don't get defrauded.

The American consumer also has been busy spending at rates that are the highest in 20 years. These figures include mortgage debt, home equity loans, and secondary mortgages totaling $10 trillion, and consumer debt of $2 trillion. No wonder Wal-Mart is doing so well and China is directly benefiting at the same time.

Inflation

Right now the Federal Reserve (the Fed) and the U.S. government are holding their breath, hoping that inflationary pressures will ease in time to have a soft landing, as the Fed is in a tight spot. They do not feel they can drop the interest rate that stands at 5.25 percent due to inflationary concerns, nor do they feel they can raise them due to economic slowdown. Their hands are tied and they are hopeful that their liberal monetary policy—in other words, the printing of excessive amounts of money backed by no real value such as gold—doesn't catch up with them.

The M3 money supply, which will be defined in a moment, has been the best measurement of true inflation in the United States, not the Consumer Price Index (CPI), as most people think, which is an estimate that the government highly understates. Unfortunately, Ben Bernanke, the newest Fed chairman, has decided that this information is no longer relevant since inflation is under control; at least that's what he would like everyone to believe. Maybe the real reason is that the government cranked up the printing presses yet again to stimulate the economy to avert a crash landing and don't want that fact detected anytime soon. It's a lot like a hot air balloon. As the balloon is coming down, the pilot always turns up the thruster to blow hot air into the fabric bag and slow its descent. Add too much hot air, and the balloon takes off again.

Here are the U.S. Federal Reserve's definition of the various money aggregates, including the M3:

M1: The sum of currency held outside the vaults of depository institutions, Federal Reserve Banks, and the U.S. Treasury; travelers checks; and demand and other checkable deposits issued by financial institutions (except demand deposits due to the Treasury and depository institutions), minus cash items in process of collection and Federal Reserve float.

M2: M1 plus savings deposits (including money market deposits accounts) and small-denomination (under $100,000) time deposits issued by financial institutions; and shares in retail money market mutual funds (funds with initial investments under $50,000), net of retirement accounts.

M3: M2 plus large-denomination ($100,000 or more) time deposits; repurchase agreements issued by depository institutions; Eurodollar deposits, specifically, dollar-denominated deposits due to nonblank U.S. addresses held at foreign offices of U.S. banks worldwide and all banking offices in Canada and the United Kingdom; and institutional money market mutual funds (funds with initial investments of $50,000 or more).

MSM (money, zero maturity): M2 minus small-denomination time deposits, plus institutional money market funds (that is, those included in M3 but excluded from M2.)

But Bernanke's rhetoric has been that threats of recession will have to sit on the sidelines while the Fed monitors its progress until inflation is well under control. In the meantime, the Fed hopes that another economic force, such as the mortgage money market, does not tip the boat. If inflation were really under control, why would the Fed be so concerned about it? History shows us that often what's really happening is the opposite of the assurances given by politicians and government. Well, if you steal from someone, you don't tell them about it. The Fed manipulates the economy through the money supply.

Let's look at some facts that will shed light on the truth. Before the M3 money supply was discontinued as a measure of inflation effective March 23, 2006, in the United States, the money supply was 11 percent, but in the fourth quarter of 2006, the inflation rate was being quoted at only 3.4 percent.

Real inflation numbers closely mirror the M3 rate as the money supply is increased. Therefore, the Fed-quoted inflation numbers do not correspond with the last known official M3 rate, and between the first and fourth quarters of the same year, they would not have changed as drastically as the conveniently offered inflation rate quoted by the Fed.

Interestingly, the 3.4 percent figure offered up by the Fed corresponds nicely with the Consumer Price Index (CPI) average of 3.5 percent inflation over the past decade. As we know, the CPI is a less accurate and more favorable indicator for the Fed's argument and their distortion of the facts.

Then, on July 18, of 2007, Bernanke addressed the U.S. Congress and stated that the current rate of inflation, as the Fed preferred to monitor it by the CPI, was only 1.9 percent during the preceding 12 months ending in May 2007. The Fed is obviously using statistics that highly underestimate the true rate of inflation to disguise the facts, and the statistics appear to be inconsistent with their own statements. Keen outside observers know what is really happening. The U.S. economy has been greatly inflated and continues to be. Today in the United States, the M3 can only be estimated since the Fed discontinued publishing this economic measurement.

And what about the ever-expanding global economy? Well, there's an ever-expanding money supply to go along with it, and it has been ramped up to alarming proportions. In these countries, the M3 money supply has increased significantly by the following percentages over just the previous year. The European Union experienced a 9.3 percent increase; Korea, 10.3 percent; Australia, 13 percent; Britain, 13 percent; China, 16.9 percent; and Russia, 45 percent.

In reality, the soft landing is a tad bumpier than the Fed had hoped. As the Fed chairman himself states, it's not over and promises to get worse. Well, he knows the truth on the real inflation numbers that he's not sharing with the public. The fact is, the economy is at the threshold of a major downturn, and it's going to effect the global economy.

The labor market is weak, economic growth is lower than forecasted, and the housing slump has been bigger and lasted longer than anticipated, which could impact consumer confidence. So far, consumer spending, as measured by one of the great economic indicators, Wal-Mart sales, has been holding steady.

But the bomb is still ticking.

Real Estate and the Mortgage Money Market

Those never-ending real estate problems are going to fester like a sore on the U.S. economy. According to the National Realtors Association, sales of existing homes are down significantly. Two of the fastest-growing real estate markets in recent years were in Arizona and Nevada. In 2007 Arizona experienced a 36 percent decrease, and Nevada, 38 percent. The hotter markets have been taking the greatest hits, which has had a net effect on real estate prices. Many homeowners have found that their equity vanished and that their real estate financing exceeded the declining current market value of their home. When equity was high, many homeowners refinanced and pulled cash out only to discover, when the markets plunged, that they were in debt beyond their equity and had no way out. Some of these homeowners opted to walk away rather than make exorbitant mortgage payments on property that wasn't worth it. They could actually improve their personal situation by dumping their property.

There's roughly $2.5 trillion in outstanding mortgages, some of which are known as subprime mortgages, which financed credit for home-owner buyers with high debt or poor credit and some of which are called Alternative-A mortgages, which are made up of not-quite-primetime debtors. These mortgages provided these two classes of homebuyers with new adjustable-rate mortgages as a means to distribute the new supply of money, thanks to the Fed's liberal monetary policy. Experts anticipate that as much as $1 trillion of these mortgages will default in 2007. In the coming years, adjustable-rate mortgage payments could go sky high if mortgage holders cannot roll over their mortgages to an improved fixed rate. A wave of foreclosures could still be on the horizon. In fact, the prediction by experts is that there will be a couple million foreclosures in the next 18 to 24 months. The mortgage money market has taken a big hit with this one. If you have a lot of cash, such as what occurs when you want to artificially stimulate the economy by printing excessive amounts of money, you need to get it into the economic pipeline. Cash does no good sitting in a warehouse. Since now there is an excess of it, interest rates need be adjusted to attract the desired level of borrowing. If you offer inexpensive money, there will be lots of takers. Just gradually lower the interest rate and people will be standing in line to borrow money to buy new homes, cars, and anything else that Madison Avenue, Hollywood, and similarly powerful influences have created a demand for in the public's mind.

Segments of the economy can be stimulated in this fashion, and since 9/11, we've seen a lot of it. Remember those interest-free car loans? And, as discussed, real estate had quite a play for a while, creating an asset bubble that ultimately popped and that is not done wreaking havoc on the economy. There are only so many truly creditworthy and employed borrowers out there. If the money supply is large enough, it may be necessary to broaden the potential number of candidates who can be recipients of this new source of funding. In other words, you might have to reduce credit requirements to a level at which you can get rid of all that new money and get those eager borrowers to take the plunge, even if it's not prudent lending, nor ultimately, good for a healthy economy.

Derivatives

And as if what I have just presented is not enough to potentially rock our economic boat, consider a market that is 27 times larger than the U.S. economy. What market could ever be that big? Global derivatives—and to the tune of over $400 trillion! This is a complex business, and it has created an underground economy. It has ballooned to astronomical proportions in a relatively short period of time. This problem child is the nuclear bomb of the investment world, and when it goes off, everything will go with it. That's one mighty problem!

If guys like Warren Buffett and those mad scientists at the Federal Reserve don't fully understand the financial engineering here, then obviously it's out of control, and it's unlikely that the general public will grasp it anytime soon. Of course, after it all blows up, we'll all get a thorough education on derivatives. We have already experienced the side effects of derivatives, which is responsible for prior economic disasters that sent shockwaves around the world more than once. The first time we took a hit was in 1987 on Black Monday. Then came the Asia crisis in 1997. Still, these dark moments are nothing like what is still in store for us. The derivatives machine gobbled up Long Term Capital Management, a hedge fund disaster that not only threatened to wipe out the U.S. financial system, but the entire world economy. The demise list reads like a Who's Who: Orange County, California, 1994; Barings Bank, 1995; Enron, 2001; Argentina, 2001–2; and that's just the beginning.

The derivatives market started in Chicago in 1973, when trading first began in the options exchange at the Chicago Board of Trade. This new investment vehicle gained rapid popularity even though most people had never heard of a derivative. Trading ballooned to over $600 billion during the deregulated Reagan era of the 1980s, and this trading activity was a precursor to Black Monday. Since that time, the dollar figures invested in derivatives have skyrocketed. By 1988, derivatives had reached the first $1 trillion; by 1994, they had passed the $10 trillion mark; and by 2000, there was over $95 trillion in derivatives held by worldwide institutions. In 2003, even the Federal National Mortgage Association (FNMA), commonly known as "Fannie Mae," a federally chartered corporation that purchases residential mortgages backed by the federal agencies, and conventional mortgages in the secondary market, got caught with its pants down when the fact that it lost $1.9 billion was exposed—sending the stock into the toilet. Now brace yourself! Since 2006, this financial Molotov cocktail went from $344 trillion to $400 trillion (July 2007).

Derivatives, often employed to protect assets against changes in value, were devised for many purposes for use by knowledgeable experts to apply in specialized areas, such as floating interest rates, currency management, interest rate risk, and swapping floating-rate debt for fixed-rate financing costs. They were intended to be a hedge against risk. In theory, derivatives have legitimate uses—but they have become a crazy means of wagering. The derivative is a financial contract that is really just a bet. Unlike Vegas, where you have to put your money on the table, when you buy a derivative, you have to place just a small portion of the bet up front. Feel like predicting the price of gold or oil? Maybe you think interests are rising and you want to wager a small amount to see if they go where you predict. What the heck, a little bet with a large potential return. Where's the risk? Derivatives are highly leveraged and make for a highly volatile and dicey business. That's an oversimplification, but that's all that's really necessary to understand, unless you actually want to get into the derivatives business. There are also exchange-traded derivatives that are bought and sold over-the-counter.

A couple dozen major banks in the United States serve as storehouses for trillions of dollars of derivatives. *When*, not if, that market implodes, it will make the savings and loan swindle of the 1980s look like the minor leagues. Between 1986 and 1990, over 1,000 U.S. banks failed. Today, the biggest holder of derivatives, JP Morgan Chase, has $53 trillion invested in them, an amount almost as large as the entire U.S. national debt of $65 trillion—and keep in mind this government debt figure includes all of America's present and future liabilities.

Recently, large holders of derivatives—major investment institutions and hedge funds—have decided that they need to reduce their risk in these shaky investments. They plan to sell off hundreds of trillions of dollars worth, and soon. If derivatives were such good investments, why do these holders want to dump them? Didn't they determine in advance how to make a profit and get safely out at the moment they went into the fancy hybrid investment game? Or, was it merely a plan to draw in investment capital, with hopes of paying off the first few "winners" as new investors jumped on board? Sounds like a sophisticated Ponzi scheme to me, and those always end the same way. When the jig is up, investors who came into the game slightly later lose their money and the perpetrators go to jail. Unfortunately, the problem is so massive that there may not be a solution. Economic global disaster may be the only way out. I wonder who has the kind of cash or assets these institutions are going to need to unload these slips of paper to reduce their exposure. Any serious effort to unload this huge, highly questionable asset could be the spark that sets off this disaster, if it isn't triggered by something simple, such as an unexpected economic force coming from another direction. Maybe this catastrophe will be the entrée to rolling out a new global monetary system.

Rapidly Declining U.S. Dollar

Then there's the declining dollar. In the first quarter of 2007, it dropped 7 percent in value against the Swiss franc, and it has performed similarly with frequency. Today, we are witnessing stronger currencies rising quickly against the U.S. dollar. The dollar's fall has caused other currencies to be buoyant by comparison. Some of the stronger currencies today are the British pound, the euro, the Norwegian kroner, the Swedish rona, and the Danish Krone, the Japanese yen, the Australian, Singapore, and Canadian dollars, and the Swiss franc. Even the Chinese yuan has been strong and is expected to strengthen against the dollar. There seems to be no end in sight as to how long or how far the greenback will decline, but according to experts, it could lose 50 percent of its value in the next five years. Already, in the past seven years, the U.S. dollar has declined 40 percent.

This kind of decline in the U.S. dollar today, the "reserve currency of the world" for decades, does not instill confidence in foreign countries and investors and can lead to economic bankruptcy. The prestigious title that the U.S. dollar has held is being threatened by the euro. What is causing the decline in value of the dollar? Newly printed money for one, which as I have mentioned is the real cause of inflation, diluting the value of all of the other dollars in circulation, thereby robbing the holders of that money and redistributing the wealth to new currency holders. The new money represents the counterfeiting of paper money with no intrinsic value. Printing new money results in a requirement for more dollars to purchase the same goods and services as purchasing power is depleted.

Another effect on the dollar's decline is that investment money can get better returns elsewhere than in the United States. Investors, whether foreign, domestic, government or private, want their investments to be secure. Unfortunately, the perception from outside the bubble is that *real* troubles are underlying the U.S. economy, in fact, perhaps the country as a whole. Therefore, money is going elsewhere and out of the U.S. dollar; investors are purchasing euros and other stronger currencies. For example, there was a huge sell-off in August 2007 by Japan, China, and Taiwan of U.S. government bonds totalling billions and billions of dollars. And who can blame them? They not only want the better returns they can find elsewhere, they want their investment denominated in a strong currency that will at least hold its value, if not also appreciate. The depreciating dollar further erodes the returns that investors hope to be making. The laws of supply and demand kick in. What happens when you have a lot of something and the demand is lower than the available supply? The price drops!

And finally, if the country's economic outlook appears grave to foreign investors, default on these debts by the government is possible although not likely, and investors may fear this prospect. Fortunately, governments can print more money to get out of debt, and suffer the consequences later. It may be just a matter of time before we experience an official government devaluation of the U.S. currency, as experienced before in the 1970s.

For the moment, the stock market is still steaming along, but that won't last and the smart investors know it. The stock market also has been stimulated by a liberal monetary policy. If this economy stalls, the dollar will lack even more luster than it already does and it will likely drop even faster, sending an alarming signal around the world.

Later in this book I discuss the U.S. dollar and how you can counter this downward spiral, and even profit personally.

Political Landscape

In this section my Americanism prevails. Today, in the United States, we find ourselves in a peculiar position: Who should we elect as President of the United States? As a body, we are overwhelmingly disappointed with what feels like failure from President Bush and his administration in several areas.

As an example, the "War on Terror" is a seemingly endless and expensive and generalized effort to fight the dark forces of the world. If we haven't caught Osama bin Laden, one human being, or at least found his corpse, then I wonder how we are to eradicate terrorists whom we are unable to identify, a great invisible but convenient enemy, possibly real and possibly the creation of some very fertile minds from the architects of change.

The threat of crime and being considered a criminal has always had a controlling effect on keeping the populace in line, careful to pay their taxes to support the law enforcement needed to keep the streets and neighborhoods safe. But are we safe? The fact that we have more people in prisons per capita than any other country may say something about the degree of freedom we really have.

Even Fidel Castro knows this ploy, and uses the contrived threat of outside forces, such as those evil capitalist rats north of Cuba, to keep his citizens buying the communist dream and to keep them from overthrowing his government. These control tactics create a stronger, united Cuba, even in the face of economic despair and rampant poverty. It doesn't have to be this way, but that's the reality.

Now we have the Patriot Act squarely in place, a document ill-conceived if one is concerned with the well-being of the citizenry, as it is essentially the anti-Constitution of the United States of America, and was put into place in the climate of post-9/11 as necessary to defend our country and protect American interests. Well, in fact, it has the opposite effect, much of which has yet to be played out. When those days come, a lot of Americans are going to have grave regrets regarding who they supported and helped finance through their generous "voluntary contributions," known better as taxes, the fuel that heats the fire. Unfortunately, I cannot say that changing presidents will make a whole lot of positive difference these days.

Here we are, again, finding ourselves at the crossroads of our future. Several presidential hopefuls are poised to give it a shot, but, when it's all said and done, in November 2008, *we the people*—or, rather, our electoral college—will elect only one of them to lead us. A question you should ask yourself is: *Whom do we trust the most?* Leaders are elected based on certain promises and perceived qualities, and always from a hopeful, forgiving, and apparently gullible public. How many times can you sell the Eiffel Tower or the Brooklyn Bridge? I believe good political aspirants require some of the same philosophies and talents as a good confidence man. And, unfortunately, in both cases you often feel like you've been stung.

In any event, the architects of change will ultimately win again. Switzerland is not the only place where secrets are kept. But, for us mortals, at least there the secrecy laws are written for us, and thus it's not a bad place to begin securing our financial futures, building a personal fortune, and defending our personal sovereignty from the winds of change.

The American political system, in particular, truly smacks of Machiavellian tactics. Generals have used these methods for centuries to conquer their enemies. Actually, perhaps that's a good idea; maybe our generals could use some of these methods to *win* a war for a change *today*. Instead, it seems the aggressive principles of cunning and deceit are reserved for the defenseless taxpaying citizen. Does it really matter whom we vote for? On the surface, it seems that we have some control and effect through our vote, but unfortunately, the puppet master has his hands on the truth. What, you ask, is the truth? For one thing, *we the people* are played from both ends to the middle. We think we're gaining ground and making progress in life, but while we are comfortable at home watching fluff on TV, we are lulled and seduced into a belief that all is fine, in the meantime the machinations of the powerful, silent, and unaccountable are weaving a web to suit their own agendas and personal goals at our expense.

What was the big rush to go to Iraq? We couldn't wait for the United Nations inspectors to complete their reports on whether they really found weapons of mass destruction or to analyze CIA claims that the presence of WMD in Iraq was real? If the UN has limited credibility, then why does the U.S. contribute $800 million a year to support its existence? In fact, without us, the UN could not economically survive, as we are the single largest financial contributor. Again I ask, why? If the UN and CIA really have validity wouldn't we have patiently waited just a little longer to get a better indication of the true situation? No! Because there's a good chance that the real agenda for kicking Saddam Hussein in the pants again was stronger than good judgment. Our commander in chief and president made that call single-handedly, because that's the outcome he, and his machine, wanted.

A former "land man" who drove his Chevy around little dusty towns in Texas in search of oil claims certainly has had a meteoric rise to the presidency. The single biggest factor in his favor, of course, was his father, George H.W. Bush, a former president himself. More interestingly, the senior Bush was a former director of the Central Intelligence Agency at a time, incidentally, when the agency was allied with none other than today's most wanted man: Osama bin Laden. Politicians and intelligence people sure keep strange bedfellows! After September 11, 2001, his son, the new president, would declare a "War on Terror."

George W. Bush has used this War on Terror to ramrod everything and anything past the American public, and it has a strangely similar ring to his father's "War on Drugs." For over a decade, George Senior had as a personal friend Don Aronow, better known as the Speedboat King, inventor and manufacturer of the cigarette speedboat and many other famous high-octane boats.

I bring this up now because it shows a pattern of how political power seems to operate in the United States. On the surface the relationship, of course, appears innocent. Everybody has friends, right? Bush liked Aronow, and he liked Aronow's speedboats—so much so that he purchased one while he was U.S. Ambassador to the United Nations. There's a memorable photograph of President George H. W. Bush, former bomber pilot, looking like any other risk taker on board his speedboat, accompanied by Aronow and a Secret Service agent. The photo opportunity was the result on the War on Drugs. Bush, who was influential with the U.S. Customs Service, helped his buddy snag a big contract to build speedboats capable of catching drug runners who were outrunning the cops in Florida and the Caribbean (in boats also built by an Aronow company). These events were an inspiration for the television series *Miami Vice*. The boat Aronow built for Customs, *Blue Thunder*, quit running during a boat parade where it was to be showcased as the

U.S. Customs Service's weapon in the War on Drugs. Its design bugs were never completely worked out, and before Aronow could make good on his contract, he was dead with a bullet in his head.

Bush's association with Aronow became an embarrassment as the investigation into Aronow's death revealed that he was murdered by another speedboat racing champion and drug smuggler named Ben Kramer, a man who had served time in prison after a drug conviction and who had ties to the Colombian drug cartels.

As it turned out, Aronow himself had been running drugs to Miami at night with a crew. The investigation revealed that he had been a homebuilder in New Jersey and had left abruptly due to a falling-out with the Mob. In an effort to get protection and support his family, Aronow consulted with Meyer Lansky. Yes, *the* Meyer Lansky, who had his own crime organization in Miami, the man known as the Mafia's financier for over 50 years. Lansky agreed to sponsor Aronow into the speedboat-building business and related drug-smuggling racket. This was George H.W. Bush's "close friend."

How is it that Bush did not know these facts? Certainly the U.S. Secret Service would have checked Aronow out closely if he was going to be spending any time hanging around the vice president. Aronow's ties were deep in organized crime and intelligence circles, and connections led all the way to the top. Now, who turns out to have been a partner with Mr. Aronow in his major cocaine-smuggling operation? Brace yourself! It was Jeb Bush, son of George H. W. Bush, brother of our current president, and the former governor of Florida. Together, Jeb Bush and Don Aronow owed their Colombian suppliers $2.5 million, and at some point they refused to pay. I wonder how ol' Jeb managed to get out of that. Been wondering about those hanging chads? Is it so coincidental that the voting controversy in the 2001 presidential election centered on Florida?

Today's politicians and government leaders appear to be operating above the law. I guess the laws are intended only for taxpayers. Remember a more recent example, the case of "Scooter" Libby? Could that have been another presidential cover-up of the type that we have grown so familiar with over the past half-century?

The War on Terror appears to be no more successful than was the War on Drugs or, for that matter, the war in Iraq, which it seems we're losing, to the tune of $10 billion a month of our hard-earned money. Or maybe they are just spending fresh cash while the ink is still drying. Now that we're in, we have a problem whether we should stay or should leave. What a dilemma! That won't deter George, though. I put my money on the war continuing through this administration. I'll take it a step further. I believe the president will strike Iran very soon. Our desire as citizens not to be there doesn't really matter. We shouldn't have supported a half-cocked plan to go to war in the first place, ostensibly because we wanted revenge on terrorists. The relationship between Iraq and terrorists is still fuzzy at best. Like other marketed "wars," this latest campaign, the War on Terror, is partly, maybe even largely, nothing more than a War on Your Freedoms in disguise. As for the Florida drug trade, eventually it moved to the Mexican border. No wonder we're having problems securing our border!

But *we the people* are not entirely gullible. In fact, it's mainly these wars that have us generally disappointed and upset with President Bush. Of course, hindsight is 20/20. But we are angry enough that most of us are prepared to make changes. Out with the old and in with the new. The rich and corporations have become targets. Well, it's not difficult, on the surface anyway, to use them as scapegoats and to help unite a segment of the American population against those "types." Then a variety of related arguments, including demonizing concepts such as capital gains earned by citizens and my favorite, tax havens that protect the assets of citizens, are marketed as threats to the system, and an attempt is made to get the public to perceive these areas as representing money robbed directly from *them*. Huh! That's humorous indeed! How in the world would money that was saved from the clutches of greedy tax collectors be construed as belonging to the rest of Americans who were not intelligent enough or visionary enough, or simply uninformed about how to protect their interests, namely their personal assets and sovereignty?

The only ones who lost out on this money are the thieves themselves. As if having your own printing presses to print unlimited funny money in the first place weren't enough. As an aside, if the currency was backed by something of real value, like gold, as it once was, I could better understand the fuss. And the deception doesn't stop here.

Now there is talk of controlling the flight of capital. A country billed as "the land of the free," should have no worries about capital that wants to compete in the real world. After all, we pride ourselves as being advocates of free markets and free enterprise. Money, like water, seeks its own level, and it will find the best and highest use for itself wherever it is rewarded better. This sounds like more protectionist thinking, similar to tighter controls on travel. What does this mean? One fast way to slow the exodus of money from a country is to impose exchange controls. Not a pretty thought!

Back to politics, and the next president. To any casual observer, most likely the stage is set for a Democrat to take office. Of course, on the surface, change is good, even welcome. But will it really help us, the citizens of this country? Or will the agenda of the next administration simply further the causes of the architects of change? Most likely, regardless where you cast your vote, as those same architects advanced their mission and purpose in the eight years of George Bush, just as they had with Bill Clinton, and George H. W. Bush. I stop here because I would rather not include President Reagan, whom I believe was truly a man of integrity, which may have been why there was an assassination attempt during his first term. Fortunately, he escaped the perils that brought down two other notables, John F. Kennedy and Abraham Lincoln, each a great individual who fulfilled his role as president with integrity. Although Reagan survived the assassination attempt, the event may have gained his cooperation and helped to shape history as planned. As an interesting footnote, Reagan wanted to put the United States back on the gold standard. Bravo! I wonder why that didn't happen.

I'll leave thoughts like these behind, as they are too deep and large in scope to be addressed adequately in this book. But before Reagan, there was Jimmy Carter, Gerald Ford, Richard Nixon, and another Texan, Lyndon B. Johnson. Need I say more? Sometimes the list of presidents seems like the cast from a whodunit. Their administrations, in part, helped to move this country away from the founding principles and toward our moment in time, for good or bad, and a clearly questionable future. In the short time that we have been alive, the current generations today have seen incredible changes and real threats to our personal liberties, which are on the verge of extinction.

Personally, I'm more interested in content than labels. But unfortunately, I don't see much substance, only some fast-talking politicians with big designs. It won't matter if we vote Republican or Democrat; Machiavellian principles are at work, preparing to conquer and divide. Unlike Las Vegas gamblers, Howard Hughes was no fool. When he wanted to control the White House, he financially supported *all* the candidates. The architects of change play it the same way. We are being squeezed like a tube of toothpaste.

The next stop: socialism. The next president, will be pressing for social changes, but with these ideas come high price tags, not unlike war. Is it sounding familiar? The question is, just who *is* winning the war? It's not us—just as it won't be with the advent of the currently touted social changes. Already, the Democrats are talking about how to raise revenues without raising taxes. Hmm—there's a thought. And recently those dirty words, "tax havens" crop up again. Led by Congressman Sander Levin and enthusiastically supported by Hillary Clinton, John Edwards and Barack Obama, Congress is pressing to pass the "Stop the Tax Havens" act. What conceit! How can they believe that the independent actions of outside sovereign nations are within their power to legislate? Scary.

In fact, it's highly unlikely they can stop or control dozens of independent countries from doing what they want to do, since, like the United States, other nations are entitled to run themselves as they choose and to protect their own interests. Our revenue problem is not the problem of all other nations and peoples. The idea of having a fair tax competition among tax men could be a Mel Brooks comedy. That hasn't stopped the Organization for Economic Cooperation and Development (OECD) from trying its hardest to convince everyone that fair competition among tax collectors is something we should care about. There they go again, the architects of change trying to plug up the natural flow of free economic forces to help financially support their goals and solve *their* problems, all the while hoping to restructure the world at your expense. Why are citizens being rallied to support such lame causes? So they can be taxed more, maybe? As obvious as it is, the vast majority of the public will not even have a chance to understand it.

So that I don't sound redundant to readers of *Tax Havens Today: The Benefits and Pitfalls of Banking and Investing Offshore,* I refer you to it, particularly Part One, which explores timely topics that every taxpayer should be aware of. These are contained in sections "Why Are So Many People Going Offshore?" "Whipping the Taxpayers into Shape,"

"The Big Squeeze," "The Changing World of Tax Havens," "The International Dragnet," "The Global Laundromat," "The Tax Police," and "Barbarians at the Gate." I invite you to have a look.

I'm not trying to pick on the Democrats; in fact, I've only ever cared about individual candidates and issues, if then, and I don't care about labels. But what I do care about are the rumblings in the jungle, the rhythm of the drums, and the chants of the natives. I'm afraid they need sacrifices! Of course, the Democrats don't want to talk about raising taxes, not just now, anyway—they want to get their man or woman elected to the presidency. The subject of raising taxes has a history of impeding progress. However, they do want to set the stage for what it is they wish to accomplish as soon as they are in control of the White House. *Raise taxes!* Yes, that's right. Why? Because they will desperately need the money, what with all their spending plans for their new social order. But didn't they say they intend to increase revenue without raising taxes? Hillary's $110 billion health care program will certainly need a fresh infusion of cash.

Isn't that the sales job? Here's the plan: Plug up tax havens, tax shelters, flight capital, and any other "loopholes"—ASAP!—*before* Bush is out of office. Then, when Hillary or Obama gets elected, the president will be pushing to raise taxes higher than we've ever experienced in our lifetimes. In this fashion, the Democrats will maximize the effect. Plug up the holes and stick it to the taxpayer. Big things are on the way!

Incidentally, while campaigning in the summer, John Edwards *did* bravely mention a plan of his to *raise* taxes. He plans to raise taxes on capital gains to as high as 28 percent. Capital gains are profits that you, the creative individual, make when you intelligently invest the money that you already earned (and *already paid income tax on,* in most cases!) *And*—here's the sales job—he's planning to give that money, which you wisely earned using your good sense and your already-taxed money, to people who don't have as much money as you. Awww! He's a really nice fellow—with some compassion, no doubt—but he wants *you* to pay for it. Even if you were to be the beneficiary of such planning, would you think it was fair?

Interestingly enough, John Edwards was quoted in *Men's Vogue* pointing out that Bush and his team have used the hot-button word "war," as in the "War on Terror," as nothing more than "high-level rhetoric to inflame the American voters to support them." Now he is claiming that, if elected, he will declare a "War on Tax Havens." See? Politicians really are all the same.

Of course, a general strategy *is* in place to restrict the U.S. taxpayers from using tax havens as much as they can, as they are certainly not going to force all those independent nations, regardless of how small they are, to give up their national sovereignty and succumb to the whims of the United States. It will be your personal sovereignty that gets compromised. But if the tax havens were ever to succumb—and anything's possible—it would take a mightier force, and there is one at work, to coerce these countries into submission. The OECD has been working overtime in the past decade to accomplish this, and today, the United Nations has aspirations of becoming the Global Internal Revenue Service. There's a truly frightening thought. If, and when, it gets us snuggly in its well-made noose, we will see taxes universally skyrocket. We will experience not discriminatory economic slavery but rather equal slavery for all.

The Un-Patriotic Act

Another strong argument for having your funds securely salted away from the prying eyes of government, and others—and not just for tax and investment reasons—is the so-called Patriot Act. Your money and assets in your own country are easy targets. When the government wants to confiscate your resources, it will find a way, it won't be asking your permission.

The Patriot Act has effectively given the U.S. government this kind of total power and control—in direct opposition of what the Founding Fathers envisioned and created for us—to take what they want, and when they choose. That includes you! Now the government has the power to legally take you out of your house, at its whim, and detain you indefinitely. Knowing this, are you going to stand by and let the government? Granted, it's your personal sovereignty at stake, but your entire existence may be on the line, not just your money, and not tomorrow, but *right now.* Why would a lengthy and broadly drafted piece of legislation empowering the government, which was supposedly about preventing terrorism, actually be two-thirds about *your money?* If you didn't know this, it is not surprising. The powers that be don't want you to know the small little details that they neatly and quickly wrapped up into the Patriot Act before anyone noticed. Why? Well, if you are planning to rob a bank, would you warn them?

This 342-page monster was introduced so quickly after 9/11—six weeks to be exact—that it challenges the imagination to think that its drafters could agree on its contents in such a short time. Makes you wonder if it didn't preexist, just waiting for the proper moment of fear and shock to quickly pass it into law. And why did most congressmen not take the time to read the most important piece of legislation that would ever pass before them? Isn't that what we pay them for? Did they already know it was coming, or, as usual, did the powers that be trust that they would fail to read this, just as they don't read other, far less cumbersome legislation prior to casting their vote? Or were the architects of change working their magic from behind the scenes? Maybe the stage was already set for the cast to follow through with a rehearsed performance. The act was made law almost instantly. Yet the hole where the Twin Towers fell over six years ago is still visible. Rather than develop the site for commercial gain, perhaps the government should designate a national monument and dedicate it to the people who died on that day.

The more governments and global organizations work to demand financial transparency worldwide so that they can know more about your private affairs, the more your right to privacy, the linchpin of personal sovereignty, is eroded. What we really need is transparency in Congress and in other dark and damp corners where the real power lurks and where secrets thrive. Then maybe we'd have a chance at ending such abuses of power, not just those ridiculous pork bills.

Speaking of those, at the moment there are 32,000 proposed plans for spending billions of dollars of your hard-earned tax dollars on frivolous nonsense. One bill alone would spend $2.3 billion to manufacture 10 C-17 military transport aircraft that the military claims it doesn't need. These bills often support activities and jobs in the districts where the congressmen reside, in hopes of getting more votes, or they serve as favors to friends or the powerful. Let's stop the waste in Washington before it stops us.

Recently, a reader of *Tax Havens Today* shared some thoughts with me. CJ writes:

> I'm always reminded of this passage by Alexander Tyler which was written about the time of the founding of our nation. To quote: "A democracy is always temporary in nature; it simply cannot exist as a permanent form of government. A democracy will continue to exist up until the time that voters discover that they can vote themselves generous gifts from the public treasury. From that moment on, the majority always votes for the candidates who promise the most benefits from the public treasury, with the result that every democracy will finally collapse due to loose fiscal policy, which is always followed by a dictatorship."

How eloquent! And Tyler's quote continues:

> The average age of the world's greatest civilizations from the beginning of history has been about 200 years. During those 200 years, these nations always progressed through the following sequence:
>
> From bondage to spiritual faith;
> From spiritual faith to great courage;
> From courage to liberty;
> From liberty to abundance;
> From abundance to complacency;
> From complacency to apathy;
> From apathy to dependence;
> From dependence back into bondage.

Thomas Jefferson summarized it well when he said that a government large enough to give you everything you want is large enough to take everything you have.

Some thoughts to ponder while you fill out your Swiss or foreign bank account application! If you would like to read some true cases of how Swiss banks have been used in the past, and why they have played an important role in the world, often helping oppressed people to keep what's theirs, I recommend you read *The Swiss Banks* by T. R. Fehrenbach, published by McGraw-Hill Book Company in 1966. This work presents a thorough understanding of the subject.

There are banks that will gladly do business with you regardless where your citizenship was issued, and I believe that will always be true. Or at least I hope so. You just need to find the right one. It has become much more difficult to locate a Swiss bank that is willing to open an account for a U.S. citizen, as you will see if you contact some of the banks listed in this book. *All the more reason why you need one.* My list is provided so that you can conduct your own banking research. This book also helps you evaluate some of the better offshore investment possibilities.. With as little as $5,000, you can be profiting from those disapproved-of foreign investments and capitalizing on those emerging markets.

Readers will discover some of the problems U.S. citizens face and the options as well as the bigger picture of how Switzerland can help you financially, and not just through its banking facilities. There are some terrific opportunities available right now, one of which I call the Ultimate Investment Plan, which I will explain shortly. Stay tuned! And, if you invest soon, you could secure yourself permanently from possible government restrictions that would severely limit your ability to get your money out of the country and safely overseas. If these restrictions happen, your physical freedom is likely to be the next thing to be restricted, ironically in the name of your *security.*

Thanks, Osama, wherever you are!

The New America

This may sound incredulous, but there has been talk of the New America. The European Union (EU) began similarly, first starting out to create a larger trading bloc, which gradually led to the EU with 28 countries bonded together by all the hallmarks of a sovereignty and sharing a single currency, the euro. Isn't that why the North American Free Trade Agreement (NAFTA) was passed, to create a free trade bloc? The architects of change might want to unite us with our neighbors, too, in our case Canada and Mexico, in the same way the EU came into being. These architects are orchestrating this plan right now, and have been working on it for decades, without our knowledge, and if so, likely we won't have much say in the final decision-making process. North America, one big country!

The EU is being used as the blueprint. Learn more about this plan by visiting www.StoptheNorthAmericanUnion.com.

If you think about many of our problems in the United States, it could seem that the reason things are going the way they are is to set the stage for this merger. It doesn't appear that our leaders really want to close the Mexican border. Okay, so maybe we have decided not to worry about illegals who are now coming into the United States and freeloading on our welfare system at the taxpayers' expense, but how are we to keep the terrorists out? Are we concerned about keeping them out, or are we just paying lip service to make it appear that we are trying to keep them out? Remember crisis? Perhaps someone else's *opportunity* to *change* things is really at work here. If it's true that the New America is really on the drawing board, then there's a good possibility that some unimaginable changes may be in the works. How do you sell a plan like that to Americans? Basically, by controlling the whole through its parts. It would inevitably mean a new constitution, just as in Europe. Do you think it will be drafted with the care that our Founding Fathers gave the original one? Do you think you'll have more rights, insuring your personal sovereignty and liberty, than you have now? The Patriot Act may just be a bridge to compromising our rights until the day our Constitution is completely replaced. The EU didn't pass the last one proposed. In 2009, when the vote comes up again, it might just pass. The New America will require only three member states to agree. Do you think Mexico is going to say no? And Canada is practically part of the United States. I don't think this will be difficult to tout. I heard through the grapevine that *they* plan to push this crazy idea through in the next five years.

And it's not surprising to find George W. Bush quietly promoting this union. In a meeting in Waco, Texas, between President Bush, the then-Mexican President Vincente Fox, and the then-prime minister of Canada Paul Martin, the three leaders of North America agreed basically to eliminate the borders in a plan identified as the "Security and Prosperity Partnership of North America" (SPP). Now, why haven't we heard more about this? And the new currency they plan to propose: the "Amero." How original!

Are you wondering how such a plan might actually be welcomed by middle class America, their main stumbling block? How about a little economic crisis coupled with a conveniently timed terrorist act? Suddenly the security and prosperity of North America may sound like the perfect solution.

A nation's sovereignty must continually be defended, not just by war, but by protecting its territory, controlling immigration, and enforcing its legitimate laws. Otherwise, sovereignty can be jeopardized. Our government leaders and representatives should not be publicly, or secretly, endorsing grandiose plans to transform our nation by merging it with other countries. In fact, that sounds a little like high treason.

Treason? Here's the definition from the *Chamber's Dictionary*: "Betraying of the government or an attempt to overthrow it; treachery; disloyalty."

I also believe that it's wise and prudent to respect the national sovereignty of other nations if for no greater reason than to provide ourselves with cheap insurance for protecting our own, just as we should in turn respect other people's histories, cultures, and religious beliefs. The first step to preserving our rights and beliefs as a nation and as individual citizens, is to respect those of others, even if we don't understand them, and even if, in our judgment, they might seem completely wrong.

Personal Sovereignty and the Urgency to Act

Claiming your natural right to personal sovereignty and taking action to secure your financial freedom and future is more of a must than an option. At the same time, however, some action needs to happen on the home front too, at least as long as we are still voters. I can't think of a better way than for all of us to send a very loud message to Congress and hold them accountable. We have been patient and trusting long enough. The United States is a republic, and a form of democracy, in which the majority of *we the people* give our representatives the power to act on our behalf. *That* is clearly *not* a license to steal from us. In that spirit, I invite you to discover how easily you can now be heard, and your participation *will* make a direct impact in Washington. Let's squash the next plan of some overpaid congressmen who think they're going to waste our money and compromise our liberties just because we gave them the power to do so and to make us look like fools.

There is a little nonprofit organization that our political leadership would like to see go away quietly into the dead of night. Fortunately, one of its cofounders, Bob Babka, is relentless in his pursuit so that the voice of Americans can be heard—loud and clear. Thanks to our newfangled technology, you can tell Congress what you think and where you stand on the issues of the day from the privacy and convenience of your home. DownsizeDC is making a *real* impact, and it's like a pesky fly in the face of Congress. You may have the pleasure in knowing your message is getting through. Collectively, DownsizeDC has already been making our opinions known and, in many instances, actually *heeded*. Visit www .downsizedc.org and www.downsizedc.com. Just five minutes of your valuable time everyday, and *we the people* can make the difference.

To learn more about your liberties, please visit www.theadvocates .org; www.cato.org; www.freedomandprosperity.org; www.isil.org; and www.freedomhouse.org.

Chapter 2

Switzerland—Alpine Financial Oasis

"Freedom can exist only in the society of knowledge. Without learning, men are incapable of knowing their rights . . ."
—DR. BENJAMIN RUSH, 1786

S witzerland has been a land of fascination, and controversy, for decades. It has a unique national history and a blend of culture and customs that come, in part, from its unique location nestled in the Alps, squarely in the heart of Western Europe. This small country covers only 15,950 square miles but boasts three national languages—German, French, and Italian—and similarly distinct regions, reflecting its neighboring countries while remaining unique, and famously politically neutral.

France lies to the west, Germany to the north, Liechtenstein and Austria to the east, and Italy to the south, and their cultures have overflowed for centuries into the soul of Switzerland. In fact, today the country is made up of three very definitive regions: German-Swiss, French-Swiss, and Italian-Swiss linguistic groups. *Schwyzerdeutsch,* a Swiss variation of German, is most popular, with 65 percent of the Swiss populace speaking it. Eighteen percent speak French; 10 percent speak Italian; approximately 1 percent of Swiss speak Romansch, an offshoot of the Latin-Rhaetian dialect; and another 6 percent speak other languages. Forty-six percent of the Swiss are Roman Catholic, 40 percent are Protestants, 2 percent are Muslims, and the balance is comprised of members of other religions and the nonreligious. The total population is a modest 7.5 million people.

Whether we have been to Switzerland or not, we all know of the fabled beauty of this country with its majestic slopes and many lovely lakes. Switzerland is a natural water source where the Alps collect and store fresh water for future delivery along its four major river arteries, the Po, the Rhine, the Rhone, and the Inn-Danube, that feed into the neighboring countries. And then there is the Aare, the largest river exclusively within Switzerland. Although the geographical limitations and the rugged topography have impacted the Swiss economy and have defined its commercial activities over time, they may also be a strong reason why international finance suits it well. There is, however, a wide economic diversity that is not just limited to secret banking, precision watchmaking, and charming cuckoo clocks.

Switzerland produces a variety of agricultural products, including wheat, sugar, beets, fruits, vegetables, potatoes, food products, dairy products, and wines. Salt is also a major product of the country, and it also is known for certain manufactured products, such as textiles, chemicals, precision tools, machinery, and pharmaceuticals. Tourism, not surprisingly, ranks as the third largest industry. And also not surprisingly, the Swiss are well educated and boast a 99 percent literacy rate.

Roots of Political and Monetary Stability

Aside from its national attributes, Switzerland also has an interesting history that has shaped the country's modern-day image. The story primarily begins with the Helvetians, a Celtic tribe who gave its name to the Swiss territory, and inhabited the region during the Iron Age,

from around 800 B.C. to 58 B.C. Around this time, they were con-
quered by Julius Caesar and the Romans, who remained for over 400
years until the fall of their empire and the rise of primarily Germanic
tribes who built new empires in Europe through the Middle Ages.
The Romans left a strong mark with the establishment of the four
main languages today and their unifying effect on this region that
helped lead into the early beginning of a league of cantons, similar to
states or regions, that, over time, grew in number. What political
unity that may have been achieved in these times began to deterio-
rate, setting the stage for the eventual occupation by the Hapsburg
family, then rulers of the upper Rhine Valley, in the tenth century.

On August 1, 1291, several districts made the first efforts to peace-
fully unite to form an anti-Hapsburg league, signing on to the Oath of
Eternal Alliance, which later evolved into the Swiss Federation. The
Hapsburgs were determined not to lose important taxpaying regions
to the new federation, and they tried to retain control, but without
success. In a reverse move, the young confederation went on the offen-
sive by taking back the city of Aarau. The French king, Louis XI,
negotiated a truce in 1474 between the Swiss Confederacy and the
Hapsburgs. Although the Swiss thus won their independence by the
fifteenth century, the country did not receive official recognition from
other sovereignties until 1648, when the all Europe Peace Treaty of
Westphalia formally accepted Switzerland as an independent nation.
This treaty was the culmination of the famous "Thirty Years War"
from 1618 until 1648 that raged throughout Europe, with the exception that Switzerland remained, the entire time, a "peaceful island," as
an early example of its famous neutrality.

Of course, local political and religious differences were inevitable,
just as in all of human history, and these kept the federation divided
until the French organized and unified the cantons and called the result
the Helvetic Republic, which lasted from 1798 to 1803. During this
period, Napoleon restored the federal government, and the territory
expanded as an independent confederation with 22 separate cantons.

In 1815, at the Congress of Vienna, Switzerland's borders and its per-
petual neutrality were first officially established and guaranteed by a federal pact, which governed until 1848 with the coming of the first Federal
Constitution. This document emerged as a result of the Sonderbund war

fought between the Roman Catholic cantons and the Protestants, and combined elements of the U.S. constitution and of French revolutionary traditions.

However, neutral or not, Switzerland was not without enemies. Also in 1815, the Swiss fought the French in Italy, took a pounding, and quickly retreated. Recognizing their military limitations, they conceded to honoring in fact the neutrality pact that they had signed earlier that year. Through this agreement, the nation's commitment to neutrality, and other unusual circumstances, Switzerland has achieved a unique political and economic stability ever since and has avoided the many European conflicts that have occurred, including two world wars. Switzerland's great prominence in the realm of banking has its roots in these historical facts.

In 1874, another constitution was ushered in, replacing the first constitution from 26 years prior, and leading to the separation of church and state. Then, in 1999, a new present constitution was adopted to replace the antiquated second constitution; parts of it no longer applied in modern Switzerland, and parts of it were in language that was barely translatable.

Of course, Switzerland's history is long—in 1999 the country celebrated its 700th birthday!—so naturally, there is much more to tell, but this gives a quick summary that brings us to the Switzerland we have come to know, or thought we knew. Unfortunately, in a step that is in sharp contrast with the nation's character over the ages, on September 10, 2002, Switzerland joined the United Nations. With that move, nearly 200 years of neutrality were completely abolished. Fortunately, at least for now and possibly for a very long time, that move may not impact many of the other beneficial aspects of Switzerland, including its bank secrecy laws, superior banking services, and investment management expertise.

The Swiss Reject the European Union

The Swiss have repeatedly voted down the idea of joining the European Monetary Union (EMU), also known as the European Community (EC). The people of Switzerland are wise to reject joining the

European Union (EU). Joining the (EU) would abolish long-standing Swiss independence and ultimately dilute Switzerland's strength and stability and its national sovereignty. Switzerland would have to ditch the Swiss franc and adopt the less attractive euro, surrender its political and monetary control to Brussels, open up its borders to residents of other EU nations, and be subjected to an uncontrollable inflow of immigrants. The Swiss federal government and the direct democracy that the people cherish would have to be relinquished in favor of the current EU government structure. Indeed, all EU countries are at risk of inevitably losing their individuality and traditions over time. Switzerland, long a low-tax country in comparison to its neighbors—a successful means of attracting business—would see taxes rise in relation to the EU's tax practices. In fact, it would only be a matter of time before Switzerland would be forced to abolish its famous Bank Secrecy Act.

Switzerland is under constant pressure from the European Union and the Organization for Economic Cooperation and Development (OECD). Even so, insiders in Zurich do not believe that Switzerland's principal areas for concern will be compromised in the foreseeable future.

No wonder the good folks in Switzerland do not want to be a part of the European Union. If it were not for the country's "direct democracy," the people's voices may not have mattered and they would likely be a part of the EU today. Poorer countries may stand to benefit from EU membership, but I cannot help but wonder what the rest of them were thinking.

Armadillo-Tough Asset Protection

Switzerland has much to offer these days. Chapter 3 outlines the rich array of services that make Swiss banking famous. Also, the chapter introduces a terrific concept little known to most people outside of Europe. I call it "the Ultimate Investment Plan," and I believe that in many circumstances, it is far and away the best way to bank and invest offshore. This plan provides the strongest asset protection anywhere—with total secrecy—while increasing your investment returns. All the while, you will be engaging in estate planning, without the usual worries. You will gain more benefits than an onshore or offshore trust or any other estate planning structure found in North America can offer. You will have an ultra-safe retirement income protected from surprise, and available anytime you choose. And, in the event of your death, your family or other beneficiaries will be covered immediately, all the while avoiding probate. Does that sound like something you could use?

Twin Democratic Republics

Switzerland has an important diplomatic and trade relationship with the United States, and is allied with the United States in numerous ways, in sharp contrast to the adversarial relationship the countries share on the subject of bank secrecy. The United States has been far from successful in its efforts to break Swiss banking silence. Although some changes have occurred in Switzerland over the years, for the most part, there is little that would directly affect you, unless you were the target of a criminal inquiry; in that case, today's bank secrecy would not protect you. The greatest concern would be the potential for future change that could significantly affect your assets and investments.

In many ways, pull up "and" the United States and Switzerland are kissing cousins, sharing politics, economics, culture, and even areas of scientific advancement. The two countries are important trading partners, and they have long groomed the relationship with each other. So close have the two been at times that they have even exchanged ideas and concepts from each other's constitutions for adoption into their own at different times in history. Funny how much similarity there is at the constitutional level while how much differently they actually function. That might make for an interesting study. Maybe Congress should spend some money to figure out where the United States took a wrong turn, instead of throwing it away on pork bills.

The two countries have fostered mutual business. Switzerland has been growing as an attractive international business base for U.S. companies and as a desirable environment for overseas living. International trade is strong between the two countries, and they are major trading partners.

In recent years, there has been little pressure coming from the United States, except for the effects of the Qualified Intermediary (QI) agreements that the Internal Revenue Service has signed with Swiss banks. Please refer to Chapter 4 for more about the QI. There is an exchange-of-information clause principally for the purpose of enforcing the double-taxation agreement.

Bankers to the World

Switzerland has earned the well-deserved reputation as "bankers to the world," in part due to the way it has handled the business of people from around the globe through crisis, world wars, and often in the face of a blaze of criticism and negative publicity. Frightened money historically has found its way there. Swiss bank secrecy has been a financial cornerstone in the world, together with a conservative national monetary policy and a long history of neutrality, attracting all kinds of business along with upward of 40 percent of the world's private assets. Unfortunately, when Switzerland joined the United Nations in 2002, it surrendered its historic neutrality. Today, Switzerland is recognized as a sophisticated international banking center with the expertise to manage assets, investments, and plain old cash to the satisfaction of its clientele, many of whom are the world's rich. Not a bad endorsement!

Until the 1930s, there was little federal regulation of Swiss banks. Swiss bank traditions were codified into the Federal Banking Law of 1935, which established the Federal Banking Commission (FBC). The FBC enforces the strict banking laws that all deposit-taking institutions and banks are required to observe. These laws have since been revised and modified to refine and ensure a more financially secure banking system. Stringent liquidity requirements are imposed, and a serious monitoring system is in place. As a result, historically very few Swiss banks have failed.

The Swiss banker has been painted as a saint and as a villain. At times, both may have been true, depending in part, of course, on the perspective of the beholder. In actual fact, the Swiss banker is basically just a shrewd, conservative money person.

Bank Secrecy in a World of Transparency

The Swiss people have always been conservative, private individuals. Traditionally, they live close to each other and do not move frequently. In fact, it is quite typical for the Swiss to live in the same house or neighborhood for generations. Neighbors get to know a lot about each other under these circumstances—that is, if they openly discuss personal business with each other. This proximity is one reason why the Swiss are very private people. They also do not take kindly to taxes or to the government putting its nose in their business. Also typical of the Swiss is that they do not typically discuss or advertise their wealth.

But, it was the rise of Hitler and the Nazis in the 1930s that really pushed the government to protect its bank's depositors, as the Third Reich sought records on accounts held by German citizens. The Swiss response—to staunchly protect the privacy of their depositors—was in the realm of a humanitarian act and of course, shrewd business, as surely Hitler would not have been happy with citizens who hid from financially supporting his massive war machine. Can you imagine Hitler for your tax collector?

Sticking with their practice of bank secrecy suited the Swiss just fine too, as it kept their depositors happy. Fortunately, Switzerland traditionally had a weak central government, as it was never empowered by its people to be otherwise. Emphasis has always been on self-government and democracy, as well it should be, and it begins at the local level. The Swiss control their government through national referendums and initiatives—a wonderful feature of direct democracy. The United States and Switzerland may be two democratic republics with shared attributes built into their constitutions, but it is apparent that, in practice, they do not operate in the same way.

In direct response to the attempt by the Nazis to muscle their way into the Swiss banking system, Switzerland passed the famous Bank Secrecy Act of 1934. This piece of legislation is the very one being enforced to this day. Bank employees are subject to fines up to 50,000 Swiss francs and six months in jail should they disclose any information on an account or an account holder; in addition, they are forbidden by law even to respond to an inquiry by anyone, private or government, without a court order. Maybe the penalties should be stiffened.

Some changes have come along the way, particularly since 1970, but basically, the secrecy laws are very effective today, except in cases of evidence of a crime *as interpreted by Swiss law.* As an example, tax evasion is not specifically a crime in Switzerland, so this would not be a good enough reason, in the Swiss point of view, to pierce their secrecy law, no matter who or which country that does criminalize tax evasion is doing the asking.

Tax fraud *is* considered a crime in Switzerland, and, of course, there could be a potentially gray area in the interpretation between fraud and evasion. Most likely the Swiss would lean toward a conservative view on what evasion means and be reluctant to open up, unless hard evidence was presented regarding the commission of actual fraud. An example of fraud in a tax case would be intentionally declaring untrue deductions to save taxes. As in all fraud cases, *intent* is the key word, and it must be *proved* for it to be considered fraud. But the test for fraud, too, has been challenged in the United States.

A Swiss banker's obligation to respect clients' privacy is not absolute, and no protection is afforded criminals. There is a responsibility to provide information in certain instances, and there are penalties against a banker for failing to meet this duty. A few of the "crimes" as defined by Swiss law that could be used to breach Swiss bank secrecy are:

- Civil proceedings (i.e., inheritance or divorce)
- Debt recovery and bankruptcy
- Criminal proceedings (i.e., money laundering, association with a criminal organization, theft, tax fraud, blackmail, etc.)
- International Mutual Legal Assistance Treaty (MLAT) assistance proceedings

The Swiss passed strict money laundering laws in 1998 that force Swiss bankers to report "suspicious transactions" that might indicate a crime. In the past, if bankers thought a serious crime was being facilitated through their bank, they might simply report it to law enforcement authorities. Reporting any "funny business" was at the bankers' discretion.

Today, if bankers fail to provide information on the account holder and the accounts of suspect customers, they face serious penalties, including prison. In the past, the opposite was true. This is a rather liberal application of the interpretation of the law in the judgment of individual bankers. The bank also has the discretionary power to freeze assets based on "reasonable suspicion" prior to any charges being leveled against an account holder. The possibility for abuse exists, but it is doubtful that this strategy would be employed, unless there was a serious offense. *That explains why the Italian mafia likes Monaco,* and they haven't signed an MLAT.

In Switzerland, well-founded "suspicious transactions" must be reported to the Money Laundering Reporting Office in accordance with the Money Laundering Act, Article 9.

The Swiss have taken a lot of heat for protecting bank secrecy from the many international organizations that I mention in this book and in *Tax Havens Today,* and many foreign governments have exerted pressure too, particularly the higher-taxing ones. But Switzerland is faring very well, considering the situation. These entities are, not surprisingly, the same ones that also apply pressure to the tax havens of the world. They sometimes use unscrupulous methods to exert their will and expect countries to bend to their demands, even at the possible expense of compromising the national sovereignty of other people. But that's a part of the plan. The architects of change are at work, hoping to mold something new from the old. Fortunately, there are countries and individuals who are not willing to compromise their national or personal sovereignty at the whims of a tax collector. Let's hope these people don't have ambitions like Hitler; I'd have to change my name to B. Traven and move to Latin America.

However, the EU has played an important role with Switzerland, and it is highly integrated in the European economy. The conservative Swiss People's Party, which has the largest percentage of support, is content with the status quo. But the leftist politicians are always angling and joining forces with leftists from outside Switzerland, such as the EU, the OECD, the G-7, or the Group of Seven, consisting of seven major economic powers, including Canada, France, Germany, Great Britain, Italy, Japan, and the United States, who are also seven of the highest taxing countries of the world, and others, who would like to abolish Swiss bank secrecy. Short of that, they would at least like to compromise it. Even though Switzerland has repeatedly declined to join the EU, the politicians from Brussels continue to exert pressure in hopes of furthering their tax collection efforts aimed at EU residents.

Unfortunately for other Europeans, in a compromise that does not disclose the names of account holders, Switzerland agreed to the "EU savings tax directive" after some arm wrestling and to avoid the overt threat that the EU would serve Switzerland with a financial boycott. The result was that an escalating withholding tax of 15 to 35 percent over the next few years would be imposed on the accounts of EU residents. After that, the tax would remain at 35 percent. This directive went into effect on January 1, 2005, permitting tax information exchange between member nations and effectively abolishing bank secrecy and confidentiality for customers in the EU. The exceptions were Austria, Luxembourg, and even Belgium—all EU member states—that ultimately chose not to allow their secrecy laws to be compromised. How long this will last remains to be seen.

The long-term outlook for Swiss bank secrecy is very good despite outside pressures from foreign governments and international organizations such as the OECD. The continued strength of the act has everything to do with the severe penalties imposed on bankers should they violate it. And this is not likely to change unless Switzerland joins the European Union, in which case, the EU will surely insist that the country abolish the Bank Secrecy Act at some point in time.

Financial transparency is being touted worldwide in the name of fighting crime and terrorism. Unfortunately, the ones who should reveal more—the U.S. Congress, the president's administration, governments in general, intelligence organizations, multinational corporations, secret societies, and plenty of others worldwide—have no intention of being transparent, and neither do the architects of change. Transparency is for you and me. Again, the terrorists may be merely a crisis management tool to accomplish the end result of someone else's larger agenda.

The dark recesses of Swiss bank vaults were once sacred places to bankers and their customers, like cathedrals are to priests and their flocks. In the long term, this will likely change. A list of Swiss depositors over the past century would read like a cast of colorful characters from a good international thriller. The secrets represented by the cash stashed in Switzerland in the past, if it had been revealed, could possibly have altered the course of history. Now, certainly, depositors are still a subject of interest. Is the intent of transparency advocates to eliminate all places of refuge for anyone but the few unknown elite?

The implication is that if you don't want to reveal all your personal information and financial holdings, you must have something to hide. When do we pull the curtain back on the architects of change and disclose the *real* truth?

Cloak and Dagger

At one point, some rumors and press emerged that insinuated that Swiss bank secrecy was being compromised in a huge way. This activity began shortly after September 11, 2001, and is said to have lasted about five years. The story is disconcerting, but fortunately it had nothing to do with Switzerland's cooperation with anyone or any compromise of the important protections built into Swiss banking.

It was reported in the Swiss press that the Society for Worldwide Interbank Financial Telecommunication, an organization known as SWIFT, was being monitored by the United States government. Headquartered in Brussels, Belgium, SWIFT is a private collective that is responsible for the electronic transfer of hundreds of billions of dollars each day in and out of hundreds of financial institutions in Switzerland, for clients, and elsewhere. When confronted by the Swiss, the United States admitted it had been gathering the information with the cooperation of SWIFT.

This financial-transaction spying was, in fact, not limited to Switzerland, but included all SWIFT transfers worldwide, a total of 9 million wires representing approximately $6 trillion daily. Naturally, the reasons given were in support of "security" and in pursuit of terrorists. Unfortunately, it's unlikely that this ambitious undertaking was limited to potential terror financing; more likely it was a wide sweep in search of anything to be used then or in the future against whomever was caught in the dragnet. There are likely numerous ways this information could be improperly used, but one in particular comes to mind. Simply stated, the U.S. Treasury would like to know who banks in Switzerland. That juicy information could then become, for example, a starting point for an audit or investigation.

Fortunately, going back to what we know about Switzerland today, that result isn't as easy as it sounds. The United States would have to prove its case before a Swiss court before there would be any potential breach of Swiss bank secrecy. And, as you will learn in Chapter 3, audits initiated by the IRS or U.S. Treasury don't have much success when a tax haven or offshore banking center is part of the taxpayer's strategy. The jurisdiction's secrecy laws and the lack of cooperation by these types of foreign financial institutions seriously impede the tax man's ability to complete the audit within the three-year time frame he is legally allotted to finish the job. Privacy does give one an advantage and helps preserve personal sovereignty and freedom too.

Now, if the account in question were cloaked within the Ultimate Investment Plan, as discussed in Chapter 6, the real owner's name is not going to appear on a wire transfer by the insurance company. Further, there would be no way to differentiate one wire transfer from another, and certainly none could be assigned to a particular individual.

Swiss Franc

The Swiss franc has been the most consistent currency on the planet for decades. You'll hear me say this throughout the book like a mantra, but there's a good reason. There are strong currencies and then there are *strong* currencies. Today, only a handful of currencies can be categorized as strong, such as the Canadian dollar, the British pound, the Japanese yen, the Australian dollar, the euro, the Singapore dollar, the Norwegian kroner, the Swedish Krona and the Danish Krone. Currencies fluctuate daily against each other, and as they do, there is the opportunity to make money. But the principal reason that most of the world's currencies are weak compared to those just named is that the rest of these countries have varying degrees of liberal monetary policies, but today, virtually all currencies are soft currencies, with nothing of real value to back them up.

What's coming next may sound long-winded, but I want to lay some groundwork for an understanding on the subject of money so you will know why the Swiss franc excels and why it can help us to stand on sound economic footing.

There's always an enormous temptation for governments to increase their money supply. It's easy! Just hit the switch, and let the presses roll!

Of course, it's almost human nature to want to spend, and it's simple to understand the temptation for those who can to just print more cash. Often, it appears that this occurs with no conscience whatsoever, except for the fact that those who order the printing presses really don't want to get caught inflating the economy. Plain and simple, the main result of printing too much of this bogus money, also known as fiat money or paper backed by nothing of real value like gold, is that it causes inflation. Regardless of what any government person or government economist declares, this is the *real* cause of inflation. And increasing the money supply is not an exact science. The outcome cannot be accurately predicted. But when those in charge want to artificially *stimulate* the economy outside of *real* growth, typically they print more money.

Unfortunately, this is not stimulation as a result of real growth created from a healthy, productive economy. It is purely artificial. And if these guys don't get the desired results, they often stimulate it further. Should the economy overheat from all this excitement, inflation can climb. In 1980 we experienced 20 percent inflation. Had it gone just a trifle higher, say 25 percent, we could have experienced hyperinflation: runaway inflation to the point of no recovery. That's when the heads of kings and dictators begin to roll from the guillotines, and governments collapse, usually followed by a new leader who brazenly does the same thing but under totalitarian rule.

In a democracy, presidents don't get re-elected, even when it's the Fed who is actually making the calls.

The only victims of this mess are the poor citizens who supported the bad habit in the first place by trusting their leaders too much and contributing generously in the form of taxes. Tax collecting is a government's primary way of generating revenue to pay its operating expenses. And since governments can *never* get enough money, they also opt to print it. When money is printed, it causes all the other notes in circulation to become less valuable and erodes purchasing power and contributes to further inflation; essentially it amounts to no more than a transfer of wealth away from the rightful owners. Literally, it's a form of stealing.

Borrowing is another option that attracts investment money through issuing debt instruments that pay a return. Of course, inevitably, repayment is required. Fortunately, as a last resort, the government can print more money. Another means for a country to fatten the treasury is through confiscating private assets.

Minimal fluctuation between inflation and deflation is desirable to maintain a stable and strong currency. A conservative monetary policy is an essential factor and contributes to building a healthy economy. But a currency may be labeled strong merely because it's strong in relation to other currencies. A currency not backed by anything of value may still appear strong if the country is experiencing real or artificially stimulated growth and productivity, which could disguise the underlying truth that the currency does not have real value. However, eventually, what goes up will come down, unless those bills represent something of real value. A country's currency should be its storehouse of value and wealth. How is this possible if the currency is not backed by gold or silver or another hard asset? Without this backing, whether the currency is going down or up, it is only play money, like the stuff you get in your Monopoly set. And it will be just a matter of time before the practice of debasing the currency leads to political ruin.

The United States dollar was backed by gold until Richard Nixon took the United States off the gold standard in 1971. Since then the country has had a fiat currency backed by nothing. That's right—even the almighty dollar! Later, when we deal with the topic of gold, we'll have a further discussion on the business of gold and money. This action alone sent the world economy spinning in the 1970s.

Many governments today are operating by the "Tricky Dick" plan. Switzerland, however, has steadily maintained a conservative monetary policy, proving that doing so is not impossible, if a government wants to exercise self-control. The problem is that the majority of voters are putting politicians in office and voting themselves financial benefits right out of the U.S. Treasury. We really need to examine our own responsibility in these outcomes. *But let's blame the politicians anyway—they deserve it too, and it feels so good.* At least it does to me.

Unfortunately, as our representatives, politicians are, in part, doing what we want them to do. Choosing a candidate to vote for is one way to get something we perceive to be in our self-interest. We find a politician who will make the promises we want to hear in order to get elected. Then we hope to hold that politician to those promises after he or she gets in office. This process happens in other countries too. What *we the people* need to do is become more self-reliant, cinch up our belts a bit more tightly, even if our lifestyles are less splash and dash as we'd like, and stop making unreasonable demands on politicians. The cost to run the government could, and would, drop drastically, requiring less money to support it. At the same time, we must make our leaders accountable, both the administration in power and the acting Congress. The problem is that it's too painful, and too many people would have to share the same desire. That's not likely; human nature will prevail. We just want to feel good as long as possible—that is, before the rug gets pulled out from under us.

Then maybe it's time to exchange our U.S. dollars for Swiss francs or another strong currency. But, you ask, who's going to accept Swiss francs in America or Canada? We know the grocery store won't, but there are ways around this apparent problem, as we will see later in the book. Meanwhile, it's important to understand that the Swiss franc is one of the best currencies in the world, even though, I am sad to say, they went off the gold standard. Until a few years ago, the franc was the most stable, best-managed currency in the world. It was also backed by a basket of real assets in other forms, conservatively invested and realistically valued on the books by the Swiss National Bank. As a strong currency, the Swiss franc had no worries and no peers. Today, a conservative monetary policy contributes to its stability. The outside world perceives that it is strong because it has a long tradition of strength and the Swiss economy is healthy, but that's it.

The new Constitution passed in 1999 stated:

Article 99 Monetary Policy

1. Money and currency are a federal matter. The Confederation shall have the exclusive right to coin money and to issue bank notes.
2. As an independent central bank, the Swiss National Bank shall pursue a monetary policy serving the interests of the country as a whole; it shall be administered with the cooperation and under the supervision of the Confederation.
3. The Swiss National Bank shall create sufficient monetary reserves from its earnings; a part of these reserves shall be held in gold.
4. At least two-thirds of the net profits of the Swiss National Bank shall accrue to the Cantons.

Item 3 refers to gold reserves, but no criterion was established for how much gold. Since the passage of this constitution, I have been assured from Zurich that the currency is no longer backed by gold. You can see from this monetary policy passage who the responsible party for this decision is: the Swiss National Bank. The country's storehouse of value has been abolished, just as what happened in 1971 in the United States. This is a disturbing fact. If an initiative were put before Swiss voters asking whether they would like to keep the real value behind the Swiss franc or not—the national storehouse of the country's wealth— I'm pretty certain they wouldn't have chosen to end gold backing for their currency. Why? They would immediately lose.

Fortunately, Swiss citizens through their direct democracy have voted down EU membership, against the will of some in the government. That's power in the hands of the people. It's too bad that the nation's monetary policy is independently administered, as in the United States, or the will of the people could have prevented the franc from falling off the gold standard. The world's currencies today are all free-floating, soft currencies; none are gold-backed and all are at the mercy of the fiscal policies and practices of their Central Bankers. The next best thing to a hard currency, one backed by gold or other real asset with proven value, is a conservative monetary policy that keeps the fluctuations between inflation and deflation to a minimum. So far the Swiss National Bank has succeeded at this. In a monetary policy report issued by the bank on March 15, 2007, inflation from early 2003 to late 2006 fluctuated from a low of 0.06 to a high of 1.33 percent inflation. That's still pretty good, as few currencies in the world have such low inflation.

Since the Swiss voters have tightened up immigration, their votes won't be diluted as quickly by foreign immigrants who have their own agendas, as can happen in time with enough immigrants in a country. A liberal immigration policy can change the face of the voting body at large. The new citizens will tend to vote for what they want, not what has been done traditionally. In Switzerland, since the voters are not making it easy to immigrate there, the Swiss ought to have a better chance to reject EU membership in the future.

The Schweizerische Nationalbank, or the Swiss National Bank, started in 1907, is the issuer of the national currency, and it functions as the central clearinghouse for all Swiss banks. If their monetary practices were to change significantly—which is an unpleasant thought indeed—then there would be need for concern. But this is unlikely in the foreseeable future. Switzerland has carefully maintained a conservative monetary policy that has created a healthy economic environment. Keeping the money supply in line to avoid wide fluctuations in the currency is critical for any country. Only in this way can a country hope to prevent inflation and create stability in its economy that affords more productivity and an increase in commerce and industry so that *real* growth can be fostered.

The reader would do well to be practical and let wisdom prevail, and as soon as possible. Translated, this means to have your cash position in Swiss francs or other strong currency. And to hedge yourself even further with a basket of strong currencies equally divided between them. You can take charge of your own destiny and create *your own personal monetary policy,* as discussed in Chapter 4. Taking it a step further, invest yourself in the real thing: gold. Later you'll learn why I would personally balance that with silver. Then reduce your own spending and cut your debt to as little as possible. As your country is debasing its currency through poor fiscal management, you will discover that you, through your own excellent management, are in a financially strong position. I will discuss these ideas more later in the book.

Just because the country's going to hell in a hand basket and the government can't control its spending, it's no reason for you to go down the drain, too. You have a choice. The long-term trend for the U.S. dollar is down. In fact, in the first quarter of 2007 alone, the U.S. dollar lost 7 percent of its value against the Swiss franc. Many experts forecast that the dollar will lose 50 percent value in the next five years. Can you afford these kinds of losses, which are happening regularly? Once the holders of the world's reserve currency, we are quickly losing that status daily as foreign governments, foreign investors, and, yes, individual Americans are getting out of the dollar for fear of its imminent collapse. It is possible that the U.S. government may even officially devalue the dollar in the coming future. Everyday that you hold U.S. dollars or other funds that have no real value and are dwindling daily, you are experiencing a loss. You need to move out of the dollar before it becomes entirely worthless. There's a strong indication that this decline will not be ending any time soon, and it may be the dollar's demise.

Your personal financial survival plan is that simple. By taking easy-to-follow steps like these, you can and *will* stop your own financial hemorrhage. Your personal worth will be intact, will stay intact, and, over time, will even appreciate in value. And that's even *before* you embark on the profitable strategies that I also present. By getting out of the dollar and into Swiss francs or other strong currencies, and then by using some of the Swiss banking and investment options detailed in this book, you will be set to weather the future with financial security and great peace of mind.

Chapter 3

Where to Begin

Opening a Swiss Bank Account

"Because of what appears to be a lawful command on the surface, many citizens, because of their respect for the law, are cunningly coerced into waiving their rights, due to ignorance."
—U.S. VS. MINKER, 350 U.S. 179, 187

B anking in Switzerland offers all of the benefits of banking that most Americans are already experiencing, plus a few more, but without most of the drawbacks that we must continually contend with. In fact, no doubt most U.S. citizens would quickly move their banking if they were offered the advantages and services that the Swiss have experienced for decades.

In fact, the single biggest hindrance for Americans or Canadians to move their banking to Switzerland would likely be the factor of distance and the feeling of not being *close* to one's money. But let's start with that thought: *Distance* might also be a benefit, as that fact, coupled with strict secrecy laws, means that it won't be so simple for an outsider—creditor, spouse, your boss, or your government—to gain easy access to your money and your affairs. That's a definite bonus, and what's more, you will be all the while availing yourself of the sophistications of a Swiss bank.

Your money could be held in a very liquid state or you could be as invested as you like. And all, or certainly a significant part, of your money can be held in a form and in an account that you can access from afar easily. By now, many Americans and others are conducting a fair amount of their daily banking online, giving them a heretofore unknown ability to do banking immediately, from home, and 24/7, without the need to travel to the bank, wherever it may be.

Further, funds in Switzerland are easily accessible any time of the day by credit card, debit card, automated teller machine, faxed wire transfers (if desired), and telephone banking. In other words, geography does not need to play a significant role in today's banking. It may feel good, though, to know that your bank is just around the corner. But nowadays banking in Switzerland is about as convenient as banking in the next town. As a matter of fact, you can conduct most of it sitting at your computer, fax machine, or telephone; occasionally you might need to courier written instructions.

The benefits of banking in Switzerland include the general advantages of banking offshore, of which there are many. These include:

- The opportunity to diversify investments
- Strategies to defer taxes
- Immediate, strong, long-term asset protection
- Tax-free compound investment earnings
- Greater privacy and flexibility
- The possibility of higher investment returns
- Avoidance of currency restrictions or other serious limitations
- Geodiversity
- Greater safety and security
- Currency and investment diversification
- Greater convenience when traveling
- Avoidance of the possibility of U.S. securities markets and banks closing due to an unforeseen national emergency

- Circumvention of potential failure of U.S. financial institutions and government agencies
- Avoidance, in some cases, of U.S. reporting requirements to the Internal Revenue Service and the U.S. Treasury
- The exercise of your rights and freedoms to do the things that are still legal to increase your financial position and security
- Avoidance of disclosure of your national or political alliances
- Positive exposure to new financial opportunities

The Swiss banks in particular, have a real advantage, in fact, a significant edge over most offshore banking jurisdictions in the world today. *That's right.* Even with the occasional controversy that has swirled around Swiss banks and the famous Swiss bank secrecy—such as the past ties to Nazis; the occasional news of colorful depositors including organized criminals, swindlers, dictators, political leaders, and others who have benefited from parking their funds in this alpine enclave—in record numbers, frightened money from lesser luminaries continues to seek the secrecy, peace of mind, and stability and financial expertise that Swiss banking offers. Little has really changed in Swiss banking in the past 60 years. The Swiss are still practicing their trade like good basketweavers ply their craft in Ecuador: providing the finest banking anywhere.

As mentioned earlier, these days it is said that as much as 40 percent of the entire world's private wealth is managed from Switzerland. That's a lot of money, and so much wealth having been deposited indicates a lot of trust. This is money that seeks:

- Easy access to world financial markets without discrimination
- Economic and political stability in an otherwise very unstable world
- The strength of the country's currency, the Swiss franc, which historically has been strong
- High bank liquidity, sometimes as high as several hundred percent
- Excellent bank management that has resulted in few failures over the course of time
- Excellent banking infrastructure
- Strong bank secrecy that cannot be matched in most tax havens
- Free movement of capital into and out of the country
- Monetary freedom unlike anywhere else

- A wide array of bank and financial services not found in banks elsewhere
- A history of standing up against the whimsical requests and high pressures of foreign governments, particularly the United States.
- The best investing skills and quality service
- A healthy respect for their clients' business, privacy and security

How does your local bank compare?

Switzerland is the third largest financial center in the world, just behind London and New York. Its banks are managing nearly $35 trillion in private assets out of nearly $90 trillion managed by banks worldwide. Switzerland is the leading money and asset haven. It is the oldest democracy in the world, from which the United States could take a few lessons. And, unlike the United States, Switzerland *is* a free-enterprise country with minimal government regulation and economic control. It has political stability, and it is fiscally conservative with a low money growth so it can enjoy low inflation—features not found in many parts of the world. There are no exchange controls restricting the free movement of capital. And, unlike most of Europe, the people of Switzerland did themselves a favor and voted against joining the European Union, thus retaining their independence, holding on to their financial standing among nations, preserving their national sovereignty, and ensuring the highest standard of banking *and* standard of living.

By starting your own Swiss banking and investment program now, you can gain immediate relief from the niggling concerns you have been harboring, those internal voices you've been hearing, and those gut feelings that keep reminding you of impending danger, including, no doubt, occasional dark thoughts of financial ruin and other nasties that could hamper your fun. Those bad feelings are real and are simply the reflection of the state of our world, of the precarious crossroads at which we know our country stands at today, and our own state of mind in which prosperity and happiness seem to elude us. With your Swiss plan in place, you will experience real financial freedom. Once you have that, you can work on other freedoms important to your happiness as a sovereign individual.

If your boat is taking on water, you need to plug the leaks, and maybe tighten the thru-hole values that are allowing water to seep into your bilge. But if the water's coming onboard quickly, there's probably no time to bail. Just grab the kids, inflate the lifeboat, and clear the decks before she goes down. At this stage, they usually go down fast. How will you fare if things in your personal life, or in the country, take a turn for the worse? Are the perceived threats real? Where are the leaks that threaten your personal existence and stability, your individual freedoms, and your financial state? In order to better secure your financial future and physical well-being, you must identify the problems quickly, stop the leaks, circumvent the troubles, and navigate the seas to safety. Better yet, you need a plan of action *before* trouble strikes and emergency provisions for when it does.

Historically, during monetary crises in other parts of the world, Swiss banks have experienced a wave of increased business. This could be a problem for anyone waiting until it's an emergency to open an account. Banks may become more selective about whose business they will take, looking closely at a person's national origin, making the opening requirements tougher, perhaps by increasing the minimum opening deposit requirement or the minimum necessary to maintain an account. If you're already established, new requirements would likely have no bearing on your account. Some of these requirements have already changed. In general, recently there has been a perceptible change in attitude toward U.S. citizens and other U.S. taxpayers. Their business is not quite as welcome as it once was, and fewer banks are open to their investments. Why wait till it's too late? The best time to plan for the worse possible moment is in advance, while doing so is still possible. Insure your future monetary freedom now!

Types of Swiss Banks

There is a variety of banks in Switzerland from which to choose: big banks, private banks, cantonal banks, savings banks, commercial banks, mortgage banks, local banks, loan associations, and other banks. From these, you should be able to locate one that suits your requirements. Switzerland recognizes the "universal" bank, which provides for a wide variety of financial services that overlap from bank to bank, and the country does not distinguish between commercial and investment banks. And the universal bank is permitted to offer private banking services. Recently Swiss banks have experienced a series of acquisitions and mergers that have thinned their ranks from about 550 just 10 years ago to around 350 today. Industry changes have helped beef up the existing banks and have made them even more competitive. The U.S. government has pressured the Swiss banking industry to discourage banks from doing business with U.S. taxpayers. This has had an impact, but it hasn't shut out U.S. persons just yet. They will just have to look a bit harder to find a bank willing to take their action.

Now, if you have a minimum of $1 million that you'd like a nice conservative-looking Swiss banker to manage, many of them would like to speak with you. If you are just looking to open a modest bank or savings account where you can park some cash for a while, you may have to shop for a Swiss bank that will accept smaller depositors. So that you are armed with good sources that will increase your likelihood of success, I have included in Appendix A, a listing of 270 Swiss banks with their names, addresses, telephone and fax numbers, e-mail addresses, Web sites, and listing of what type of bank they are. After you have found a few worth considering and made contact, go to www.fitchratings.com and check out their financial prowess in comparison to the others.

Big Banks

There used to be three big Swiss banks, known as the Big Three: Swiss Bank Corporation, Credit Suisse Bank, and Union Bank of Switzerland (UBS). Over time, two additional banks joined the ranks, Bank Leu and Swiss Volksbank, to create what became known as the Big Five.

The landscape has changed a lot since then. The "Big Five" eventually became the "Big Two," after UBS, gobbled up Swiss Bank Corporation, transforming UBS into a mammoth in the world of banking. UBS manages $2.12 trillion in assets worldwide. In 2007, Credit Suisse merged its five independent banks to become Clariden Leu. These are truly global giants. Although large and powerful, they offer every type of banking service imaginable. As they are also known as universal banks, they are, interestingly, less liquid than some much smaller Swiss banks. Liquidity will be discussed shortly. UBS and Clariden Leu are not *pure* banks, and therefore, they are very active as foreign exchange dealers, stock brokers, and bullion merchants. They have subsidiaries around the world in many related financial, investment, commercial, real estate, and commodity industries that complement their diverse banking activities. They are publicly traded on SWX Swiss Exchange, and they seek business from around the world.

One significant drawback to these banks, and other banks that have branches or divisions in other countries, especially in the United States, is that the host government can exert pressures on the foreign bank due to the bank's presence on U.S. soil. Recently there has been an overt effort to obtain otherwise secret information on Americans with accounts in Switzerland. In theory, this action could happen elsewhere, whenever a government feels it needs to obtain otherwise confidential records on their citizens. There are enough banking choices in Switzerland so that you should not feel compelled to do business with any banks that have operations in your country. Doing so could prove fatal to your privacy.

On that note, I want to remind readers that "U.S. persons" are required by law to declare signatory power over a foreign financial account by filing the annual Treasury Form TD F 90.22-1, *if* the account has an aggregate value over US$10,000 or equivalent in another currency. By filing, clearly, your account becomes known to the government, and this information could be considered a red flag. However, remember that filing *does not* indicate any illegal activity. And by filing the form, due on June 30 for the previous year, you need not worry that you will raise anything more than possible suspicion, if the government is paying attention at all. And in the case of Switzerland, unless there is some real criminal activity that *is considered as such by the Swiss,* whether your Swiss account is known to exist or not, your government and the rest of them you left behind are not going to be able to touch your money or your information. The only potential exception to this is the future possibility that your government—and I am primarily thinking of the United States—could force its taxpayers to repatriate any funds and investments held overseas. I'll continue with this disturbing thought later in the book. But since Switzerland has not signed a Tax Information Exchange Agreement (TIEA), the United States won't be able to get your account information easily. (Chapter 8 describes the TIEA.)

Check the banks that are of interest to you and determine if they have facilities in your country. If so, keep shopping; you'll eventually find one that suits you. Also, the deposit requirements will vary, and be less at some, and more at others. For instance, UBS will open an account for you with US$25,000. Expect the deposit requirements to be higher with most Swiss banks—US$50,000, $100,000, or even $250,000— although you can open an account with far less at some of the banks.

Private Banks

Private banks are a separate category of bank. They are unincorporated, general or limited partnerships, and unlike most banks in Switzerland, they are not universal banks. Even the genteel business of private banking is changing today. Once a staid, traditional business, the private banking game has gone global. Neighborhood banks that once offered the Swiss and nearby Europeans cozy sanctuaries for building their estates far from the prying eyes of their own governments have recently been branching out in search of more members to join the "Millionaire's Club."

This is an area of specialization known in the business as investment portfolio management, where frequently $1 million is required for a discretionary account. The world has become much wealthier, and Swiss private bankers are getting more innovative as to how they attract potential business. And the business they want is the multimillionaires, the global elite from the far corners of the world. In its 2006 Global Wealth Report, Boston Consulting Group estimates that there are 7.2 million millionaire households.

At one time, the focus of private banks was stocks and bonds, but today they are heavily invested in hedge funds, private equity, and institutional investments. Switzerland is also ranked number three in commodities trading. Its increasingly diverse investment selection appeals to rich foreign investors. Today's private Swiss banker, a new breed born from generations of banking dynasties, is no longer satisfied with staying put in the land of fine chocolate, precision-made watches, and noisy cuckoo clocks. Rather he has branched out to Asia, Latin America, the United States, and even China in an aggressive effort to capture new business.

Swiss bankers are also motivated by competition. Aside from the other quaint little banking and asset havens of Liechtenstein, Andorra, and Austria nestled in Europe, Dubai and Singapore are also doing very well at appealing to the needs of rich foreign investors and are proving to be effective private asset managers themselves. Private Swiss bankers take pride in affording their clients with personalized service and the best of what Swiss banking is about. Generally, the older banks are more conservative. Private bankers can tailor your investments to meet your desires, and as a rule of thumb, they strive for capital preservation, asset growth, and maximized investment returns without taking unnecessary risk.

Today, to open a private banking account, you usually have to make a personal visit, so that you can meet with your future banker and discuss your needs. In fewer cases, it is possible to open a discretionary account entirely by mail. Private banks do not provide demand and savings accounts typically associated with general banking, as they are not authorized to solicit deposits. If you want those services, contact a universal bank, like a big bank, or a cantonal, savings, or other bank. For private banking, a minimum of a least US$500,000, but typically $1 million or more may be required. There are exceptions, and I know of one that will provide a discretionary account with a minimum of US$200,000, but in this case, you will have to travel to Switzerland for a private meeting.

Cantonal Banks

Switzerland is geographically divided into 26 cantons, individual regions each with a high degree of political and economic autonomy. The individual cantonal governments authorized and often provided the initial capitalization for local banks, which once were the actual issuers of the currency and coin in their respective cantons. Today, these banks are principally made up of general commercial banks, but they also include some savings banks, mortgage banks, and loan associations. Cantonal banks exist mostly to provide banking services and financing needs to the local business and real estate trades and assist local government funding. They also accept business from overseas.

Although there is no deposit insurance, such as a Federal Deposit Insurance Corporation (FDIC), as we know it in the United States, the cantons themselves guarantee all bank deposits. The initial deposit requirement is likely to be low. Cantonal banks would be good places to begin your search for an appropriate Swiss bank, and typically they offer a wide variety of services. It's likely best to approach banks outside of the cantons of Zurich or Geneva, where the majority of high-powered bankers reside, as the requirements there probably are higher.

Savings Banks

Savings banks offer a variety of savings accounts, even check-writing services. Their primary focus is to encourage thrift in the community and use the funds on deposit for lending for the benefit of the local community. Unlike cantonal banks, savings banks are not organized by the government. They do accept business from overseas. Expect a reasonable minimum opening deposit, and remember that deposits in a cantonal savings bank are guaranteed by the canton.

How to Select a Swiss Bank

This book gives you contacts for most of the main branches of all types and sizes of Swiss banks located throughout the country. As you don't reside in Switzerland, location would be of minimal impor-tance. The larger Swiss banking centers include Zurich, Geneva, Basel, Lausanne, Berne, Lucerne, and Lugano. The most significant difference among these areas are the language and customs that influ-ence the different regions of Switzerland. The German-speaking region in the north includes Zurich, Basel, Lucerne, and Bern; Geneva and Lausanne are found in the French-speaking region in the west; Lugano in the canton of Ticino is in the Italian-speaking region in the south; and Romansh is spoken in San Moritz to the southeast. Fortunately, most bankers in Switzerland are multilingual. Bankers in Zurich and Geneva typically speak fluent English, as in many other Swiss cities, and German, French and Italian are common, of course, especially in their respective regions.

Although their English may be difficult to follow, if you are flexi-ble and like the challenge, it can be fun speaking to foreigners who are making wholehearted attempts to speak your language. Generally, I've found that their intent is well meant, even at moments when it may sound unfriendly, cold, or short. I would not take it personally. This applies also to written English translations of correspondence. The important thing to know is that, generally, the Swiss are quite understandable and definitely service-oriented. Fortunately, they are also very civil and efficient people and take their business and your business and your money seriously.

In the smaller banks, from the moment you contact your bank-to-be, you will be turned over to a person who will be *your* banker. Unless the person changes departments or leaves the bank, he or she may be the only person you ever deal with at the bank. So, if you can establish a good rapport with this individual, your banking experience will likely be more personal and efficient. In fact, life with your new Swiss banker should run very smoothly. That person will be very plugged in to you, who you are, what your interests are, your previous communications and instructions, and how you handle yourself. They may even get to know your voice. Of course, if your Swiss bank is a private one, you will have what is known as a relationship banker who will handle every detail of your account and know where you stand with your investments. In larger banks, although you may be more like a number, the service will generally still be of very high quality.

Liquidity

One important factor in banking in Switzerland versus the United States and many other places is that the banks are financially sound. The number-one factor in selecting a Swiss bank may be the liquidity of the bank itself, especially if you are concerned about the possibility of bank failures or a catastrophic international banking crisis, which may be possible if the derivative market blows sky high or other world events come to pass. As there is no government agency that guarantees deposits and the Swiss federal government itself guarantees only some deposits—and even this could change—the strength of your bank may be of greatest importance to you, especially if you're keeping your entire fortune in it. But the fear of losing your money in a Swiss bank should be minimal, because, unlike in the United States, where American depositors have witnessed the failure of hundreds and hundreds of banks in the not-so-distant past, and many more in the 1920s and 1930s during the Great Depression, Swiss banks rarely fail. Now, isn't that good to know? The possibility of bank failure happening again in the United States and perhaps elsewhere is very real.

As mentioned, the exception regarding the lack of guarantee for deposits in Switzerland, is that, the deposits in the canton banks *are* guaranteed by the regional canton governments. These banks range from small to large, and they can provide a wide range of quality service. You may find that a cantonal bank will service your general banking requirements best. Also, they are not likely to have overseas branches, and therefore, any presence in your country.

Liquidity is defined as the ability to pay off current liabilities, that is, depositors, in particular, and other obligations, particularly short-term ones, in general, with liquid assets, either cash or assets that can be quickly liquidated to satisfy withdrawals by customers on demand and meet the bank's ongoing operating expenses. Of course, long-term obligations must be met too; however, that is of less consequence in the immediate moment, as banks typically have used these funds for long-term investments that provide a higher return. When the investments are liquidated, they offset the inevitable demand of long-term deposits. If a bank ultimately cannot give its investors their money that is held in cash accounts and in non–time-deposit-type accounts on demand, then they will have disgruntled customers, and worse. To be liquid and able to meet these standard demands and obligations as they arise in the short term does not require banks to hold that sum in cash alone. Funds also can be held in other forms that can be made immediately liquid or converted into cash within the very short term. Banks have a variety of options available to operate profitably and remain liquid, including keeping cash on deposit with other banks to make transfers and spread risk, but only within demand accounts so as to provide liquidity. Also, they may grant call loans or margin accounts to borrowers, which are profitable for the banks and that borrowers must repay on demand. These loans are collateralized, and the collateral, such as securities and precious metals, are in held in the bank's vault. More on margin accounts follows in this chapter.

It is unlikely for a Swiss bank to run into trouble due to poor management. Government examiners scrutinize the banks' financial statements extremely closely. And, as mentioned, the cantonal banks provide added security for depositors. And, of course, the Swiss are much more prudent than U.S. banks with their decision making. One Swiss bank was begun in the 1970s by an American, Paul Erdman, who was representing a California bank that got into a little trouble. Erdman later became a best-selling novelist, writing his first novel, *The Billion Dollar Sure Thing,* while sitting in a Swiss jail. In Switzerland, incidentally, it doesn't matter what caused a bank to fail; the head of the bank will be held accountable and responsible first. But those were unusual circumstances and an exception to the rule of superior management of Swiss banks. By the way, all of Erdman's novels are entertaining and based on Swiss banking, something he knows a lot about.

Swiss banks are required to publish financial statements periodically, typically twice a year, depending on their size. The standards for financial reporting vary by country, and, unless you are an accountant, the reports can be difficult to understand, making the liquidity ratio not easy to determine. However, the ideal situation is to have a bank, that if caught in a global banking disaster—and it would have to be global because it would be next to impossible to have an isolated Swiss banking disaster—could not only pay off all its obligations, but likely even remain in business. That's the safest bank with which to do business. This bank would have to have *at least* 100 percent liquidity; and even one that wasn't quite that liquid probably would survive a major problem. However, 100 percent or, better yet, greater liquidity would insure that customers would recover all of their deposited funds even if they all showed up at the same time to withdraw all their money. And, under an extreme scenario like this, if the bank had well in excess of 100 percent liquidity, it's possible it could continue operating with no help from government. Not bad. That's the way to run a bank!

A few banks boast liquidity ratios of up to several hundred percent. Big banks, although more leveraged, have the advantage and ability to access cash faster and from more places. And banks with a higher percentage of liquidity, even if short of 100 percent, stand a much better chance of surviving a real crisis. You can obtain a current financial statement from your bank of choice. If it's in English, it's a sign that the bank might consider accepting an account from an American or Canadian. You can also review it yourself or find someone, such as your accountant, to determine the bank's actual percentage of liquidity. A better measure of a bank's strength is *liquid* assets (very salable assets like exchange traded securities and other highly marketable assets), not *semiliquid* assets (those whose value may change by the time they are sold, or that most likely would not fetch their real value in a fire sale, or that are difficult to unload because there's not much of a market). Leave out those types of assets when dividing the liquid asset figure by the current liability figure to arrive at the percentage of liquidity.

On a Personal Note
When my grandmother closed the First State Bank of Williams, Montana in the 1930s due to the death of her father, and my great-grandfather, H. L. Barber, the controlling shareholder of the bank, it was liquidated to the profit of all shareholders. This bank had survived the depression! A lot of banks weren't so fortunate in those days. If H. L. had still been alive, he'd have kept it going, as it was the central source of financing for the two Montana towns he founded, Williams and Manson, and it supported many of the local farmers and businesses. Unfortunately, when he died and the bank was closed, the towns, which he had still owned much of, began a gradual decline. But, his bank was proved to be liquid, and his depositors did not lose a dime.

Types of Swiss Bank Accounts

This section presents a sampling of the types of accounts that a Swiss bank might offer. The process of opening a Swiss bank account is simple once you've found a bank to your liking that is also ready, willing, and able to do business with you, based on the level of your deposit and your possible status as a "U.S. person." Now, with your new Swiss bank account, you will have immediately achieved several important accomplishments. Once your funds are moved into the bank, you have gained international diversification of your financial holdings and engaged strong asset protection for your cash, investments and other valuables. And, instead of being able to hold only U.S. dollars, you can choose from virtually any major world currency. You have also just availed yourself of the wide array of financial and banking services that Swiss banks offer. Let's take a look at some of the types of accounts you'll find. Please note that I have not included specific interest rates as these are subject to change and would vary by bank.

Current (Demand) Account

The basic account in a foreign country is a current account similar to a checking account in the United States. However, checks generally are not available. The account could be denominated in any one major currency offered by the bank. Additional accounts normally are required for each additional currency. Current accounts are non–interest-bearing accounts.

Deposit, Private, or Personal Account

Deposit, private, or personal accounts are interest-bearing accounts, similar to savings accounts or passbook accounts. The bank might offer a variety of major currencies that you can hold. Interest rates are notoriously low and are offset by the safety of the funds. Being generally very solid and liquid, Swiss banks attract depositors even though they don't offer much in the way of interest in return.

Savings (Passbook) Account

A savings (passbook) account pays interest. Again, usually interest paid in Switzerland is on the low side. This is the price investors pay for stability. These accounts provide ready access to your money. The bank may send you a monthly statement or you may be offered a passbook.

Fixed Term Deposits

Fixed term deposit accounts pay a higher rate of interest than other types of accounts. You are required to leave the funds on deposit for a certain term, and in return you are paid a higher interest rate. Funds cannot be accessed on demand, only when the term comes due.

Multicurrency Account

A multicurrency account is a demand account like a checking account but is denominated in multiple currencies. Checks are generally available and can be written in any of the currencies offered. Before the euro was introduced, this type of account was especially handy when traveling in Europe. Multicurrency accounts are non–interest-bearing.

Twin Account

Twin accounts include the features of both a demand account and a savings account. Often a bank provides two accounts that are linked to one another. They may also be denominated in different currencies. The savings account will pay low interest.

Commercial Account

The commercial account is similar to a personal current account but is used for receiving deposits and making payments for a business. It is usually a company's general account. A checkbook is usually available. Banks that offer commercial accounts are likely to provide other business-related banking requirements, including investment assistance, currency transactions, lending facilities, financial information, access to Swiss capital markets, equity-based compensation, structured financing, syndications, and trade finance. Your Swiss banker can also tailor a financial solution to your requirements.

Certificate of Deposit

Certificates of deposit (CDs) may be denominated in a choice of major currencies. They are usually bearer form, and as such, they are easily transferable. Foreign-currency CDs are also available for different periods of time, up to five years. Usually there is no withholding tax on them and you can be earning interest payments *tax-free*. CDs pay higher interest rates than savings accounts. Interest rates will vary by bank.

Eurocurrency Deposits

Large sums are required for Eurocurrency deposits, so naturally the interest rates are higher. A Swiss bank will act as agent to place the depositor's money in the Eurocurrency market. Also known as Eurodollars, they are simply U.S. dollars on deposit by American banks with a foreign counterpart or one of their foreign branches in Europe. Also, some

Swiss private banks and London merchant banks specialize in Eurocurrency placements. Swiss holding taxes are not imposed. They are not regulated by the U.S. Federal Reserve Board or U.S. Securities and Exchange Commission.

Money Market Account

Money market accounts offer a higher interest rate than typical savings accounts. The best part is that your earnings are tax-free. Funds may be deposited and withdrawn without restriction. Several currencies are available. The denomination of the currency can change anytime you choose. Larger banks offer this type of account. Benefits will vary by bank.

Margin Account

A margin account is actually two accounts, a custodial account for holding the security or precious metal and a current account, providing a statement indicating the money you owe. In many cases, and without needing to be based on credit criteria or decisions, the bank with loan up to 50 percent against your asset, which the bank holds as collateral. Margin accounts are a good way to increase your investments or holdings when all is going fine and a fast way to lose the same when the trend is in reverse. The bank wins either way.

Precious Metals Account

A precious metals account is for the purpose of buying and selling gold, silver, platinum, and other precious metals on your behalf. The bank will store the precious metals in its vault for a small fee, or you can rent a safe deposit box from the bank and place the precious metals in the box yourself. You can also purchase the metals on margin, often up to 50 percent. In these cases, no credit check is required as the metals are used as collateral and kept in the bank's vault.

Fiduciary Account

A fiduciary account is ideal for investing anonymously, as the bank will keep assets in its name. As all the investments are made outside of Switzerland, you avoid Swiss taxes. Fiduciary accounts are worth looking into. You direct your Swiss investment manager regarding your investment choices.

Investment Accounts

Larger banks and private banks often can provide investment accounts to invest in mutual funds and commodities in your name. The funds will have different performances and may be denominated in different currencies, which has an effect on your investment returns. It is best to denominate your investments in the Swiss franc or another strong currency, such as the euro.

Managed Accounts

Managed accounts are popular with high-net-worth individuals. These accounts are the specialty of private banks. They will invest and manage funds and assets on your behalf in their name. In some cases, they will act on your instructions by letter, phone, fax, or in person. The minimum in Switzerland to open this type of account is usually the equivalent of US$1 million. There are exceptions to this requirement; sometimes a bank will allow a minimum of US$500,000. I work with one private bank that will accept a minimum of US$200,000. Banks justify the $1 million minimum by saying that they need this much in order to get the best investment diversification for the client, which may be correct. But well-heeled, high-net-worth clients are their preference. The best private banks strive to provide a high level of quality service and create a diversified portfolio of highly liquid investments, such as a basket of strong currencies and a multi-asset investment strategy with minimal risk. These accounts are frequently referred to as discretionary accounts, personal portfolio management, investment portfolio management, personal asset management, international investment management, or private asset management.

Custodial Account or Safekeeping Account

Custodial or safekeeping accounts are accounts that are segregated from the bank's own assets. The bank manages the assets on the customer's behalf. This type of account could even amount to the bank holding a sealed envelope or package that contains important documents or valuables on behalf of the client. The bank's service fee is based on a percentage of the value or is a set fee if there is no established value.

Other Accounts

Banks may offer other types of accounts, such as youth or senior savings accounts designed to provide unique benefits for their intended customers. Your bank representative will gladly explain the many accounts offered.

Giro Accounts

Swiss banks do not typically provide checks with an account, but instead use other methods as already discussed. The reason that checks are not common is, in part, because the Swiss have another system in place outside the banking system, known as the giro system, which is administered by the Swiss postal system. Basically, a giro account is a special checking account system used by locals to pay their bills and amounts smaller than they would normally keep in a current or savings account. The Swiss National Bank and all other Swiss banks have a giro system that interfaces with the postal giro system. Payments and balances between banks are easily cleared through the Swiss National Bank.

Safe Deposit Boxes

A safe deposit box in Switzerland is a sound way to physically safeguard your important documents and valuables. The biggest challenge is to physically get to your box. A trip to Switzerland may not be in the cards, and when you need something from it on short notice, retrieving it could be costly and inconvenient. A box in Switzerland would be good for long-term important papers, jewelry and precious metals, and so on. You could keep original documents there and perhaps retain a photocopy for reference in a safe place near you. The box would be a very safe place to keep things, and only you or your authorized party would have access. Of course, if necessary, you could give someone, including your attorney, if you trust him or her, a limited power of attorney to open the box and act on your behalf. Doing this could compromise security but may be necessary or convenient. The box is not reportable, and the only way to gain access would be by Swiss court order, which is not likely to happen. An alternative to a safe deposit box, or at least temporarily until you can get to your box, would be to establish a safekeeping or custodial account to hold your assets at the bank. You could send your assets by registered and insured mail, along with your instructions; they would remain in the custodial account until you get to Switzerland to place them in the safe deposit box yourself. Remember, when sending valuables and instruments exceeding US$10,000 out of the United States, you must declare them as required by U.S. Customs.

In the event of death, your heirs would have a chance to gain legal access to your safe deposit box through a Swiss court. Probably the existence and the contents of the box would remain "unknown" to your government and would effectively circumvent probation in your home country. Where there's a will, there's a way.

Credit Cards, Debit Cards, ATM Cards, and VTM Cards

Credit cards, debit cards, and automated teller machine (ATM) cards are often available from Swiss banks, especially universal banks and banks with commercial-type operations, including local and cantonal banks. A credit card is separate from any accounts and is issued based on personal or business credit. However, some banks offer a secured credit card whereby an amount is held on deposit and a credit limit is granted. Usually this limit is based on a percentage of the amount of the deposit. In other words, a card that the bank requires to be secured by 150 percent of the credit limit would mean you would have to deposit $15,000 for the privilege of charging $10,000. Naturally, you would receive a monthly statement, which you would have to pay like any other bill. If it is not paid within the terms on the card's agreement, your credit may be negatively affected if reported to a credit bureau. Prompt payment or paying off balances would have a positive effect on your credit. Of course, the deposited amount is security against the outstanding balance, so if you don't pay your credit card bills, eventually the bank will attach the deposit and apply it to the bill.

A debit card is an alternative choice to a credit card, and it is attached to a corresponding bank account. You use it like a credit card, but the funds are debited directly from your bank account. The card usually has the symbol of a credit card company, such as Visa, Master-Card, American Express, or other company, and it can be used wherever these symbols are found. These cards work fine, except you should use good discretion as to who has authorization to charge on the card, as your bank account could be drained by a thief. A Personal Identification Number (PIN) will allow you to get cash at ATM machines bearing the appropriate symbols.

Also, keep in mind that the card *is* connected to a bank account, and as mentioned, by law U.S. taxpayers are required to disclose such foreign accounts each year to the U.S. Treasury on form TD F 90.22-1, if the aggregate annual amount exceeds US$10,000 or its equivalent. Make sure you keep good track of the exchange rates throughout the year if your money is held in a foreign currency, so that if you wish to stay under this limit, you don't unknowingly exceed it by mistake due to currency fluctuations. Also, most of these credit cards companies are American and keep their records in the United States, within arm's reach of certain people, as some citizens have learned the hard way.

By squeezing the credit card companies at home, the U.S. government has been able to discover the existence of certain foreign bank accounts of U.S. taxpayers, often of persons who had not filed the required Treasury form for whatever reason. Hundreds of thousands of Americans have been themselves compromised in this manner. This is foolish; the penalties are too severe not to file the Treasury form. There is more on this subject later in the book in Chapter 5 under "U.S. Taxpayer Requirements." Then, of course, by filing, you might be waving at least a tiny red flag. You should weigh the risk against the potential gain or the potential loss.

Finally, many foreign banks will issue debit cards that are *not* attached to American credit card companies; rather, they are cards they issue themselves or that are serviced by a company within their jurisdiction. They may call them "courtesy cards" or "convenience cards," or something similar. These cards will allow you to access your funds at most ATM machines around the world, but without a record back home in the United States. The drawback usually is that you can use them only to access cash; you cannot present them for purchases.

All forms of ATM cards are attached to a bank account. By using a PIN, you can access funds from your account from anywhere in the world where the appropriate symbol is found.

The VTM or Visa Travel Money card is handy when traveling and an alternative to cash. It is not attached to a bank account but works like a debit card. The card is issued by a foreign bank that is part of the VTM program. You may be able to find one issued by a Swiss bank. The maximum amount that can be placed on the VTM card is US$10,000, However, you can apply for multiple cards. Although it's not a credit card nor a debit card, usually minimal information is required of the holder, including that the issuing bank may want a professional reference on you and, possibly, proof of identity. A VTM is electronic money and can be used only in ATM machines or similar electronic devices that can scan. Therefore, your transactions are anonymous. Your personal information is protected if the bank is located within a tax haven jurisdiction with strict bank secrecy, such as one of my annual T-7 list of the best tax haven countries.

Other Swiss Banking Facilities

Banks in Switzerland offer many types of services because Swiss banks, with the notable exception of private banks, are universal banks, which allows them to perform many functions outside of traditional banking as we know it. Not all banks operate as universal banks; some prefer to specialize in corporate business such as mergers and acquisitions; investment banking; commercial finance; custom financing based on industry demands; foreign trade financing; securities; futures; currency; precious metals; commodities trading; and forward contracts.

Aside from the banking services already mentioned, typical banking facilities and services include personal loans, mortgages, lines of credit, commercial loans, foreign currency exchange, letters of credit and other trade financing, money transfers, bank drafts, traveler's checks, credit cards, debit cards, ATM cards, safe deposit boxes, and more.

Opening Your Swiss Bank Account

Before opening your Swiss bank account, there are 20 things that you should consider.

Personal Visit to Switzerland

The way most people are accustomed to opening a bank account is to personally visit the bank. Of course, nowadays people frequently do this online. A personal visit to your new banking center, Switzerland, would be a very pleasant experience. You could take your next "vacation" there. You could visit banks along the Zurich's Bahnhafstrasse, a beautiful boulevard known for its banks. You also could explore a few of the cantons where you will find more local types of banks, big and small, that welcome overseas business and don't require large minimum initial deposits. You could literally shop for your bank and find the most suitable match. Your trip would likely be very productive and rewarding. And, in this way, you could ask all the questions you like of your new "personal" banker. You would come back having a much stronger sense of the country and having established a nice, personal, face-to-face relationship with your Swiss bank and personal banker. While there, you could open a safe deposit box and drop your important documents and valuables into it before you return. *Mission accomplished!*

However, a personal trip is not required in all cases. Some Swiss banks will open an account for you from long distance.

Opening Your Account by Mail

A common way to open a Swiss bank account is by mail. It's fairly private, convenient, and much cheaper. You can get the required documents together in your leisure, and the bank can fax any required bank forms to you or you can download them from the bank's Web site, all in the privacy of your home. Naturally, if you are worried about the bugs on the telephone line or about just how secure the Internet really is, and if privacy is an issue, the most discreet method might be by mail. The Swiss are very good at doing business by mail, and they know how to use the mails for the sake of a client's privacy; *this is automatic.*

For example, when you receive a letter or statement from your bank, it will be by air mail, in an innocuous-looking envelope with no bank name visible anywhere, bearing a nondescript address, with a postmark that may be the most revealing identification on it, and well sealed. To the untrained eye of most Americans, it would generally be difficult to determine from where it was sent. Swiss bankers have also been known to use their home address instead of the bank's address when sending mail to customers. Now, *that's* a commitment to their profession!

Mail Spies

But a sharp-eyed postal person or government agent trained in the ways of spying on your mail can spot this kind of mail. If they are authorized to do so, they have ways to take a peek at the contents. I'm confident that this kind of activity is occurring in the United States and elsewhere as I write, but it's like playing the odds—the minimal risk of using the mail versus not having a Swiss bank account. If by some chance you were unfortunate enough to be spied on, yes, the government might suspect you have a Swiss bank account, but that in itself is not a crime. That's where the trail ends, too, because even if they know which bank your account is in, they won't be able to get anything out of the bank, unless you should commit a crime that's also a crime by Swiss standards.

In recent years, due to 9/11 and in the name of "security," postal employees have been trained to spot suspicious mail and a variety of things that might be of interest to the government. This government snooping falls into the gray zone along with other shady government activities that are now justified and supported by the Patriot Act. All of this skullduggery is in the name of your "security." Now, do you feel more secure? It's a sign that you probably *need* a Swiss bank account, or better still, the Ultimate Investment Plan (or possibly both) as described in Chapter 6.

Your Identity

There is a means to help further ensure your mail privacy. Some excellent foreign mail services are out there, known in police vernacular as *mail drops*. Fortunately, there is nothing illegal about them. Although many folks use them in the normal course of doing business, often they also are used by suspicious characters. But before a Swiss bank will open your account, you will be required to prove your identity with the bank, under the "Know Your Customer," or "KYC" rules, which most everyone follows these days. This requires a notarized copy of your passport with an Apostille issued by a Swiss embassy or consular general's office, thereby proving your identity, and a copy of a recent utility bill showing your name and physical residential address, thereby proving where you live. The bank is not interested in your Social Security card number or any other government's tax identification number. And, unlike many tax-haven banks, a Swiss bank will not request a notarized copy of your driver's license. In some cases, a bank reference letter or a professional reference letter from your accountant or attorney may be requested, or both.

These items are the basis for satisfying the bank's due diligence required by law. The address on your utility bill will be the address the bank uses for corresponding with you, including where it will be sending your account opening forms, if that is how you wish to receive them, and where it will send you the letter indicating your account number after it has opened the account. So, you definitely need to be using an address where you will receive the mail. This will be your address of record.

However, once your identity and residential address are established, you *can* instruct the bank to send all correspondence and statements to another address—your new mail drop. You could inform the bank that you wish to do this for privacy reasons. As long as the bank has proved your residential address for due diligence reasons, it should have no problem with such a request. Using an alternative address for privacy reasons will generally be sufficient to throw off anybody but the most determined mail spy from the fact that you are routing mail from somewhere else, which might be an indication that you have something to hide. As your mail drop will gather and forward your mail, there will be no indication on the outside that your mail is from Switzerland. Thus, you have immediately increased your privacy with just this one step.

Setting Up a Foreign Mail Drop

You can instruct your mail service to use only their address, and not their business name, on the envelope. A name like Mail Forwarding

Services, Inc. would more clearly indicate what you have set up. You would also want the mail service to seal the envelope very well. Many of these services do this automatically, since they are in the business and they know many of their customers want privacy. If they are not naturally cautious, you might ask if they would take extra care. I know of one service that forwards mail in innocuous-looking beige envelopes that are practically hermetically sealed. The cost of these services might run a couple hundred dollars a year by the time you include the postage costs to remail to you.

Canada is a nice friendly place and there's nothing too suspicious-looking about a piece of mail arriving from there to the United States, or for that matter, vice versa, and the remailing postage fees will be less expensive. There are hundreds of these services worldwide, and a few good sources for finding them quickly. Go online to www.escapeartist.com/global/maildrops.htm or purchase a directory from Eden Press. They have two titles, *The Eden Directory of Private Mail Drops in the U.S. and 90 Foreign Countries* and *The Worldwide Maildrop Guide*. Contact the publisher: Eden Press, PO Box 8410, Fountain Valley, CA 92708 U.S.A. Telephone (800) 338-8484 (toll-free); Fax (714) 556-0721. Their Web site is www.EdenPress.com. Eden Press also has an interesting catalog loaded with books and publications on privacy and other subjects to do with dwindling liberties and other timely topics. Of course, these additional steps to secure greater mail privacy take additional time, but they may be worth your effort and the expense to get them in place.

Bank Requirements and Steps to Open the Account

The actual process for opening an account could not be easier. With your two pieces of identification in hand, as explained, you are ready to begin. In most cases, the bank will give you a questionnaire or application to complete in advance and request that you return it with your identity documents. The bank's forms are self-explanatory and usually brief. These initial forms can be delivered to you by e-mail, by fax, or by mail; in some cases, you can download them from the bank's Web site. You can request the account opening package be sent to you using these methods or by telephoning the bank. You'll want to indicate what type of an account you would like and what currency it should be denominated in. You'll also want to ascertain the minimum amount required for the initial opening deposit. At some banks (usually cantonal or local savings banks), the account can be opened with no minimum, but in most cases, US$25,000, $50,000, $100,000, and even more maybe required. If you have questions regarding completion of the forms, you can communicate back by any means mentioned, or telephone your bank representative and ask. If you don't want the call to appear on your phone bill, use another means of telephoning.

Before sending your identity documents and completed bank forms, be sure all required forms are properly completed and signed. Then return them by air mail, if you're not in a hurry, or by over-night courier service. FedEx and UPS are very good to these countries. *Do not send your initial deposit at this time.* Wait for the bank to contact you. You can call to confirm that the package was received and all is in order, which is a good idea in case something is missing and to save time if there is a problem, or you can simply track the package using the airbill tracking number, making note of who signed for it, or simply wait. Either way, you will be hearing from your banker within two weeks or so, depending on air mail delivery time. If everything is acceptable, the bank will send you a personal letter with your new account number. It will also send you a couple of standard forms that will require your signature, such as a completed signature card, and it will ask you to return these at your earliest convenience. These forms usually are completed by the bank, or there may be a little information that you must insert. In the meantime, even before the bank might receive returned forms, you are allowed to transfer funds to your account for deposit. Again, it is best to return these completed and signed forms promptly, and by overnight courier service. For additional privacy, I would suggest using a private courier service, such as FedEx or UPS, and not your country's postal system.

Transferring Your Initial Deposit to Your Swiss Bank Account

Once your identity is established and the bank has issued you an account number, you are in business and will be treated like a valued customer, not someone on the outside. The only matter left to do is to transfer your funds to the bank. To receive immediate credit, these funds will have to be cash or cash equivalent such as an international money order, bank wire transfer, or cash at the counter. Checks have to clear first, which often takes several weeks. Bank drafts have to be sent for collection but are better options than checks, and the clearing time should be shorter. Most major banks have a correspondent banking relationship with a Swiss bank, and the draft can be sent there for payment. At the time of purchase, the draft can be denominated in the currency you are using in your account. That way, you know exactly how much is deposited because the exchange rate is based at the time of purchase, not when received by the bank, after fluctuations in the exchange rate are likely to have occurred. Although the fastest and most efficient way to move funds is via bank wire transfer, an international or postal money order offers the most privacy. I've already stated some precautions regarding reporting requirements, so take heed. Also note that under mandatory KYC rules, banks may request details on the source of funds that will be deposited in the account.

Alternative to a Bank Wire Transfer

An alternative to sending a wire transfer from your bank direct to Switzerland would be to engage the services of a foreign exchange firm that does international wire transfers on behalf of clients. These companies are licensed to handle funds. Their proficiency and expediency in handling international wire transfers exceeds most banks, a fact that better ensures the correct and speedy arrival of the funds. There is nothing worse than dealing with a missing wire. I've seen wires that could not be located for six weeks. I've had to call every day to keep the sending bank on top of the problem and make certain it didn't forget my request. There is typically no pressure on the sending bank to track your funds expeditiously, and in the meantime, you lose the use of your money.

Interfacing with this third party provides you with another level of privacy. The firm is the one that actually is remitting the funds to Switzerland, unbeknownst to your sending bank. The cost is inexpensive. There are other companies that can provide these services, but I recommend this one:

Asset Strategies International Inc.
1700 Rockville Pike, Suite 400
Rockville, MD 20852-1631
Telephone toll-free (800) 831-0007 or (301) 881-8600
Fax (301) 881-1936
Web site: www.AssetStrategies.com

You can calculate currency conversions by going to Xtrade at www.xe.com/fx or visiting www.x-rates.com.

Value Date

Your Swiss bank's bookkeeping system is based on the value date. This date is the actual date that a transaction is credited or debited from the account. For example, if you make a deposit with a personal check, the value date will be when those funds have become "cleared" funds and are credited into the account. The date will be expressed the way Europeans usually date everything, first with the day, then the month, and finally the year. The date July 2, 2008, would look like this: 02.07.08. The value date is applied differently depending on the transaction. For example, a currency exchange transaction would be value dated on the day the exchange took place. The same would apply if the transaction were to purchase gold. If you are borrowing money from the bank, in the case of a margin account, the value date would be the date from when interest is computed. And, in reverse, if you deposit money in your interest-bearing savings account, the value date starts with the day interest is first earned. With bank wire transfers, if your written instructions are dated July 2, but you missed the bank's cutoff time for getting wires sent out, the value date would be the next day when the wire is actually sent. On an incoming wire, the date will be the day it is to be credited. On the sender's copy, you'll notice a value date set in the near future. If the funds do not arrive or are not credited by the receiving bank by this date, the receiving bank is required to pay interest effective as of that date, an incentive for the receiving bank not to hold on to the money too long and to expeditiously credit it to the beneficiary account. And, if you go to the bank's counter and make a cash deposit, the value date should be that day; however, if you miss the official cutoff time for deposits credited that day, likely the value date will be the next day, although the receipt in your hand will shown the date on which you made the deposit.

Commercial Account Requirements

For a commercial account, such as a corporate account for an offshore corporation, the bank first requires the same identity documents for each signer on the account, along with certified copies of certain corporate documents, together with a Hague Apostille, obtainable from a Swiss embassy or Swiss General Consul's office in your country. Like an individual, corporations can choose from a number of different types of accounts. The account opening will require bank forms to be completed, and the process will be similar to opening a personal account.

If you were opening a Swiss corporate account for your Belize international business corporation (IBC), here's what you'd need in addition to the identity documents and standard bank forms to be completed and signed. You can get these documents from the government bound together in a nice presentation to give your banker.

- Apostille
- Notarial (notary) Certificate
- Registered Agent Certification
- Certificate of Incorporation
- Memorandum of Association and Articles of Association
- Signed letter attesting to who are the director(s) of the corporation

Additional costs can be associated with opening a corporate account. Those fancy documents will cost you US$400, and some banks will charge a document-verification fee. One Austrian bank I know charges US$400 to verify documents.

Online Banking

Your Swiss bank will likely have online banking available as an optional service. Logging on requires a secret pass code. You can arrange for online banking at the bank or you can go online, where the procedure is explained. You will have to provide certain information online, and a pass code will be sent to your address of record or other address where the bank has been requested to send your mail. When you receive this pass code, you can go online and follow the bank's instructions to access your account. This procedure may vary by bank.

Written Instructions to Your Bank

The bank has your signature card on file, so when you wish to instruct the bank directly to execute a transaction instead of going online—say to request a bank draft or a wire transfer or send instructions on your investments—you can write the bank a letter, mail it, or rush it by overnight courier service. Expect two days for overnight courier delivery from the United States or Canada. Upon receipt, if the funds are available, the bank will act on your instructions immediately. The instructions should be specific and accurate. Send an original letter, be sure you sign it, and keep a copy for your records.

Wiring Instructions

If you want to instruct your bank to wire funds to another account, you will need to furnish the bank with the recipient's bank wire coordinates. The person who is requesting funds from you will provided these coordinates. Your instructions should be as detailed as possible, providing complete information on the receiving bank and any correspondent bank, and the full account information of the beneficiary (i.e., the one receiving the money into the account). Special bank numbers will also be required and will vary depending on the country and the banks involved. These numbers include the IBAN (International Bank Account Number), the SWIFT (Society for Worldwide Interbank Financial Telecommunication) code, the transit number, the ABA (American Banker Association) number, the presort code, and so on. The coordinates are like a road map of where the funds will need to go to get to the other person's account. Always double-check these numbers for accuracy and double-check from the party providing the wiring instructions that they are complete.

Faxed Instructions

Another way that is quicker than courier delivery service is to fax the bank the written instructions, but this method may be slightly higher risk, particularly if you are worried about telephone spies. The fax can be the same letter as the one you would have mailed or couriered. Some banks require you to sign an indemnity to protect them should someone fraudulently send a fax concerning your account and succeed at milking it. Other banks have an improved fax system; once you've made it known that you want the capability to instruct them by fax, after getting the indemnity signed, the bank mails you a sheet of numbers. Every time you send a faxed letter of instructions, you must include the next number in succession. Then you scratch that number off the list, and you use the next number on the next faxed instructions, continuing this process until all the numbers have been used, at which time the bank will gladly send you more. Another variation is that when you request to be able to fax instructions, the bank will ask you to provide them with a pass code. You put this code in your letter to be faxed. The method with the series of numbers seems to be the most secure.

Payment Order

The payment order is a bank form provided to an account holder for completion and return, and it instructs the bank to make a payment by some means. The order could tell the bank to send a wire transfer, issue a cashier's check or bank draft, or move funds to another account within the bank. It is a standardized order in which the spaces must be filled in and the boxes checked so that nothing is overlooked. The account number is provided by the account holder and the funds are debited to complete the transaction in the currency in which the account is denominated. The funds could also be converted into another currency.

Perfectly Legal Secret Account

As I have alluded to previously, having a secret bank account may be perfectly legal. A good strategy might be to have two accounts. The first is the Swiss bank account that you actively use, which means you

probably will be moving more than US$10,000 a year through it and
are required to report it annually on U.S. Treasury form TD F 90-22.1
if you are a "U.S. person." As you have learned, this form is a red flag
to the government that there may be some kind of suspicious activity.

However, if you have an account that never exceeds the $10,000
limit, you never need to report it. You can even open it with a minimal amount—if you can find a bank that will accept such a low opening
amount—and maintain it as basically inactive for a rainy day. It could
be your lifeboat account. It would be best to have this account with a
second bank. And when do you usually need a lifeboat? You'll know
when the time comes! But then, depending on the scenario, you will
have a place to move monies to, even significant amounts should the
circumstances warrant it, that is completely unknown. Who knows
what lies ahead? Your funds could go quickly from the one account to
the other for safety purposes and give you some breathing room to
make future plans based on the circumstances. It's part of your financial emergency plan, like knowing where the fire escape is in a hotel.

Tax Evasion or Tax Fraud?

The U.S. Treasury form TD F 90.22-1, as previously discussed, is
designed to detect illegal activity such as money laundering, and more.
Although government agents won't be showing up in black SUVs to
question you if you do or do *not* file this form, you will want to file
because of the potentially heavy penalties for not filing. As I have stated,
filing this form makes the government aware; that's all. If it raises questions in someone's minds, it's possible that it might be investigated. But
an awful lot of these forms are filed every year. The filed annual Treasury form would likely have to fit a pattern that specifically involves you
before it might receive any individual attention. However, the government will not be able to get information from your Swiss bank, because
the United States and Switzerland have not signed a Tax Information
Exchange Agreement (TIEA); if they had, Switzerland would be
required to open up like a clam at a clambake. As mentioned, the only
chance that the Swiss might assist the United States would be if a law
were broken elsewhere that is also the law in Switzerland.

With regard to taxes, tax evasion is not considered a crime in Switzerland, although I strongly suggest avoiding it, since there could be stiff penalties at home if caught, including prison and fines. Getting caught not filing the Treasury form and being found guilty of tax evasion or tax fraud would get you more time in jail than Paris Hilton recently experienced; and most likely, a lot more. Also, tax *fraud is* illegal in Switzerland. As an example, tax fraud would be if you failed to file your annual tax return or lied on your deductions to fraudulently reduce your tax liability, as discussed in Chapter 2.

The problem might be with the perception of the difference between actual fraud and just evasion. You could find yourself in the gray zone of interpretation. Let's say that the U.S. government wants you badly for tax evasion, but it can't specifically find a technicality in which it could sling tax fraud at you. So, it might stretch its reasoning capacity to gain a sympathetic ear from Switzerland. In an attempt to make a strong argument for the case of tax evasion, an agent might state that the government has been defrauded. Keep that in mind if you're thinking of hanging your hat on the fact that tax evasion is not a crime in Switzerland.

Worried about an Audit?

A *New York Times* article dated May 3, 2007, was headlined: "IRS Curtails Many Audits in Tax Havens." In summary, the story said that although the U.S. Internal Revenue Service believes that as much as $40 billion is being moved offshore annually from U.S. investment and business income, the tax havens—including Switzerland, of course—and their bank secrecy have hampered the normal audit process, which requires about two and a half years to complete.

Often the IRS ventures into fishing expeditions to see what it can dredge up, but the fact is, even if IRS agents have a clue of impropriety or are confident that there's tax evasion, often they choose to terminate the audit prematurely or not pursue the issue at all. Why? When they discover that a taxpayer has an offshore corporation or an offshore bank account, agents realize it's not going to be easy to finish their examination within the three-year statute period allotted them for conducting an audit. And that includes tax havens where there is an exchange-of-information clause in a tax treaty or in which countries have signed a TIEA. Tax havens are slow to cooperate or provide little, if any information. Of course, the seven excellent tax havens and off-shore banking centers, discussed in Chapter 8, have not signed a TIEA and will not provide any information to the IRS at all.

Without the cooperation of the foreign jurisdiction to provide what could amount to evidence, concluding a proper examination for auditing purposes is very difficult. Although successful audits of people with money offshore have revealed they owed twice as much as the average taxpayer, the irony is that the average sum they owed was just $5,800. As that sum sounds low, there must be a lot of taxpayers offshore, individuals and corporations, who are tired of the government and leadership squandering their hard-earned tax dollars.

Chapter 4

Investing through Your Swiss Bank

"To consider the judges as the ultimate arbiters of all constitutional questions is a very dangerous doctrine indeed, and one which would place us under despotism of an oligarchy."

—THOMAS JEFFERSON

Many types of investments can be made through your Swiss bank. One common way is to invest using one of your accounts, such as Swiss francs bought and held in your Swiss franc–denominated bank account, whether it is a demand account, savings account or fixed account; or gold and silver bought and held in your precious metals account; or stocks and bonds traded through your securities account. The end result is that the investment is held in your name in your account.

Another excellent way to make the same investments is through the bank, in which case the investment is held in the bank's name, not in yours. This certainly has some advantages; in particular, you would be investing anonymously. You can accomplish this type of investment with a fiduciary account with the bank. Refer to "Types of Swiss Bank Accounts" in Chapter 3. Another way to invest in restricted and forbidden investments is through the Ultimate Investment Plan described in Chapter 6.

A foreign investor can avoid the Swiss 35 percent withholding tax on interest and dividends paid by Swiss banks, companies, and the government itself if the investments are properly structured. Your banker can give you advice in this area and on which investments will avoid Swiss taxes, such as investments outside of Switzerland. You can avoid this tax altogether by investing in non-Swiss foreign securities. You also can invest in precious metals tax-free when utilizing a fiduciary account. Many funds in Switzerland are highly invested in foreign investments, because Swiss bankers know that their foreign customers like avoiding Swiss taxes.

Switzerland has over 70 tax treaties, commonly known as double-taxation agreements, and there is a U.S.–Swiss treaty and a Canada–Swiss treaty. From a tax standpoint, these agreements are attractive as they save you from paying taxes twice—to the Swiss and to your own government. More on tax treaties is found elsewhere in this book in Chapter 5 under "Tax Treaties."

Your Swiss banker can act as your agent in the acquisition and liquidation of any asset or investment on your behalf. Should you have any questions, once your account is opened, feel free to ask him or her. Bankers can give you specific answers based on the services offered by their bank. You have many Swiss banks to choose from (see Appendix A for a list), but for quick reference, here is a Swiss bank with offices in Geneva and Zurich that specializes in online trading, including stocks, exchange-traded funds (ETFs), currencies (Forex), contracts for difference (CFDs), and futures:

Synthesis Bank
15, Rue des Alpes
Case Postal 2164

CH-1211 Geneva, Switzerland
Telephone (41 22) 317 95 68 / (41 44) 266 22 66
Fax (41 44) 266 22 67
Web site: www.synthesisbank.com

You can open a personal or corporate account online. The next sections describe some of the investment choices available today that will work in harmony with your Swiss bank.

Stocks and Bonds

Contrary to what you may be accustomed to, Swiss banks also can act as your securities broker and provide you with an account for trading purposes. Generally, this is a *cash account* used for maintaining funds for the purpose of buying securities and for depositing the proceeds when sold. Customers may deposit funds at anytime into this account, but the prevailing restrictions on withdrawals will determine when you can take money out. Brokerage fees also are paid from this account. If the withdrawal limitations are not convenient, you can use a *current account* instead. The account pays no interest, but the balance is available for withdrawal at any time. Another option is the interest-bearing *deposit account* used to settle buy and sell orders. There are restrictions on the size and timing of withdrawals, and advance notice would be required to make a withdrawal.

After purchasing securities, if they are not to be held in the trading account, as would be the case if you were buying and selling frequently, the stock certificate or other instrument can be physically delivered to you. If you do not want to take possession, you can establish a safe custody account, and the bank will hold the securities and provide you with a receipt acknowledging that it has custody. The bank also assumes responsibility for receiving interest and dividends and depositing them into the cash account automatically. The bank receives and handles all notices from companies, clearinghouses, and the like, and any action required is at the direction of the customer.

There are two types of safe custody accounts. The most common is the *collective safe custody account,* where the securities are held together with the bank's own securities for the customer's benefit. The customer's securities are not identifiable by serial number when held in a collective depository, as in this instance. When foreign securities are purchased, the same service may be offered, and the securities will be held in your bank's name by the correspondent bank in a foreign country, where the securities were purchased. The other type of safe custody account is the *separate custody account* for customers who want securities held in their own name, not the bank's name, or who wish to have the securities held apart from the bank's securities. In this case, the customer knows the serial number and is required to pay storage fees at the bank or the foreign correspondent bank.

Naturally, stocks and bonds can be purchased through your trading account worldwide and through any exchange in the world. One of the leading stock exchanges, ranked eighth largest in the world and one of the most technologically advanced, is the SWX Swiss Exchange (SWX), owned by a group of Swiss banks. There are also plenty of good Swiss companies to invest in, and a few of the world's largest companies are based in Switzerland. To avoid Swiss taxes, it's best to invest in Swiss securities from offshore, not through a Swiss bank or Swiss brokerage firm. Your banker will be familiar with many of these firms, and the bank's investment research department can provide valuable data. You also can trade securities online through Synthesis Bank in Geneva.

Swiss Bank Bonds

Bank bonds, also known as *cash bonds* or *term savings notes,* are medium-term obligations issued by Swiss banks for periods of three to eight years. Due to the fixed time period, banks can offer higher interest than on deposit or savings accounts. This type of bond is available in increments of 1,000 Swiss francs. The interest earned is paid into your current account at the end of each year. The longer the bond period, the higher the percentage of interest paid. Ask your Swiss banker for details regarding the bonds his or her bank has to offer. There is no secondary market available for readily trading these instruments; they have to be held to maturity.

Forward Contracts and Margin Accounts

Forward contracts, also known as futures, and margin accounts are excellent ways to hedge against a currency asset like the dollar, for example, that is frozen due to a fixed-time situation or tied up in another fashion. If the dollar asset's value is declining or you're convinced it's going to decline, and you can't liquidate your investment soon enough to avoid a loss, perhaps a significant one, a forward contract or margin account could be the answer. These contracts or accounts can be used to purchase greater amounts of precious metals, securities, or currencies than your cash position normally would permit.

Forward contracts and futures trading are sophisticated investments and require expertise. They are a means to invest in commodities, financial instruments, and currencies with a relatively small amount of cash, for the purpose of taking delivery of the asset at a price agreed to in advance. They often are used as hedges against interest rate or price risk.

In the case of a margin account, you may already own the investment, which would be placed as collateral for a loan of up to 50 percent of the value of the asset, or you could purchase it on margin to maximize your leverage. Of course, the more leveraged you are, the riskier the transaction is. Things may not go in the direction you expect, which could cause a margin call—a request to increase the collateral—or the bank may become owner of your collateral. Margin accounts are not available through all Swiss banks. No credit criteria are required, as the asset is collateralized and in the bank's possession. The margin account is a custodial account and segregated from the bank's own assets, which means, if the bank fails, the asset remains yours.

A forward contract or future provides leverage like the margin account except you are not taking ownership of the investment. Instead you prearrange to take delivery of the asset on a future date at a fixed price (the *spot price* or today's price). You anticipate that you're going to be correct in what the price will be and thereby make money. You also incur interest and storage costs as if you were in possession of the asset until the delivery date. For instance, if the contract was for gold, someone has to store it during that period at their expense. The interest is earned on the sum of the contract as if the money to purchase the commodity were borrowed—a small price to pay for the leverage gained. The forward contract or future usually lasts for a short period, one month to a year.

Because a dealer market exists, forward contracts are liquid; they are traded daily like stocks with bid and ask prices on regulated futures exchanges. The price difference between today's spot price and the price on the delivery date is known as the *premium*. The longer the term of the contract, the greater the premium, which diminishes over the course of the contract. A security deposit is a guarantee called a *margin,* which is required by the bank regardless of the fluctuation of the investment. Other forms can be pledged as a security deposit besides cash—including interest-bearing accounts and other liquid assets. The bank may require as much as one-third to half of the value of the contract for the security deposit, and this can be applied to the purchase, if you so choose. At the end of the contract or on the delivery day, you can take possession of the asset by paying the preset price or selling the contract to the bank, which pays the current market price of the asset. Usually the seller of the contract exchanges it for a new one rather than taking actual delivery. Because the premium has vanished at this point, you'd have to add the premium amount to the price if you wanted to purchase it. This delivery date should correspond with the end of the fixed-term of the investment you were originally hoping to hedge against loss. If all went well, the forward contract or margin would offset any anticipated losses in the illiquid investment or whatever you were holding. Your Swiss banker can explain the merits and virtues of these devices, or you can trade futures through an online trading account established with Synthesis Bank.

Worth Pondering

Keep this in mind: If you had borrowed money in a weak currency—say the U.S. dollar—and it dropped in value over the period of a loan, and you kept your cash and other liquid assets in a strong currency like the Swiss franc and accessed these funds as needed to make the payments when required to service the dollar-denominated loan, the loan would cost less to repay. How much less? It could be significant. The difference between the decline in the currency the loan was in and the value of the stronger currency could add up. For instance, if the stronger currency stayed constant, never rising in value, versus the declining dollar, the difference would be a savings, or profit, depending on how you look at it. But if the stronger currency also rose in value against the declining dollar, that would increase your savings or profit that much more. If both currencies were going in opposite directions at the rate of 10 percent, you would make 20 percent on just the difference in values of the currencies involved. Of course, this is a simplification for illustration purposes; the loan would be being paid over time as the currency gradually declined in value, and, if the other currency was going up, the rise in value likely would also be gradual and spread across the period of the loan. To figure the percentage of gain or amount of profit, you could calculate the difference, which is your gain as each payment was made, and at the end of the loan period know how much you were ahead and for what time frame. Now, imagine this same scenario, but that the borrowed dollars were used to buy gold, and gold was increasing, possibly for the same reason the strong currency was increasing. You could really score.

Precious Metals

Why own gold and other precious metals? For decades the United States was on the gold standard. A strong currency backed by gold, in conjunction with a conservative monetary policy, helps create a solid, stable currency. It also leads to national economic stability and real economic growth and minimizes the wide fluctuations of inflation and deflation. In 1971, President Richard Nixon took the United States off the gold standard. In the same era, he devalued the U.S. dollar in two separate moves, by 10 percent each time. He may have ended the Vietnam War, but he didn't do much for the U.S. economy. A currency with no real value, one that is not backed by gold or something of sustaining value, is basically a fiat money. In the past these countries often have inflated their currencies until they struck hyperinflation and then when the whole thing crashed, they quickly rolled out another currency to replace it, backed once again by nothing of real value. The new fiat currency would soon go the way of the old one. The money was worth no more than the cost of the paper, ink, and labor necessary to print it.

But in the United States we have sustained a long period with a free-floating currency for reasons many nations cannot boast of: an economy with real economic production, generally strong financial markets, and the ability to defend ourselves against most other nations. The "bomb" has even contributed to national and economic stability. These factors and more have helped the nation sustain a period in which America's superiority, know-how, and enterprise keep us afloat, along with a feeling that we can do no wrong. All the while our currency is bolstered by nothing more than perception and other people's willingness to take it as a form of payment. But this concept will only work as long as the perception lasts and you can keep paying your bills.

Today, all currencies are soft currencies, free-floating in relation to each other in the present global soft-money cycle that hopefully, one day, will change. If it does, we will enter a new hard-money cycle that the world has experienced in the past, and such a cycle can contribute to global prosperity and peace, and among people, an increase in morality and civility. A return to the gold standard is overdue.

Unfortunately, our national debt is so high—higher than most people realize, as the numbers are not accurately reported today—that we are barely able to service the debt. In other words, we're on the brink of *not* being able to keep up with our bills. We are heading down a path that many other countries have taken to their demise. In the process of trying to keep up with our past mistakes, we print more money—the direct cause of inflation. Currently many people believe the Consumer Price Index (CPI) accurately reflects inflation, but this is a distortion of the truth, as, at best, it is a considerably understated estimate by our government. The M3 money supply, as earlier defined, has been the best measurement of true inflation in the United States. Unfortunately, Ben Bernanke, the new Federal Reserve chairman, has decided that this information is no longer relevant since inflation is under control; at least that's what he wants everyone to believe.

But if we cannot read inflation easily by the signs from the prices on the shelf or from those dubious government charts and figures, then there is another more obvious way, as inflation is not level. It crops up here and there, as a very visible asset or equity bubble that can readily be seen. Remember the equity bubble in 1999? How about the housing market bubble in 2006? Can you see the next one coming? Maybe the $400 *trillion* derivatives balloon will play havoc with us. And we're not the only ones playing this liberal monetary policy game. Maybe the Federal Reserve banks of the world are in concert with each other. *The Chinese stock market looks like an overblown big red balloon.* Yes, there have been rallies in the dollar since Nixon's days, but then the dollar recedes again, like a tide against the other currencies exposing the strongest among them against our weak dollar.

The Swiss franc has a long history of being stable. For years it was backed by more than 100 percent in gold reserves to offset the number of Swiss francs in circulation, and the gold was only one of a basket of valuable real assets that backed the Swiss franc, the franc representing the stored wealth of Switzerland. Unfortunately, as you have already learned, this is no longer the case. On the positive side, the Swiss still have a conservative monetary policy that keeps inflation nil and the franc very stable, although it may be slightly softer than it was and, of course, it's no longer a hard currency. Still, it is definitely one to include in your currency basket, along with half a dozen or so other strong ones today including the euro; British pound; Japanese yen; Swedish Krona; Danish Krone; Norwegian Kroner; Australian dollar and the Canadian dollar. Of course, this list can change over time. Together, these currencies can create stability and long-term appreciation. The currencies selected should be held in equal proportions. With your basket of stable currencies along with precious metals, you will have succeeded at creating personal economic stability even without your government's assistance.

A Case for a Return to the Gold Standard

Today, countries should strive to support and promote their individual sovereignty as nations, and seek their own economic solutions for stability and growth, rather than submit to grandiose ideas served up by international organizations that solicit membership to unite countries into a larger body. These tactics are for greater control in the hands of fewer global elite, and they allow for the prospects of further limiting citizen's liberties and imposing more taxation and bureaucracy. The EU, the

NAU, the OECD, the UN and other stealthy bodies bearing initials, are a step not to "globalization," but for the potential of a one-world government. International commerce has been around for eons, "globalization" is a disguise for the true intentions of the "architects of change."

A healthy nation does not need to render its national sovereignty to be exploited by international elitists. But, today, the world has exhibited growth and prosperity, generally speaking—on the surface, that is—but in reality the world economy is built like a house of cards. In order to establish a sound economic foundation for a nation to create *real* economic growth and prosperity, which could lead to a real economic boom, based on sound economic fundamentals, a nation would be wise to follow successful patterns in history. An example would be how Germany and Japan prevailed after World War II.

Sound economics originate from proven policies and practices that foster economic stability and growth. This is as important as having a strong military, as it helps to ensure national sovereignty and continuum. An example is the prosperity that the United States experienced between 1865 and 1914, as mentioned in the Preface. At that time, at the close of the U.S. Civil War, taxes were nearly non-existent—the federal income tax was not passed until 1913—and the world economy was positively impacted by the great American economic boom.

Whether there are any other nations who would consider this idea, or not, the United States today could certainly stand to gain, resolve many of its underlying economic problems and possibly avert the huge pending economic disaster that's brewing. The United States could be the benchmark and lead the world to return to a hard money cycle by backing the U.S. dollar with a gold standard. This would truly stimulate the world economy into a potential golden age of real stability and prosperity that we have never seen before. A sound strategy to accomplish this mission would be required—in addition to a return to the gold standard, the painful acts of slashing government spending, and drastically reducing taxes permanently would be required, together with implementation of a conservative monetary policy that we commit to hold onto. The U.S. government and the Federal Reserve would have to work in tandem to maximize potential economic benefits. The outcome would be global prosperity. Maybe "we the people" could apply some pressure in Washington and force the issue of a gold standard and sound fiscal practices.

Until that idea succeeds, if ever, your own private monetary policy is critical to personal financial survival and success.

Ways to Hold Precious Metals

There are physical possession possibilities for your investment metals, each with various benefits or drawbacks, and then there are indirect investments in gold, silver, platinum, and palladium that come in the form of mining stocks and related paper investments.

Physical possession may sound most desirable and convenient. It certainly is nice to look at gold and silver in your hand, as coinage, ingots, medallions, or bullion. Physical or near-physical possession would be those metals you keep at home, in your local safe deposit box, at the office, or buried under a rock at your vacation home. Your metals are essentially in your possession, unless, of course, there is a natural, government or terrorist emergency that prevents you from getting to your valuable assets.

Let's say a natural disaster strikes, such as a massive earthquake in California, which many people anticipate any moment. Gold is not going to be your first priority, although you might soon need it for your economic survival. Unfortunately, you cleverly stashed it under a large rock deep in the woods behind your cabin in Wyoming. Now all you have to do is get there. That may be very difficult to do, as many residents of New Orleans realized. Then, if you need to cash out to get some fast money in your hands, you would need to find a coin or bullion dealer nearby. The logistics of such plans begin to mount against your best efforts and seemingly well-laid plans.

Let's say that scenario sounds too impractical. Instead, you've opted to put your gold in the local bank, in your safe deposit box. Sounds safe, right? But any number of things could go wrong. A creditor, the government, or an ex-spouse, through a court order, could gain access to your box and its contents before you have a chance to clean it out. Maybe the banks were closed over the weekend or on normal business days due to "national security" reasons. Certainly there are provisions in the Patriot Act for such situations. Maybe the banks are on shakier ground than you imagined, and your bank unexpectedly closes. Maybe your bank was horribly overextended in derivatives (a couple dozen of the biggest U.S. banks are) and that house of cards crumbled, as it is bound to do. Maybe the economy reaches proportions beyond your understanding and suddenly the government *orders* the banks closed. What if terrorists succeeded in striking the New York financial district? If an attack was big enough, it could send shock waves across the nation, through its banking system and financial markets, and around the world. You may not be able to visit your bank, because the doors will be locked, at least for now. Or your bank may not be able to withstand such pressure and close for good, as the entire financial system would likely be threatened, possibly the entire economy.

Did you anticipate 9/11? Did your great-grandfather anticipate the Great Depression and the closing of banks? Are we going to anticipate the next disaster that threatens our personal lives? In our bones, we know there's trouble brewing, but can we accurately predict it? Events like these and adverse government actions usually strike like a bolt of lightning. So, feeling prepared? And is physical possession the best choice? What if, after you bought all that gold and silver, which as a U.S. citizen today is perfectly legal, then stashed it conveniently somewhere in the United States and awoke one morning to discover that the government has outlawed private ownership of gold and silver? Do you doubt that will happen? It's happened in our past, and it could happen to a citizen of any country. President Gerald Ford passed a bill allowing U.S. citizens to own gold effective December 31, 1974. Before that, ownership was illegal, but not always. The Gold Reserve Act of 1934 outlawed private ownership of gold in the United States, with some minor exceptions such as jewelry, for industrial applications, and for miscellaneous practical purposes. Since today ownership is legal, the question is: *When* will it become illegal again? The key word is more likely "when," not "if." The pendulum swings both ways.

This is not a book on gold or other precious metals per se, but there is a strong point to be made here, since the subject of gold ownership has everything to do with your financial survival and success. Therefore, keeping close possession of the bulk of your earthly holdings, such as gold and silver, may not be the wisest idea. A small amount of silver coinage, such as "junk silver," or old U.S. coins that contain 90 percent silver content, for example by the bag, to use for immediate purposes at home in bad times would be a very good idea; it's easy to store and convenient to get your hands on in short notice. The small amount of silver in the coin will be worth much more, of course, than the face value of the coin. It actually could save you in extreme moments. But the rest of your holdings should be as safe and secure as possible and should include a degree of diversification.

Precious Metals and Your Swiss Bank

Obviously, I am making a solid argument for precious metals not only for investment diversification reasons, but for hedging against economic bad times and whatever could trigger such events. Advance planning is most definitely required and is one of the reasons why a Swiss bank should fit into your plans. Granted, you won't be able to put your hands on it, and holding precious metal is certainly a pleasure, but, while aspects of your life might be in serious trouble, you will have peace of mind knowing your last-resort investment plan is securely intact, albeit somewhere else. And that somewhere, we have already learned, is about as good as it gets. By utilizing a Swiss bank account, you can trade precious metals like stocks, or, as a customer of the bank, you can open a safe deposit box to place them in, along with your other valuables. Some Swiss banks are major bullion and coin dealers, too.

You might have to go to Switzerland or entrust someone else to do so for you, or better yet, have your bank trade your metals per your instructions. Or your bank can make your purchases and hold them on your behalf in its vaults with its gold, but segregated. Your precious metal trades and holdings will be reflected on a statement that will be sent to you periodically. If you need to liquidate, you are in an excellent position to do so, regardless of where *you* are physically. Had to leave the country in a hurry? No worries; you could be sailing in the South Pacific and order your bank to sell and transfer the funds wherever you desire. You probably would prefer to access the cash from long distance, using any of numerous means, so you could continue to keep your money safe and in a nice strong currency.

Accumulation Plans

An accumulation plan is a method by which to buy precious metals for investment purposes and as a hedge against inflation and economic uncertainty through a forced savings plan. Some banks offer these plans. The plan may be a gold accumulation plan, where every month or established period you contribute a pre-established amount. As an example, you may agree to kick in $250 a month for the period of the plan, maybe for a year or two or even longer. The plan can be tailored to your requirements. You can adjust the amount to whatever you are comfortable with and to how much gold you want to have acquired during that period. The gold is purchased at the market value on the day of purchase. The advantage is that it's secure with a Swiss bank; there are no physical storage problems for you to deal with, and you have no worries or expense to do with handling, shipping, and theft. The plan can be for a single purchase or multiple purchases over time. It's like a savings account, except it doesn't earn interest and you are acquiring gold instead of accumulating currency. It is a good method for small investors to acquire precious metals. You can discontinue the program at any time. Purchases are whole or fractional as they are based on the dollar amount, not on the ounce. Orders are combined daily by the bank executing the purchase; therefore, customers benefit from the lowest purchase price, giving them more gold for their money. The bank buys on the wholesale bullion market, and the commission rates are heavily discounted. All these cost savings are passed along to you. And you do not incur any of the usual small-order charges. With the accumulation plan, you have ownership, but your physical possession is in Switzerland.

Perth Mint Certificate Program

Another excellent way to own precious metals, without burying them in the backyard and having to worry about them, is to purchase Perth Mint Certificates. These certificates represent real ownership in whatever metal you purchase, such as gold, silver and platinum, in either coin or bullion, but the metal is kept safely at the Perth Mint, a government-guaranteed program of the Western Australian government (Standard & Poor's AAA investment rated) and insured by Lloyds of London at their expense. With the Perth Mint Certificate Program (PMCP), you are the owner of the metal represented by ownership certificates. The certificates are easy to purchase and liquidate. Western Australia is politically and economically stable. The certificates may be purchased in increments of as little as $50 each and may be held by an Individual Retirement Account (IRA), a foreign trust, a foundation, an offshore corporation, or bought through your Ultimate Investment Plan in Switzerland. A minimum investment of US$10,000 is required. The metals are safely stored in a government vault, not just a foreign bank in Australia. The certificates are issued in the name of the purchaser, and each certificate is numbered. The mint uses a system of code numbers to ensure client confidentiality and security. The certificates are nonnegotiable and non-transferable. You can have them in your possession when you travel, and you are not required to declare them as a financial instrument on the U.S. Customs form when leaving and entering the United States.

Perth Mint Certificates may be purchased through an authorized Perth Mint dealer. Three are listed below. You may visit the Perth Mint at www.perthmint.com, and you also can sign-up for e-mail notices of precious metals offers. The Perth Mint is accredited by the London Bullion Market Association, the New York Commodities Exchange, and the Tokyo Commodities Exchange. As another benefit for Americans and Canadians, the mint does not maintain any presence in the United States or Canada. An American could purchase from Kitco in Canada, giving their purchase a little more privacy, or a Canadian could purchase from Asset Strategies in the United States. You also could send your certificates to your Swiss bank and instruct your banker to hold them for you in a custodial or safekeeping account until you decide to do something else with them, such as put them in your safe deposit box when you visit. You also have the option of purchasing the certificates in Zurich from EurAxxess AG, an authorized dealer, and picking them up there for deposit into your Swiss safe deposit box.

In Switzerland
EurAxxess AG, Zurichstrasse 103
CH–8123 Zurich, Switzerland
Telephone (41 44) 980 4281
Fax (41 44 980) 4255
Web site: www.euraxxess.com
E-mail: info@euraxxess.com

In the United States
Asset Strategies International, Inc.
1700 Rockville Pike, Suite 400
Rockville, MD 20852-1631
Telephone (301) 881-8600
Fax (301) 881-1936
Web site: www.assetstrategies.com

In Canada
Kitco Precious Metals, Inc.
620 Carthcart #900
Montreal, Quebec H3B 1M1 Canada
Telephone (514) 875-4820
Web site: www.online.kitco.com.pmcp

Precious Metals–Backed Electronic Currencies

Since we are on the subject of various forms of gold and ownership of
other precious metals, I want to mention the electronic currencies backed
by precious metals. These include, but are not limited to, e-Bullion, Gold
Money, and e-Gold, all of which can function as alternatives to the banking
system. Although the U.S. government has recently indicted the principals
of e-Gold, in an effort to discredit these types of nontraditional systems, it
has not put them out of business. E-Gold has probably been around the
longest of all the electronic currencies and is therefore a bigger threat to
the government. Adverse government actions help discourage people from
using these systems. The government also uses these tactics to uncover
people whom they are convinced are not paying their taxes. Offshore bank
account holders with offshore debit and credit cards have experienced the
same scrutiny in the recent past, and so have some PayPal customers. Expect
more of the same in the future. I suspect the government will take this
kind of activity to a higher level when it figures out new ways to do so.
The case with e-Gold is pending, but the outcome is likely to be similar to
the examples just mentioned, with nothing concrete achieved except an
attempt to shake up these various types of payments systems that may be
perceived as threats. Still, it's annoying.

E–Bullion, Gold Money, and e–Gold are all worth learning more about. Their Web sites are www.e-gold.com, www.e-Bullion.com e–Gold and www.goldmoney.com.

Two large publicly traded gold mining companies are major shareholders of Gold Money, DRDGold Limited, a South African mining company, and IAMGOLD Corporation, a Canadian mining company.

Gold Futures

Gold and other precious metals can be traded on futures exchanges worldwide, as mentioned earlier. Several Swiss brokerage firms are listed in Appendix B if you would prefer to use their services. But your Swiss bank can execute any of these transactions and give you good advice as well. You also can conduct futures trading online with Synthesis Bank.

Gold on Margin

You also can purchase precious metals using leverage. With a margin account, you can increase your holdings with the same amount of cash by up to 50 percent. You would need to consult with your individual Swiss bank as to what its requirements might be. Remember, there is a greater degree of risk purchasing gold this way, as the margin is collateralized by your holdings stored in the bank's vault. If there's a margin call, you'll be asked to increase the reserve or forfeit your investment. Ask your Swiss banker for your bank's policies.

Gold and Other Precious Metal Mining Stocks

There also are gold and other mining stocks in North America and elsewhere. There are some good ones, but remember, they are not the real thing. That is, they are not gold or other metal, but rather securities traded on a stock exchange. Gold and metal prices generally have a direct effect on these stocks, and they could rise significantly with the increase in the price of the investment metals and even an increase in the price of oil. However, the investment is in the company, not directly in precious metal itself. This point applies to the other investment–grade metals and the companies that mine them. Still, they are worth considering, and they are another means of diversifying your gold or precious metals portfolio or your investment portfolio in general.

Although the following companies are not being offered as recommendations, they are worth looking into for investment purposes:

Newmont Mining (NEM-NYSE)

Here are the major gold producers worth following:

Anglo Gold (AU-NYSE)
Barrick Gold (ABX)
Freeport McMoran (FCX-NYSE)
Gold Fields (GFT-NYSE)
Goldcorp (GG-NYSE)
Kinross Gold (KGC-NYSE)

Some secondary mining companies:

Agnico Eagle (AEM-NYSE)
Alamaden Minerals (AMM.TO)
Aurizon Mines (AZK-AMEX)
Bema (GBO-AMEX)
Buenavista (BVN)
Cambior (CBJ-AMEX)
Claude Resources (CGR-AMEX)
Desert Sun Resouces (DMS.TO)
Glamis (GLG-NYSE)
Iamgold Corp (IAG-NYSE)
Madison Enterprises (MMR.V)
Nevsun Resources (NSU)
Northern Lion Resources (NLV)
Northgate (NXG-AMEX)
Orezone Resouces (OZN)
Queenstake (QEE-AMEX)
Virginia Gold (VIA.TO)

In silver mining, look into these companies:

Apex (SIL-AMEX)
Coeur D'Alene Mines (CDE-NYSE)

ECU Silver (ECU.V–CDNX)
Endeavour Silver (EDR.V–CDRNX)
Gammon Lake (GRS–AMEX)
Hecla (HL–NYSE)
IMA Exploration (IMR–AMEX)
Pan American Silver (PAAS–NasdaqNM)
Silvercorp Metals (SVM.TO)
Silver Standard (SSRI–NasdaqNM)
Silver Wheaton (SLW.TO)
Sterling (SLG.V–CNDX)
Western Silver (WTZ)

In gold and silver:

Bema (BGO–AMEX)
Golden Star (GSS–AMEX)
Miramar (MNG–AMEX)

In copper, gold, silver, and zinc:

NovaGold (NG–AMEX)

In silver and copper:

Phelps Dodge (PD)

In gold and copper:

Northern Dynasty (NAK–AMEX)

In uranium, investigate:

Camico (CCO–TO)
Cogema, a division of AREVA (ARVCF.PK–OTC)
Denison Mines (DEN–TO)
Energy Resources of Australia (EGRAF.PK–OTC)
Western Mining Corp (WMP)

In copper:

Ivanhoe Mines (IVN–NYSE)

There are also Gold Exchange Traded Funds (GETFs), an index or special portfolio that trades like a mutual fund. These funds own certificates of physical gold that are on deposit and insured. They have been traded only for the past few years. A few worth considering are:

American Century (FSAGX), an open-end, no load mutual fund
ASA Ltd. (ASA), a closed-end mutual fund invested in South African mining shares
Central Fund of Canada (CEF-TSE)
Gold Bullion Securities (GOLD-GBS)
i-Shares COMEX Gold Trust (IAU-NYSE)
Streettracks Gold Trust (GLD-NYSE)
Tocqueville Gold (TGLDX), an open-end, no load mutual fund

As with gold coins and bullion, GETFs could be confiscated by your government. Therefore, it's best to own them outside your own country and purchase them through your Swiss bank or, for the sake of anonymity, through your Ultimate Investment Plan. GETFs are bonds, and the investor's rights are those of a creditor, not a shareholder.

Gold-Backed Certificate of Deposit

A U.S. bank in Florida called Ever Bank has a clever certificate of deposit (CD) that is backed by gold. It sounds good, if only it were offered elsewhere, as in Switzerland. Of course, in Switzerland, your bank may be more than 100 percent liquid and you could choose any number of strong currencies to denominate the CD in, so this concept may actually be overkill there and really of interest only in someplace like the United States. But if you do find a Swiss bank with a gold-backed CD, please let me know. The major drawback to the Ever Bank plan is that the investment is held in a U.S. bank. Also, you're locked in for a fixed term. If something unexpected should happen to the U.S. banking system during that time, as they say down South, "You're easy pickins."

There are other ways to invest in precious metals than directly. If owning the real thing is of importance to you, and you can ensure access to your valuable commodity without fear of loss or confiscation, then physical ownership with safe storage methods is probably the most secure way to go. Be sure it's somewhere safe—that is, outside of your own country. That's another good reason for your Swiss bank.

Foreign Currencies

The importance of foreign currency today starts with the state of the United States dollar. Those readers who are not U.S. citizens or don't use U.S. dollars should take a close look at your own government's currency and see how it fares. If your country's Central Bank has a conservative monetary policy, you may be fine continuing to hold their currency without too much financial risk. If not, you will want to reconsider it as your primary currency asset choice, unless it is showing strong characteristics and preferably is appreciating against other currencies.

In the case of the dollar, 1913 might be called the beginning of the end. That was the year that Congress passed the Owens-Glass Act, and the Federal Reserve System was created as we know it today. The Federal Reserve is a single national banking system empowered to regulate the banking industry, act as a clearinghouse for the movement of funds within the system, and decide on the nation's monetary policy, including money management and the issuance of government securities.

Federal Reserve notes soon became the national currency, replacing all others in existence at the time, and they were redeemable "in gold and any lawful money." That meant any money the Fed printed, gold and silver coins and bullion, and silver certificates. Originally, the Constitution mandated that only gold and silver coins could be used as legal tender. In other words, the coin *was* the stored value; there was no need to redeem it.

Incidentally, it was also in 1913 that Congress passed another piece of prime Grade A legislation, the Sixteenth Amendment to the Constitution of the United States, making income tax permanent. As you may remember from history class, the public was assured that income tax was only a temporary measure. Within just five years of its passage, in 1918, the U.S. Treasury collected its first $1 billion in a single year.

The United States Mint introduced the first U.S. currency known as the gold certificate, and it was represented that the certificate was redeemable for a specific amount of gold on deposit at the United States Treasury. The Mint also issued silver certificates. The gold certificates continued in circulation until 1934. As we discussed earlier, that was the year that the Gold Reserve Act was passed by Congress, making it illegal for us to own *any* gold. Incidentally, the silver certificates continued until 1963. With the swipe of a pen, the word "gold" was removed from the notes. The new language on the next generation of bills stated:

> This note is legal tender for all debts, public and private, and is redeemable in lawful money at the United States Treasury, or at any Federal Reserve Bank.

Then, in 1963, the new language was further edited to remove any promises of redeemability, with just the first eleven words remaining on the face of the notes. This happened in the same month that President John F. Kennedy, who ironically had wanted to abolish the Federal Reserve, was assassinated. Kennedy also wisely wanted to slash taxes.

President Richard Nixon, old "Tricky Dick," dropped the final gauntlet by officially removing us from the gold standard, gutting the almighty dollar, again with the stroke of a pen. Today, our money is a fiat currency that, until recently, has endured amazingly well for decades, with no *real* stored value to back up the paper and ink. But for years, it's been in a gradual decline. It was only a matter of time before our weakness began to show, principally due to having a liberal monetary policy. Basically, our currency is backed by people's perception of its strength and worth, somewhat of an illusion, and their willingness to accept it as payment for goods and services. Since there's nothing backing it, there's no limit to how much may be printed. If it were to be backed by 100 percent gold, the gold would have to exist and be held somewhere. But the nation would have only so much gold, or it would have to acquire more to print more money and still have it fully backed by gold.

It's interesting to note that in order to have a gold standard whereby notes may be convertible into a fixed amount of gold, 100 percent liquidity is not necessary to achieve the desired results of currency stability, although it would certainly be ideal. The fact is, historically a small amount of gold in reserve can create the same effect. The only time that the gold standard would be exposed to an inability to meet its obligations would be if enough people tried to redeem their notes to physical gold that was over and above what was held by the Central Bank as reserve. The Bank of England succeeded in achieving a gold standard with very little gold in reserve, but, the convertibility of notes to gold built confidence and England's economy boomed as a result around 1880 and until 1914, and the world economy was positively impacted.

How much credit can a country have in the eyes of foreign investors when the United States is $65 trillion in debt? We're on the verge of having to print money just to service the debt. In the private world, you and I would be told we're bankrupt. It's no wonder that foreign governments and others holding U.S. dollars and dollar-denominated investments are dumping them as I write, by the tens of billions. They may also suspect we're considering a devaluation, but news like that is usually hush-hush until it's yesterday's news.

If our wealth is being eroded before our eyes by the simple act of having U.S. dollars, then we have a dire need to hedge against its fatal fall and find a safe harbor. This could be in the form of stronger currencies of other countries, preferably backed by gold or silver, known as the stored wealth of a country, and/or in the *real* thing that currencies were intended to represent to begin with—ownership of gold and silver itself.

Unfortunately, until a country is bold enough to return to a hard money system, the only available option today is a strong, soft-money currency that exhibits signs of stability and appreciation, since no currency today is backed by gold or silver. As mentioned, the only other alternative is to invest directly in precious metals. Preservation of wealth is critical to your future. If your slice of the American pie no longer tastes good, you better look around for another recipe. Otherwise, you may find yourself with no pie at all.

It matters less how much you have than whether you can keep it and, it is hoped, even grow it. The transition to a digital cashless society may or may not work. But gold and silver are always solid storehouses of value. If the global economic system fails, we may find ourselves thrown back into the days of Robinson Crusoe economics. I don't know what your talents are, but at least I'm pretty good at spear fishing. The best answer to the current trend of "tax and inflate" would be to return to the hard-money cycle and drastically reduce taxes to genuinely stimulate economic growth.

Not all currencies are created equal. Only a handful of currencies are stable enough for real consideration for holding or for denominating your investments. Which currencies do you think will float your currency basket the most? Did someone say the United States dollar? *Wrong!* Even the mighty U.S. dollar, the reserve currency of the world for decades, does not belong in our basket. That's the sorry news today. Because of strong negative effects causing the U.S. dollar to decline noticeably against other currencies, foreign investors including the Chinese are seeking non-U.S.-dollar-denominated investments. Besides, most likely you want to bet *against* the dollar, to protect yourself and possibly even make money.

Why is the buck not getting any respect? Maybe foreign governments think they can sink our ship through economics! We've been getting attacked from a lot of directions since 9/11. However, money seeks its own level, like water, and it will go where the returns are greatest and the financial environment is the safest. The Chinese handwriting reads like permanent spray paint on the Great Wall. No one wants to get stuck with a lemon. The rapidly declining dollar throws too much imbalance in otherwise perfectly good investments, and its downward spiral may end with a whimper. Seek currencies that:

- Show strength and appreciation
- Are backed by a conservative monetary policy
- Come from a healthy growing economy and stable government

Switzerland has been very successful in creating stability and a currency that appreciated against most others, in other words, over time, the value of the currency rose. For example, as the dollar declined it has put upward pressure on the franc, the euro and some of today's other more stable currencies.

Here are some of the strongest currencies in the world today. Literally, they represent only a handful of the hundreds of nations on your Rand McNally globe, but they represent the crème de la crème. Drum roll, please. May I present:

- Canadian dollar
- Euro
- British pound
- Japanese yen
- Australian dollar
- Singapore dollar
- Norwegian kroner
- Swedish Krona

- Danish Krone and
- Maybe the Chinese yuan (I include it here for the purpose of illustration)
- Swiss franc

My, that's a short list! This list is not necessarily in order of strength. Over time, this list will need revisiting, as the strength of currencies changes like flowing water. For now, though, this combination offers excellent strength. As a currency declines and another strengthens, it would be worthwhile to revisit your basket and rethink your collection. You may want to consider requesting the advice of a currency expert with a proven track record of success if you intend to speculate, and not just hold currencies.

Imagine, even the Chinese yuan, their currency, is listed here as a possibility. Why? A strong yuan could be possible only because of China's strong economy; or at least that's how their economy is perceived at this writing. Of course, this could change, and could possibly be negatively impacted if the United States went into a recession. Our economy gives many the impression we're strong, too, but a closer look reveals real problems. China is possibly overinflated and overvalued, and a huge correction may be on its way. Granted, China's looking like an economic powerhouse, even overshadowing our own seemingly largest economic expansion ever, but what does all this mean? The Chinese currency is considered strong because of the nation's immense economic growth in recent years, whether real or artificially stimulated, but this does not automatically make the country stable, either as a nation or as a currency. There's a lot of hyperbole about China, but maybe there *has* been a real economic shift from West to East. The nations of Asia are doing very well overall with no sign of their economies nose-diving soon. Japan, however, may be poised to explode for the good, and the yen will likely take a free ride. These are thoughts to consider when currency trading or for long-term currency appreciation and equity investments.

China has become the fourth-largest economy in the world. That would certainly contribute to the strengthening of the yuan against our weakening dollar. Or maybe it's the hype and hoopla of the Beijing

Olympics in 2008. No doubt China is out to make a first-world impression for this big date. For now, however, the yuan might be a candidate for a basket of strong currencies that can make for a safer haven for frightened money than a single currency can offer. But if their currency is to stay strong, the Chinese need to turn their printing presses off too, and soon, since in 2007, the nation's inflation rate was 16 percent, according to their M3 money supply.

But the combination of a basket of promising currencies coupled with ownership of gold and silver could be the backbone of your investment portfolio. As for China's future, without our spending on all those made-in-China goods, I wonder how their economy would fair.

There are several ways to invest in currencies and multiple currencies. You could hold them in your Swiss account or accounts in the various strong currencies as suggested here, or another combination to suit your preferences. You will certainly be liquid, and that is important in the current economic climate, as it would be in bad times. The key here is strength— you want to be holding strong currencies and have your investments denominated in strong currencies. If you are a U.S. citizen or other U.S. taxpayer, you should invest outside the United States. If you are a Canadian, invest outside Canada, and probably outside the United States, too.

Another way to get a play in currencies is not to actually own them but to take options on them. If you are highly leveraged, your profits can be fantastic. Initially, if you buy only puts and calls, you only risk the premium you paid per each to purchase them. Two other ways are currency futures and spot Forex. Risk management is crucial to success, but the financial payoff can be big. Your investment will be highly leveraged, and, unless you are a professional in this business or have been doing it a long time with success, it would be wise to use the services of a top currency trading advisor. If you play this market right, you may discover that it's not as volatile as the stock market. And you can trade round the clock, five days a week. But this is currency speculation, as opposed to owning and holding a basket of currencies as a hedge for financial safety purposes.

As with precious metals, there are exchange-traded currency funds (ETFs). You can buy and sell through your Swiss bank, Swiss brokerage firm, or one of the nifty Swiss insurance wrappers that I call the Ultimate Investment Plan. Seven ETFs are traded on the New York Stock

Exchange, and as you can see from the list in the next paragraph, many of the strongest currencies are available. This is an excellent way to invest with no minimum requirement. The share units in the ETF represent ownership of the currency, not just a future. This form of currency investment is also liquid. ETFs are low-leverage investments, and each share is 100 units of the respective currency.

Two points to think about is that ETFs are traded in the United States, which for me is a negative, and you would likely want to use an offshore entity for investment purposes. If you are considering investing in ETFs, then check these out through your bank or broker: Swiss franc currency trust (FXE); euro currency trust (FXE); Canadian dollar currency trust (FXC); British pound currency trust (FXB); Australian dollar currency trust (FXA); and the Mexican peso currency trust (FXS).

If you follow the advice of professional currency traders, you stand an excellent chance of learning how to invest in the currency markets, without excess risk, and you'll have the potential to make a lot of money as you sleep. There are several good places to start. You might look into the *Money Trader*. Subscribers get insider advice and wisdom from experienced currency pros, Kathy Lien and Boris Schlossberg. Visit www.money-trader.com. Gary Scott, a very successful investment advisor and one who fancies the currency markets, offers the Multi-Currency Investment Service. Visit www.garyascott.com. Jack Crooks is a sharpie in the business. He can help fast-track you on the road to extraordinary profits with his Crooks Currency Forex service. Visit him at www.crookscurrencies.com.

Global Investor magazine claims Jyske Bank in Denmark is one of the best-managed European equity funds with 19 international equity funds. Most of these are top producers and generate 44 percent to 89 percent returns. With Jyske you can leverage your investment dollars up to four times. Contact:

Mr. Thomas Fisher, Vice President
Jyske Bank
Vesterbrogade 9
DK-1708V, Copenhagen, Denmark
Telephone (45 33) 787 812
Fax (45 33) 787 833

Web site: www.jyskebank.com
E-mail: fischer@jyskebank.dk

As this bank is located outside of the United States and Canada, it would be a good way to invest indirectly in currencies. You could do it through your Swiss bank.

A couple of other angles for currency trading and investing include buying short-term government debt in your currencies of choice—the strongest, of course. But an easier way might be to invest in the Merk Hard Currency Fund (MHCF), a no-load mutual fund. Merk's goal is to invest in strong currencies that have the best possibility to appreciate against the dollar. The countries whose currencies are chosen have more conservative monetary policies than most, ensuring greater currency stability. The fund amounts to a basket of currencies and therefore that achieves the desired results of this method of investment and is probably more attractive than currency *derivatives*. The fact is that you are buying into a security, not the commodity itself. This is something to consider when you are evaluating the various possibilities for maintaining a basket of currencies. The MHCF is well managed and as liquid as the currencies in which it puts your money.

You can establish a currency trading (Forex) account or trade spot gold and silver at this brokerage trading firm in Geneva:

ACM-Advanced Currency Markets, S.A.
50, Rue de Rhone
1204 Geneva, Switzerland
Telephone (41 22) 319 22 09
Fax (41 22) 319 22 01
Web site: www.ac-markets.com

You can also conduct Forex trading through Synthesis Bank in Geneva, listed earlier in this chapter.

Commodities

The long-term investment trend, like the one we experienced in the 1970s, is toward commodities and away from equities. The commodities bull market is in its early stages so there are tremendous opportunities.

Due to liberal monetary policies, many countries are debasing their currencies in relation to the hard assets found in commodities. Professionals and astute investors are making tremendous gains.

If you want to make money in this specialized business and create your own lucrative portfolio, one commodity investment service worth investigating is *Commodity Trend Alert*. Mr. Eric Roseman has a proven track record. Contact him at:

ENR Asset Management
2 Westmount Square, Suite 1802
Quebec H32 S24 Canada
Telephone (514) 989-8027
Fax (514) 989-7060
Web site: www.globalmutualfundinvestor.com
E-mail: enr@qc.aibn.com

Another service to consider is headed by John Pugsley, author of the former bestseller *The Alpha Strategy*. Pugsley is very bullish on natural resources. He'll help you discover commodity and small-cap stock opportunities with tremendous potential that your broker hasn't heard of. Pugsley is also chairman of the Sovereign Society listed in Appendix C, and membership is highly recommended by the author. Visit his Web site at www.stealthinvestor.com, and the Sovereign Society website at www .sovereignsociety.com to learn more.

Warrants and Options

A *warrant* is a security giving the purchaser the right to buy a stock, metal, or other commodity for a specific price any time until a specified date. Warrants are good only until the exercise date; after that they are worthless. Warrants do not pay dividends. They give the investor the opportunity to purchase the stock, metal, or commodity for less than might be quoted during that period, but they usually are offered at above-market price. They are exchange-traded securities. The price fluctuates much like stock prices, but the cost to purchase warrants can be considerably less than those traded high during the exercise period. The object is to gain leverage. The longer the period is to exercise it, the better chance you'll have to make a profit or sell the warrant itself, possibly also at a profit.

An *option,* also known as a *call,* is a contract granting a right, not an obligation, to purchase or sell assets during a specific period and at a prearranged price. Options frequently are associated with stocks, but they also serve to provide a hedge in currency trading, futures, and commodities. The price fluctuates based on dynamics like those in warrants. But unlike a warrant, which is issued by a company, an option is a security issued by a market trader and is good for a shorter period than a warrant. Options can be traded with the assistance of your Swiss banker or Swiss brokerage firm.

Jack Crooks of Crooks Currencies is an expert in the currency options game. He will share with you how to apply the high profit potential of options to the immense opportunities in the Forex market. Learn more about his currency option service at www.crookscurrencies.com.

Mutual Funds and Electronic Traded Funds

There are all types of mutual funds and electronic traded funds, and investors often choose them as alternatives to assembling their own portfolio of securities. Of course, you could have a portfolio of mutual funds too. There are proponents of mutual funds, and then there are those who favor a careful selection of stocks to address an investor's very individual requirements. In recent years, the Gold Electronic Traded Funds have emerged, and they provide a means for trading mining stocks, not just gold stocks. They are becoming popular as an alternative form of precious metal investing or to provide greater diversification outside of possession of precious metals. Unless you wish to study individual stocks, mutual funds and ETFs are a possible answer, although they need to be analyzed just as carefully.

International funds are mutual funds targeted at foreign investment and often at emerging markets. They have done very well at times. Morningstar (www.morningstar.com) provides the most comprehensive rating service of mutual funds. If you want real professionals to manage your investments, this is when a discretionary account with a Swiss bank is nice, and a discussion with several potential private bankers will give you a good idea if they match your investment philosophy and ultimate goals. Of course, you can trade international funds yourself through your Swiss bank without having them professionally managed. Open a securities trading account with your Swiss bank or with Synthesis Bank in Geneva. Refer to Chapter 3 under "Managed Accounts" for more information on these types of banking services, and also under "Types of Swiss Banks," also in Chapter 3, as these banks specialize in managed investment portfolios.

Two investment services to guide you to profits include the Global Market Investor, plugging you into the most promising global ETFs available, and the Global Mutual Fund Investor, tracking the world's top-performing mutual funds. Contact Mr. Eric Roseman at the address listed in the "Commodities" section.

Here are four emerging market giants to consider if you would like to diversify your portfolio and improve your odds. Their markets are growing with gusto and actually may develop into more than just bubbles. That remains to be seen, of course, but for now they are worth considering, as they show signs of greater growth potential:

1. Brazil
2. China
3. India
4. Russia

To learn more about funds that are invested in these countries, visit: www.funds.morningstar.com and www.investmentsuk.org.

Real Estate Investment Trusts

Here's perhaps a better way to invest in real estate than owning it yourself, aside from buying some good expat property, and it's also a way to capitalize on specific markets. Real Estate Investment Trusts (REITs) issue investment certificates that are exchange-traded, making them highly liquid. Through REITs, you can invest in real estate in many international markets without the drawbacks of actual real estate ownership. Singapore's market has done well, as have many Asian countries recently, and they promise further growth, especially Malaysia and Hong Kong. In fact, the region has also been a hot spot for all types of funds and international banking. Japan is poised to take off and conditions are promising for the yen, too. A bottom is forming in the German real estate market, and the profit potential there is tremendous.

Conservative investors might want to have a piece of Switzerland. Although it's not practical for foreigners to be Swiss real estate investors, as you will learn in Chapter 7, some Swiss companies specialize in Swiss real estate traded on the SWX Swiss Exchange. Unfortunately, there are no REITs in Switzerland. You would want to invest in these companies from offshore and outside of Switzerland, although your Swiss banker could give you good information on the companies to consider.

An example of one successful REIT to look at, although it was launched only in 2002, is CapitalMall Trust (CMT), traded on the Singapore Stock Exchange (www.ses.com.sg). One the city-state's oldest REITs, it has outperformed all others.

Real Estate

Real estate in the United States has the potential to be a bad investment, particularly in certain areas of the country. Many factors could play on market prices, beginning with the impending and expanding problem in the mortgage money market that has not fully played out. The U.S. real estate market has times of being a very illiquid market, too. For example, your mortgage may be in the way of a sale—there's nothing more illiquid than pulling money out of your own pocket in order to sell your real estate to someone else.

Then there are potential natural disasters waiting to happen, as we witnessed in New Orleans. Should we experience a large enough terrorist strike, the effects could hamper real estate, as could any unrest, including Bagdad-style car bombings or other random acts of terrorism around the country. The overall economy has everything to do with this market as well, and *that* can also be affected by terrorism. The real underlying economy upon which our house of cards is built today could topple very easily with any number of events, as discussed earlier.

It may sound pretty far out, but the potential for government confiscation of your property is definitely real. Clauses exist in the Patriot Act that provide for such drastic measures. Sound crazy? Visit www.fear.org, the Web site for the organization called Forfeiture Endangers American

Rights (FEAR). There you will discover how the government today is doing just that: confiscating private property and other assets without due process of law, in the name of crime and security. It sure makes me feel secure! I'd rather have my Asian and German REIT certificates squirreled away in Switzerland.

Frankly, the best real estate investment in the United States today is perhaps just to own a home for the sake of personal enjoyment and as a place to raise your family—that is, if you want to stay in the country. If such ownership gives you peace of mind, it's probably worth it. And, if you're fortunate enough to make money with it, that's a nice benefit. But real estate shouldn't be viewed as the best or only serious investment. There are too many other profitable ways to invest that are highly liquid. The days of flipping properties are probably behind us. Frankly, that practice was typically the negative result of an over-stimulated economy or a direct result of an increase in the money supply, which created an asset bubble and gave people false, or temporary, hopes of quick riches. If you are going to own real estate, keep your home mortgage to a minimum. Otherwise, you may find at some point that your property is worth less than you owe. This is happening in the real estate market today.

You can't literally move property, so it's not practical to take it "off-shore," and it does not lend itself to my offshore investment philosophy and strategies, which are among the reasons I wrote this book. Any asset in the United States, regardless of how it's titled, is at risk from lawsuits, forfeitures, and confiscation. Your mission should be to structure your investments, including those that are real estate–related, in a safe and sound manner to help preserve your personal sovereignty, financial freedom, and ultimate happiness. Asset protection is essential.

Today, the best real estate investment opportunities lie outside the United States, as I have mentioned. Canadian real estate is doing well, and so is the Canadian dollar. And there are hot spots around the world that offer dynamic real estate opportunities for expatriates, such as in Panama, Belize, Ecuador, Argentina, and many others even Eastern Europe. Interesting real estate investment opportunities abound. At the same time you could be enjoying living overseas, you could be profiting from foreign real estate investments, all the while successfully structuring your personal financial and investment life and gaining real asset protection and impenetrable estate planning.

You would also be able to exercise the $80,000 loophole, per person, and legally beat income tax up to that level. And with the tax savings, you'll have more money to invest. Plus, in many of these places, you can have excellent quality of living—possibly better than you now have—and definitely for a lot less money. If these ideas appeal to you, for an excellent place to begin discovering what you've been missing, visit www.internationalliving.com and find out why 250,000 Americans are leaving the United States each year, and this number is expected to increase in the next year or so to 350,000. If you want suggestions on some reputable foreign real estate developments, drop me an e-mail at barberfinancial@hotmail.com or President@BarberFiancialAdvisors. com. I'll give you some referrals of excellent developments I know something about. In the near future, my company's Web site may also have links to foreign real estate opportunities for offshore and expatriate investors.

Your Own Private Monetary Policy

In today's world, there are insidious factors working against you all the time, many of which you have little or no control over. But in the realm of your own personal economy, and against the endless ebb that erodes your financial well-being—namely your savings, your investments, and your net worth—there are still ways to create financial stability and even prosper. You must recognize the problems, take control of the ones you can impact personally, and implement a plan of action to free yourself from government, and capitalize on outside economic forces. There are some outstanding solutions to help you shore up against the losses from inflation, taxation, confiscation, and risky investments and secure your personal sovereignty and financial freedom.

Inflation is a nasty, silent, alien culprit that we have experienced repeatedly in the United States, even today, and in other countries, and it's been around throughout history. It constantly works against you, robbing you of your hard-earned money. Taxation eats away at the fruits of your labor, and the bureaucratic animal never rests—it just wakes up to go at it again, more and more. These two factors have had a tremendous negative affect on societies, but a spectrum of economic and political troubles should raise an alarm in a normal person. As mentioned previously, governments can also confiscate, which is happening in the United States and is a huge potential threat. Visit www.fear.org to learn more on this practice. As individuals, we have very little direct effect on the outcome of our country, our enemies, or the world at large. In fact, at times even maintaining our own peaceful existence can be a challenge.

Fortunately, there are some things that *we can control,* and those are the areas where we need to focus. If you agree, then action is required. No one but you can solve the problem. This book will assist you with developing a plan, but we must first make a pact of honor with ourselves and agree not to do the very thing that sent us searching for answers in the first place.

We are sovereign individuals. You, I, and every person on this planet has natural sovereign rights. They are not granted to us by any government. Government is there to serve us, the ones who empowered the government and continue to support it through our tax dollars. Our elected representatives are there to act on *our* behalf according to our wishes. Unfortunately, these people have little conscience, it seems. They are more akin to pathological liars, telling us one thing to please us and then doing something different. This process has been going on for so long we've been lulled into complacency. Meanwhile, they feel free to mismanage the nation through careless fiscal management and bad stewardship and to embrace a self-destructive liberal monetary policy. Is that what we want for ourselves, our families, and our grandchildren?

The fact that you are reading this book is a sign that you are self-motivated and driven to seek solutions, probably not to save the world—as nice a thought as that may be—but to save *yourself* from impending financial disaster, if not all-out doom. Saving the world can be achieved one person at a time—beginning with oneself. Charity begins at home. Without taking care of you and yours first, you will have little success trying to find help or to help others. If at this point you still have energy, it *would* be a good time to extend yourself and be charitable within your means. The solution lies within you and your personal resolve to make some simple but intelligent moves that will build a strong foundation that can withstand good times or bad. If the government and reserve bankers of the world cannot create monetary stability at home or elsewhere, then we, acting as our own individual sovereigns, need to establish our own personal monetary policy capable of withstanding the bad decisions of others. A strong personal foundation contributes to a more peaceful global co-existence with other persons and nations.

That may sound absurd. If the big boys of finance and government can't work it out, how could *we* possibly make a difference, even in our own lives? But that's what makes this plan even more fun—the fact that we can implement a simple but very effective *conservative* personal monetary policy, and we don't have to be rich to do it. And, best of all, it *will* make a difference to *you*. The core of your plan is not churning off a printing press, but it consists of *sound* economic principles that have been here since the dawn of mankind. Like Einstein and the law of compound interest, it existed before *we* existed. As a personal sovereignty, like national sovereignty, you need to preserve that entity (you) and make certain that you remain economically sound and stable so that you can create *real* growth for yourself over the course of time and through productive investment. In the process, you will find *greater personal freedom*.

We have reviewed the advantages of Swiss banking. It's difficult to argue with the benefits, even if there are outside pressures on the country. Today, most countries have fared much worse, but the good news is that it looks as if Switzerland intends on keeping its sovereignty independent and stable through a conservative monetary policy, keeping its currency strong, preserving bank secrecy, and continuing to foster the banking and investment sectors. That is why Switzerland can be your little Fort Knox, just like the U.S. storehouse of national value that at one time backed the United States dollar.

Your personal monetary policy should start with a safe place to store your valuables. Here I'm talking about Switzerland for all the reasons covered so far. Then you need to put solid, stable assets into your vault that will be the basis of your financial empire, regardless of its size. You can make adjustments as you go to suit your outlook and pressures from the outside. Sound fiscal management is your goal in support of your own personal sovereignty and your own ability and fortitude to weather the unforeseeable and unpredictable.

Therefore, you will build a personal asset base in Switzerland by starting with the world's strongest and most stable assets to ballast your economic ship, and this vessel is going to deliver you to safety and ultimately to financial prosperity. We have already discussed Switzerland, the Swiss franc, some of the world's other strongest currencies, and gold and other precious metals. Plus, we've considered other possible investment opportunities and ones that we could no doubt do well with in the future. Regardless, however, whenever you expand your investments, you must stabilize your Swiss investment portfolio.

Let's look at that portfolio, our mainstay to smooth sailing. Your investments can be held in a Swiss bank or structured like the Ultimate Investment Plan under your direct control, or managed by the world's best asset managers in Switzerland. The Ultimate Investment Plan is a superior asset protection structure, through which you can shield your assets and investments while they quietly appreciate, and conduct your banking in secrecy, all the while simultaneously engaging the best in estate planning available today, a key component of this plan. The Ultimate Investment Plan is discussed in Chapter 6.

In any case, your investment portfolio should be weighted to provide stability and exceptional growth in good times. In bad times, you not only want your portfolio to be buoyant and outperform riskier investments, should they falter, but you also want to capitalize on the various crises that are trying to destabilize you without the risk. Your ballast will keep you afloat, but in economic bad times, it doesn't falter—in fact, it has the chance to make you rich. The reason why is, that while many other forms of investments might lose a good portion of their value, possibly even certain ones in your own portfolio, your hard assets that comprise your financial ballast will stabilize the shock of a crisis and maybe even skyrocket in response.

For instance, gold and silver could go up 10 to 20 times, even conservatively. Any number of events could make that happen tomorrow—in part because these investments are undervalued now, especially silver. But a variety of factors can influence your investments, negatively and positively, and bad economics and financial mismanagement are but a couple of the ways. As you know, politics and government actions have the potential to wreak havoc on your personal economy. You can make your own list, but here are a few to think about that can cause the hard assets in your portfolio to outperform everything else you are holding.

Imagine oil going through the roof. In Sweden today, people are paying $9 a gallon for gasoline. A little monetary crisis would work to send oil prices up. How about a Chinese stock market crash; do you think it'll have any bearing on Wall Street or the U.S. economy, or vice versa? What if suddenly our little democracy crumbles overnight like what happened in the Soviet Union? Maybe derivatives will take us out, or maybe our government's poor, irresponsible fiscal management. Any of these circumstances could cause gold and silver to go 50, 75, and 100 times their present values—and this may even be an underestimate! Where do you think these commodities will be if Iran strikes Israel, Russia strikes Europe, we strike Iran, and the Al Qaeda get control of Pakistan and its nuclear weapons? These are not stretches of the imagination. They are potential threats right now that could come to haunt North America and send commodities through the roof.

Where do you think the price of food and oil will be if these things happen? These are not even the worst-case scenarios; they are real possibilities. And any of these events could spark counterresponses. If there were a severe global economic crisis, only the strongest currencies may stand a chance, but if backed by a hard asset—real value—they would be bellwethers of stability. Precious metals are real wealth, and you can begin with gold and then silver.

So, the ideal investment balance is critical, in good times or bad, and the ratios are subject to analysis and personal opinion. But for my money, I want about 40 percent of my entire portfolio weighted by my ballast. And for the ballast, I would want 40 percent gold, 40 percent silver, and 20 percent in a basket of strong currencies. As for the remaining 60 percent of the portfolio, 30 percent could be invested in strong mining stocks, Gold Electronic Traded Funds (GETFs), maybe some Real Estate Investment Trusts (REITs) in Asia and Germany, Asian equities including Japan, and other investments with relatively low risk, good returns, and a promising future based on the scenario of an economically volatile future.

Then, the remaining 30 percent could be in more volatile investments with high profit potential, maybe even leveraged: alternative energy stocks, oil and natural gas through energy trusts, natural resources, commodities, currency trading, and options, and possibly hot markets like China, India, Russia, and Brazil. Also you could consider the undervalued soft agricultural commodities such as orange juice, sugar, coffee, cocoa, and others. Changing weather patterns are causing significant price increases in these commodities, there is increased demand by a growing global population, and war and terrorism could drive these commodities through the roof. We all have to eat.

Your investment portfolio should be adjusted over time based on how well each one is doing and on economic and political events that can directly affect them. But your ballast should always remain a constant percentage of your overall portfolio. With 40 percent ballast, you'll never be too top heavy, but this is subject to your own investment philosophy and perception of the future.

But in all cases, I would seek the advice of experts in the individual investment fields, some of whom I have mentioned in this book. Keep in mind that the long-term investment trend appears to be in commodities and away from equities. When you make your investment decisions, you'll want to base them on the long-term prospects of the broader investment outlook. We are in a period similar to the 1970s, with a serious credit crunch, a rapidly declining dollar, liberal monetary practices, rising inflation, war expenditures, the development of a commodity versus equity cycle, high interest rates, and prospects for devaluation and price controls, which could make the coming years more spectacular than even the 1970s. If you are a member of Sovereign Society, you can follow its TSI (The Sovereign Individual) portfolio and it has produced excellent returns. Visit www.sovereignsociety.com. Membership is inexpensive!

But before you start shrewdly investing your money, you must cut your personal spending. This is a critical aspect of any conservative monetary policy, because you certainly do not want to operate like those out-of-control politicians. Next, you must pay down your debt or liquidate bad "investments" of all kinds, especially if you had to borrow to make them.

Your investment portfolio *must* contain gold, silver, and strong currencies. That's the foundation you want to build from. With spending cuts, debts reduced, and your investment ballast in place, you will have stabilized your personal sovereignty and will be a liquid entity able to withstand gale-force winds. Only after the ballast is in place can you begin considering other investment options. They must start with more conservative investments as mentioned, ones that offer good returns, and then you must work your way up to the riskier ones that offer tremendous profit potential, with reasonable risk. In that way, you are not going to be top heavy with high risk.

Here are some of the factors working in favor of your hard asset ballast and why these few investments will not only weather unforeseen economic problems but stand to do exceptionally well. Precious metals have taken a bad rap from Wall Street and bankers—but why not?—Wall Street only has paper to hawk. Would you talk up the merits of a Rolls-Royce to a car buyer if all you had to sell were Volkswagens?

Your Swiss-style conservative monetary policy starts with gold. Gold has been creeping up in price since 9/11 from $272 on Saturday 10, 2001, to $737 in September, 2007, nearly a 200 percent increase, a sign of security in gold and real insecurity in the economy, even in the face of so-called economic expansion and prosperity. The question could be: Have we created real growth and prosperity? Gold is now more realistically priced, but in my opinion it is still highly undervalued. Think big, thousands of dollars per ounce may be coming.

Although it has shown a more gradual rise in price in recent years, silver is poised to take off. Inventories of silver, produced years ago at cheaper costs, have basically run out. When high demand meets low supply, there's no place for silver to go but straight up. There's an organization of silver users that also works to downplay silver's importance as an investment metal in hopes of keeping the price lower for commercial purposes. What does that tell you? Today's silver is undervalued because there has been deliberate effort to keep the price down. The demand is great, and increasing, but the supply is drying up. New silver cannot be produced fast enough to keep up with demand; this is a little-known fact. In other words, the possibility is there for *great* profits and an excellent hedge against a weakened currency, and worse prospects.

One of the great benefits of precious metals and currencies is that they can be owned anonymously, like the perfectly legal Swiss bank account. Few things today give you real privacy. And privacy helps ensure your personal sovereignty. That is why governments want to abolish paper money; ownership of investment metals may be next. Gold and silver offer real value. Real value means you have real power and the ability to preserve your individual sovereignty—and that ensures your personal freedom. What most people don't realize is that all of these things are being challenged and compromised daily. This process will continue until one day our freedoms will vanish. There's a high price to pay when you become reliant on government. Fortunately, your conservative personal monetary policy, structured safely in Switzerland or perhaps over several strong and stable assets and money havens, will sep-arate you from the vast majority who are not getting the picture.

But the day may come, after we've been looted six ways from Sunday through inflation, taxation, and confiscation, that a new monetary order may be ushered in to replace our current monetary system. Our paper currency will go the way of Mr. Ford's Model A, perhaps in favor of dig-ital currency. Some changes in our Constitution may be in order to restrict our freedoms and abolish ownership of gold and guns. Maybe the U.S. Constitution will just be scrapped when the European Union–like government sets up shop as North America, Inc., to become the seeming answer to all our problems. Your financial privacy has already evaporated entirely thanks to the Patriot Act, and only a concerted effort on your part to get your personal sovereignty in order will provide you with personal and financial privacy and freedom. Imagine what they might be dreaming up for the new citizens of the North American Union (NAU). For a glimpse into this concept, visit www.Stopthe NorthAmericanUnion.com. And, other grim prospects are possible. Will you be standing by watching, or will you be somewhere enjoying the bounty of your assets and advance planning?

Chapter 5

Banking Policies and Regulations

"Those who would give up essential liberty to purchase safety deserve neither liberty nor safety."

—Benjamin Franklin, 1759

S wiss bankers act as financial counselors; they have as much experience on the subject of banking and all types of investments as anyone, anywhere. The Swiss themselves view their individual bankers as private counselors to assist them with suggestions on their banking requirements and on where to invest based on their individual situations and requirements. And when it has been decided what the client desires, it's the bankers responsibility to assist in executing their investment wishes—like a pro. This "free advice" is standard to clients. The banker's judgment is deemed to be valuable to their customers.

This goes beyond the standard banking experience you are accustomed to in the United States. A Swiss banker's investment advice is available to customers of the bank, regardless of the investment sum, and it's expected to be sterling. And when customers are ready to proceed with their investment plans, their banker is standing by to execute them on the customers' behalf, since the bank also functions as an expert securities broker, currency trader, and commodities dealer. Customer can buy and sell at their own discretion or in concert with their banker's advice. Swiss banks also can execute buy and sell orders through your accounts established with the bank, or if you are a bank customer, they can buy and sell on your behalf in the name of the bank, thereby keeping your name out of the picture.

Swiss Regulators

Regulation of banking and financial markets in Switzerland is strictly enforced, but the country does have a strong tradition of self-regulation that has worked effectively for years. Self-regulation has been conducted successfully by professional organizations with a vested interest in maintaining order within their industries and through their own regulations and supervision. These organizations have attained recognition as conducting themselves irreproachably. At times Swiss legislators have officially required that organizations be required to be self-regulated, at which time, the appropriate leading professional organization has then been appointed to carry out these responsibilities and functions. Self-regulation, if administered diligently, is an excellent way to keep unnecessary bureaucracy out of your industry and potentially elevate it above what might come to bear with excessive bureaucracy. Switzerland has accomplished this nicely, in connection with well-regulated financial industries, and this area is another reflection of how well Swiss democracy works. These organizations have passed their own standards of conduct and codes of ethics, and they abide by them rigorously.

Here are some of the self-regulating organizations in the banking and financial sectors today.

Swiss Organizations
Swiss Admiesdssion Board
Swiss Association of Independent Asset Managers (VSV)
Swiss Bankers Association
Swiss Banking Ombudsman
Swiss Exchange (SWX, Eurex, Virt-X)
Swiss Funds Association

Outside International Organizations
Bank Committee
Financial Task Force on Money Laundering (FATF)
International Association of Insurance Supervisors (IAIS)
International Organization of Securities Commission (IOSC)
International Securities Markets Association (ISMA)

The official Swiss government agencies that preside over the Swiss banking and financial markets include the Swiss National Bank, Swiss Federal Banking Commission, Swiss Takeovers Commission, and the Money Laundering Control Authority. These Swiss regulators enforce the federal legislation governing the banking and financial markets, and the Swiss financial industry has very strong legislation and the laws are strictly enforced.

The main federal legislation in place includes:

- *Federal Banking Act of 1934 on Banks and Savings Institutions,* including all subsequent adopted amendments, which regulates the banking industry
- *Federal Act on Stock Exchanges and Securities Trading of 1995,* regulating securities trading principally on the secondary market
- *Federal Act on Investment Funds,* completely revised in 1995
- *Federal Act of 1997 on the Prevention of Money Laundering*

Other federal laws also impact the financial markets. Naturally, the Swiss also have their own tax laws that affect investors. Being international in nature, the Swiss financial industry strives to maintain international standards in its financial markets.

Financial Actions Task Force

Switzerland is a member of the Financial Action Task Force (FATF). The original purpose of this task force, when it was conceived by the G-7 during a 1989 summit meeting, was to prevent money laundering by drug cartels using the international financial system. The FATF's authority was enhanced in 1990 when the "40 recommendations" were passed to impose further restrictions; subsequently 9 more recommendations have been added regarding terrorist financing.

Financial institutions that are FATF members are cooperating to gather financial data through their financial intelligence units (FIUs) for monitoring purposes so that they can comply with the FATF. Switzerland has developed a new specialized centralized intelligence agency to compile such financial data for analyses and, where appropriate, to turn it over to respective government authorities for investigation and prosecution. The Egmont Group, an organization of financial intelligence units has been created, comprising 101 member nations for the purpose of information exchange, education, and training. The Swiss FIU is the Money Laundering Reporting Office Switzerland (MROS) established in 1998. The power of MROS lies in the Money Laundering Act; it is an administrative authority only, with no power to police or prosecute.

Fortunately, Switzerland is not a party to the Mutual Legal Assistance Treaty (MLAT), which, incidentally, is not a treaty at all. Forty-eight countries have signed onto this agreement, which was created to help law enforcement in criminal investigations, except tax evasion cases. The most disturbing aspect of the MLAT is that it lacks regard for due process of law, which requires "probable cause," an important aspect of the U.S. Constitution known as the Fourth Amendment. Here's another example of an international organization or, in this case, an international agreement overriding your well-founded U.S. constitutional rights, but then, thanks to the Patriot Act, we're losing those too.

Money Laundering

Today, money laundering is a hot topic everywhere. It's a subject that everyone ought to understand better. You may be already asking yourself how money laundering might apply to you. Although the Organization for Economic Cooperation and Development (OECD) tries to say that tax havens, including banking and financial centers like Switzerland, are conduits for laundering money from ill-gotten gains, the irony is that this could not be further from the truth. The fact is, more money is laundered through the OECD member nations and the United States of America than what is being laundered through all the 40-plus tax havens of the world put together! As for terrorist financing, all such funds uncovered to date came through either an OECD member nation or an Islamic nation. I covered this important topic and some others that relate to how your personal sovereignty is being threatened at the international level through governments and organizations like the OECD, and their stepchild, the FATF in my previous book, *Tax Havens Today.*

The scope of the FATF has gone beyond controlling laundered drug money and terrorist financing; now it also incorporates any suspicious transaction that might be crime-related. The net is getting wider, and the definition of money laundering itself is so broadly written that an ordinary, law-abiding person in many countries today could be accused of money laundering. Legislation regarding money laundering and other areas supposedly intended for a narrowly defined threat but ultimately intended for expansive purposes has the potential to affect everyone and be extremely harmful to your personal sovereignty.

Qualified Intermediaries

Here's a prime example of the United States trying to exert its control and influence not only over its own citizens, but into foreign countries and foreign business.

There are many international securities and markets that U.S. investors are restricted from investing in, because these investments are not allowed to be sold in the United States on U.S. exchanges or through U.S. brokers. Sharp investors have been getting around this restriction for years by investing from offshore, through either an offshore bank or a foreign brokerage account, often in the name of an offshore corporation. This does not seem to be a problem for the U.S. government, possibly because these investments may not necessarily be purely for tax reasons. And offshore investments would be more difficult to control, since the investments are outside the United States.

But American investors have also begun investing back into U.S. markets for the purpose of letting their profits rest offshore in a low-or no-tax haven to avoid capital gains taxes. What other reason would you have for investing in this manner when you could just open an account with Charles Schwab? I suppose you could claim asset protection, but the Internal Revenue Service (IRS) clearly interprets it as an attempt to evade taxes. Well, the IRS does not take kindly to being cheated by taxpayers out of their hard-earned revenues. The IRS has devised the Qualified Intermediary (QI) to uncover those investors who are making it a practice of investing back into the United States anonymously while simultaneously not paying their taxes.

For those foreign institutions that sign a QI agreement, the QI regulations impose far-reaching requirements to disclose the identity of any U.S. account holder. As the QI agreement only benefits the U.S. government and the respective banks of the account holders, it's hard to understand why any foreign institution would sign one. The motivation must be financial in nature, and/or a response to pressure from the almighty U.S. Treasury department. These financial institutions have literally signed an agreement to act as compensated auditors or at least spies for the IRS. Recipients of U.S. source income find themselves forced to withdraw their investments from the United States that they hold offshore, due to the OI, or have their identity disclosed to the IRS and face the music, including a penalty of over 30 percent on the cash flow of their investment. The financial institution would act as a tax collector of the funds.

In this way, the IRS could also snag people who are required to file the annual U.S. Treasury Form TD F 90.22-1. Its stiff penalties for failure to file can include up to five years in prison and up to a $500,000 fine. People who are trying to evade taxes certainly wouldn't file this form, which advertises their accounts to the government.

Having a foreign bank account and investing overseas *is* exercising your sovereign right, and your sovereignty cannot be legislated. *Remember,* when banking offshore, the best places today for Americans and Canadians are the T-7 tax havens, none of which has signed a Tax Information Exchange Agreement (TIEA) with the United States. The TIEA is another device designed to skirt around a foreign country's secrecy laws and get the cooperation of a foreign financial institution to provide all the information it has on you and your financial accounts. Please refer to Chapter 8 for more information on the T-7 tax havens.

Fortunately, not all foreign banks are jumping on the bandwagon to play pseudo-cop and risk their images and reputations. This type of agreement is very serious exercise of U.S. power and its influence, and it's a sad commentary on foreign concerns that would treat their customers, U.S. persons or not, in this manner. You can get around this problem, and this book gives you some good ideas. You can also consult with a professional. As you can see, you don't want to get caught with an undeclared foreign financial account or have your account information showing undeclared earnings turned over to the IRS.

U.S. Taxpayer Requirements

It's with great pleasure that I explain the reporting requirements for U.S. taxpayers here, because there are so few requirements. The Ultimate Investment Plan, described in Chapter 6, gets you around the typical reporting requirements if you have a foreign bank or financial account, a trust, or a corporation.

Even with an offshore account or offshore entity, you would still have had to do the required filings *and in some cases* hire expensive accountants, lawyers, or other advisors to assist with complex international tax planning issues. These issues include the controlled foreign corporation, the foreign personal holding company, the personal holding company, the passive foreign investment company, the matter of accumulated earnings. And, we must not forget Subpart F income of the Internal Revenue Code, and a plethora of forms to navigate, some of which would definitely need filing—or else.

Here is what you *do* need to concern yourself with when you have a Swiss or other financial account: Treasury Form TD F 90-22.1— Report of Foreign Bank and Financial Accounts (FBAR). A U.S. taxpayer must file this form annually, disclosing any financial interest in or signing power over a foreign bank account or other foreign financial account if the aggregate value of the account exceeded US$10,000. Multiple accounts can now be reported on the same form.

The FBAR reads, in part:

> F. Bank, Financial Account. The term "bank account" means a savings, demand, checking, deposit, loan, or other account maintained with a financial institution or other person engaged in the business of banking. It includes certificates of deposit. The term "securities account" means an account maintained with a financial institution or other person who buys, sells, holds, or trades stock or other securities for the benefit of another. The term "other financial account" means any other account maintained with a financial institution or other person who accepts, exchanges, or transmits funds, or acts as a broker or dealer for future transactions in any commodity on (or subject to the rules of) a commodity exchange or association.

Structuring

Although "structuring" does not specifically apply to Switzerland but does apply to banking in the United States and is serious enough to need pointing out. Under a 1991 amendment to the Bank Secrecy Act of 1970, the Financial Record Keeping, Currency and Foreign Transactions Reporting Act, "structuring" is basically the conscious act of avoiding the system set up to detect money laundering, which is illegal. This type of activity includes structuring deposits to avoid the $10,000 currency transaction reporting that the U.S. government requires of banks. When a bank files this form, known as Form 4790, it can be a red flag that a suspicious transaction may have taken place. In an effort to get around this detection illegally, certain bank customers may structure transactions in hopes of avoiding attention.

Say you have a lump sum of whatever amount. If you break it down into amounts smaller than $10,000 each and deposit these in various accounts rather than depositing the single sum in a single account (which would require the bank to file Form 4790), or if you delayed depositing such lesser amounts into one or more accounts, spreading them over time to avoid the $10,000 threshold, then you are structuring. This act in itself is illegal and carries stiff penalties. Structuring can be done by an individual acting independently or with any number of others assisting in the process, which is known as smurfing. Wire transfers received into your account are also deposits.

It is legal to have multiple bank accounts. It would not be defined as structuring if you chose to keep them under $10,000 each; thereby the bank would not be required to report them. Structuring was not addressed in the Bank Act of 1970. If you have foreign currency accounts—which is a good idea, especially if holding stronger currencies like the euro, British pound, Swiss franc, Singapore dollar, Canadian dollar, the Australian dollar, the Norwegian krone, and so on—be sure that you correctly calculate the exchange rates, as the $10,000 figure is based on U.S. dollars. If you keep the account topped off, the exchange rate could throw you over the limit and you could break the law inadvertently. This law is too serious not to pay close attention.

Although structuring will typically have no bearing on your Swiss banking activities, the moral of the story is not to send money home from Switzerland in a way that can be defined as structuring. In fact, don't send money home from Switzerland *period*. You are trying to keep it offshore!

Tax Treaties

Tax treaties are important to understand. The United States and Canada have a double-taxation agreement with Switzerland, which helps you avoid being taxed twice, that is, once by Switzerland and once by the IRS or CRA. That's because Switzerland withholds 35 percent on your investment earnings. The only way to recoup that money is to declare it. The amount of the withholding tax is deducted right off the amount you would owe the IRS for that year. Check with your accountant or the taxing authority of your particular country. You can also get a refund direct from the Swiss.

Swiss double-taxation treaties are in effect with the United States and Canada and numerous other countries. These treaties include exchange-of-information clauses that allow several possibilities for exchanging information between countries, such as routine or automatic transmittal information, requests for specific information, and spontaneous requests. This information exchange is mainly to assist with treaty enforcement. But what is really disconcerting is the Tax Information Exchange Agreement, which, as we have seen, is not a tax treaty at all, but rather a way for the IRS to obtain confidential information, even information normally protected by secrecy laws, from another country that is party to such an agreement. The United States and Canada have not signed a TIEA with Switzerland, but both have signed a Mutual Legal Assistance Treaty. More information on the TIEA and MLAT is presented in Chapter 8.

Chapter 6

The Ultimate
Investment Plan

*"No one shall be subject to arbitrary interference with his privacy,
family, home, or correspondence . . ."*

—ARTICLE 12, UNIVERSAL DECLARATION
OF HUMAN RIGHTS, UNITED NATIONS

H ere it is: the Ultimate Investment Plan. This is the best asset
protection structure available anywhere today, and there are
several variations to pick from to suit your requirements. This
strategy blends some of the most sophisticated concepts that are available
in certain critical areas of personal finance, including Swiss annuities,
portfolio bonds, and life insurance. These Swiss financial-related insurance products have passed the test of time and provide iron-clad asset
protection. All three of these insurance products have their own benefits

and share some similarities to each other. Yet all three are simple structures, easy and reasonable in cost to maintain.

Swiss banking is the core of the Swiss financial community, with
several hundred successful banks providing an array of banking, investment, and financial services. But the golden umbrella might be the
mammoth Swiss insurance industry. There are 20 companies, but they
have immense reserves and financial clout, and they are famous for their
creative applications of what is normally considered a very dry, staid
business: insurance. This could be the first time you will actually get
inspired about an otherwise—to most people—dreary topic. Pay close
attention. In my humble opinion, insurance just might be the single best
answer to guarantee your financial success and stability and the reason
why you have a tremendous chance, even in today's unpredictable world,
to avail yourself of the best offshore financial opportunity out there: the
golden Swiss-made waterproof umbrella.

The Swiss Federal Bureau for Private Insurance (FOPI) is the watch-
dog of the Swiss insurance industry. It enforces strict Swiss regulations
that are uniformly administered under Article 34 of the Swiss Constitution, which was passed in 1885. Financial conservatism is the rule of the
day. FOPI monitors the performance of insurance companies and their
investments, determining that they are operating and investing without
undue risk-taking. These companies must have strict standards for diversification, security, liquidity, and yield. The industry also regulates itself,
generally operating very conservatively, and it has a collective desire to
maintain strength and stability, a tradition and present-day view in the
Swiss financial center. In the end, Switzerland might find itself as the last
financial bastion, or at least one of a few, in the world that could withstand a global economic meltdown.

The FOPI and the insurance companies routinely undervalue the
true net worth of investments, and the investments are in very liquid
forms. The companies also have an excellent record for getting a healthy
return on their investments with minimal risk. Because of these conservative and shrewd accounting methods, the insurance companies, like
many Swiss banks, have hidden reserves, and it is possible that under the
worst global economic scenario, the Swiss insurance companies could
meet their obligations and remain liquid even if they lost half of their
book value. Of course, they might do exceedingly well on their precious

metals holdings alone and find themselves in a position to buy assets for pennies on the dollar. Think about this when you are putting together your personal investment portfolio. Remember the ballast?

The Ultimate Investment Plan defies most of the concerns associated with going offshore and making money. Those can include niggling fears of a safe place to put it, getting the most in return, keeping taxes to their lowest, staying ahead of the crooks, avoiding the threat of financial penalties or jail time for making an innocent mistake, being exposed to financial ruin by the whim of a bad court decision, or being the recipient of some negative ramifications from your government gone wild. *There is nothing more dangerous to your personal well-being and financial health than being the citizen of a declining world power.*

Fortunately, there's still time to get the best that going offshore has to offer. But there are real indications and rumbles that loopholes are going to be threatened with vigor and that taxes may increase more than we can imagine; such thoughts have recently passed through the loose lips of some liberal politicians. These concerns may be the least of our worries. We know that the barbarians are at the gate; 9/11 was the beginning of that trend, and it promises to get worse. Can't you just feel it in your bones? It's known as instinct. Your next thought, and instinct, should be one of survival. The Mexican border is a joke! Frankly, so is the Canadian border. Al Qaeda, or anyone else for that matter, may already be within American borders, planting their dastardly seeds of revenge. According to *The Week* magazine, news source to American movers and shakers, the A-bomb used on Hiroshima was a rather simple, lightweight device. The components needed to build one today are readily available in the United States.

I will leave you with those thoughts, as we move on to explore new ways to aid you in your quest to escape the bondage of our times and gain personal and financial freedom. Leave it to the Swiss!

Secrecy Factor

Whether you purchase a portfolio bond, an annuity, or life insurance, you gain the same secrecy as you would get with your Swiss bank. In fact, not only is your insurance company bound to this secrecy by law, but since the bank accounts and investments are held in the name of the insurance company, your assets and investments are literally anonymous, which completely alters their legal nature and the treatment of the assets. You are not obliged to meet any U.S. reporting requirements as you must when you are a controlling signatory over a foreign financial account, a significant shareholder in an offshore corporation, or a grantor in a trust. Swiss insurance companies, by law, are not allowed to report the purchase of any policy to anyone, including individuals, companies, or governments. Secrecy should begin with *you* by not divulging the existence of any Swiss investment. Remember, the subtitle of this book—*An Owner's Manual to Quietly Building a Fortune*—also reflects Swiss philosophy and practice. The Swiss don't want their government or even their favorite neighbors knowing a thing about their personal finances and wealth, and they are typically hush-hush about their money, as are their banks, by law. For one thing, it's difficult to go after something that no one knows exists, such as your Swiss investments.

Investment Safety

We have already learned about the stability and security of Switzerland, one of many good reasons why the country has succeeded in attracting a large portion of the world's private money for investment and management purposes and for investment into the Swiss banking and insurance industries. Switzerland is one of the safest and most stable countries in the world with a history of over 700 years. In its 150-year industry history, not a single insurance company has failed, and very few banks have, either. Swiss insurance products also have individual safety features, which we'll review in a moment.

World's Best Asset Protection

With your new Swiss insurance product, you gain the best asset protection available anywhere, in part because you no longer own the asset; the insurance company has it titled in their name. You simply have an annuity, bond, or policy with the company. Beginning 12 months after your annuity, bond, or policy goes into effect, your Swiss insurance company will protect you from any creditors. The one-year delay is to avoid suspicion of making a fraudulent conveyance. Your assets are protected under Swiss law and cannot be seized by creditors or become part of a bankruptcy proceeding. In fact, your assets will be entirely judgment-proof. You cannot get this protection in your home country. And your policy will stand up to any U.S. court order to seize your policy or its assets. Switzerland will not assist a foreign court or honor any court order. Any assets held in a bond, an annuity, or a policy will be very difficult to take a run at, particularly if no one knows it exists. Swiss policies should not be considered the last resort to hide assets, but rather as part of your overall asset protection program, which is purely legitimate and thus protected by Swiss law.

The best strategy is to keep all the assets within Switzerland. By keeping the bond, annuity, or policy deposited in a Swiss bank safe deposit box or with a Swiss attorney or other Swiss fiduciary, you maximize asset protection even for those assets held outside of Switzerland. In the case of life insurance, one other requirement for assurance of asset protection under Swiss law is that the benefits and beneficiaries must be stated; however, owners can change the beneficiary clause at any time. Important to understand is that if the beneficiaries are your spouse and/or descendants, and not a third party, the insurance policy will be protected by law from creditors of the policyholder whether the policy is revocable or irrevocable. Even if the policyholder goes bankrupt, the assets are protected as they bypass the policyholder and automatically transfer to the beneficiaries as the new owners.

The question of forced repatriation, that is, the demand by your country to bring your money home, has received increasing attention recently. Reputable Swiss investment counselors who represent many big Swiss insurance companies claim without hesitation that these insurance policies would escape forced repatriation, as in the scenario of your government passing exchange controls that prevent or limit you from taking money out of the country. If your government makes such a move, likely it would also attempt to get your investment capital back into the home country from foreign banks and other financial-related institutions. The reason the government could not enforce this is that the insurance policy is a *pending contract between you and the insurance company*. This feature is important to you and should be a strong incentive for considering

Swiss insurance products for real asset protection. If you had any type of Swiss bank account outside of an insurance policy, you could be required by law to repatriate the funds under this type of scenario, but not the funds held in a bank or brokerage account within an insurance policy. Because these assets are not technically in your name, you do not retain control over signing power of the accounts.

One last thought on asset protection. If a foreign court tried to force a Swiss policyholder to revoke a beneficiary named earlier so that the policy assets could be incorporated as part of a foreign bankruptcy estate, the policyholder might prefer to comply rather than break the law. However, even in this case, the insurance company might not cooperate, especially if the policy were an *irrevocable* one, as repatriating a customer's assets by the insurance company would defy the contractual arrangement and purpose of the policy. In this case, the foreign court would be unable to penalize the policyholder for not complying, as the policyholder may have acted as the court requested but the matter was out of his or her hands. Courts can't force people to do something that is out of their control.

Swiss Legal Proceedings

Most creditors will be readily discouraged from pursuing your assets and investments if they discover you have them salted away in Switzerland. Further, to begin the process of chasing your assets, they would need to know with which insurance company you have dealt. Definitely keep this fact to yourself; it's the cheapest insurance. Creditors would have to retain a Swiss lawyer, and they can charge up to thousands of dollars per hour. The lawyer also would typically require an advance deposit—likely at least $15,000 on deposit before he or she would proceed. When a lawyer finishes explaining the process for obtaining an order of attachment, creditors may decide to save their money instead. An attorney retained for this purpose is required to try to secure an attachment order, but that hardly means he or she will succeed, and the lawyer knows it. There must be an enforceable judgment or a recognition of debt making a specific claim. No fishing expeditions are going to fly here. If there are grounds, then the cantonal authority has to place the order that the policy be attached. Creditors will have to advance the court costs, and a cash deposit will again be required. Naturally, the policyholder will want to object to the proceedings and he or she has 10 days to file a protest with the court, at which time creditors must initiate a civil lawsuit, which will not be cheap. It is the responsibility of the creditors to prove fraudulent conveyance, and if proved, the Swiss court could invalidate the policy. Every step could be the end of a creditor's efforts to continue this contest. To avoid such a scenario, the best strategy is *not* to discuss any policy with any third party who doesn't absolutely need to know of its existence.

Swiss Franc

The Swiss bond, annuity, and policy can be denominated in a choice of currency, but I must say, it would be foolish to denominate any of them in U.S. dollars. You would be virtually defeating your purpose, and instead of experiencing appreciation over the long term, you would achieve the opposite. As previously discussed, there are a handful of strong currencies that your insurance vehicle should be denominated in. The Swiss franc is one of them. Historically it has been price-stable. Thanks to the Swiss National Bank, it has been the best-managed currency in the world. The Swiss conservative monetary policy is still in force today. Unfortunately, a few years ago Switzerland stopped backing the Swiss franc with more than 100 percent gold and a basket of other conservative liquid assets that served to offset the currency in circulation. A result of this move is that the franc has softened somewhat, but the conservative monetary policy has helped keep Swiss inflation to a bare minimum. Between the beginning of 2003 and the end of 2006, inflation fluctuated between 0.06 and 1.33 percent, based on a monetary policy assessment of the Swiss National Bank released on March 15, 2007. That's the good news, and it has a strong bearing on the fact that the franc still is a stable currency, one suitable for our basket and a candidate for denominating your insurance portfolio, annuity, or policy. The most important consideration is the strength of a currency and the possibility for appreciation over the time frame of your investment.

U.S. Tax and Reporting Requirements

Swiss insurance companies do not issue U.S. reporting forms to the U.S. government or withhold taxes of any kind on earnings from Swiss investment-related insurance products. There are *no* reporting requirements to the U.S. Treasury or the IRS. The bond, annuity, or policy is not considered to be a foreign bank account, and the policyholder's relationship with the insurance company is not considered to be with a foreign financial institution. And there are no reporting requirements to Swiss authorities.

No U.S. income tax is due and payable during the life of a *variable* annuity or life insurance policy; it is due only when the income phase begins or when the policy is liquidated. However, a *fixed* policy is not tax-deferrable on accrued income, as it is defined as a debt instrument and also an insurance contract. The IRS addresses this under "Tax Treatment of Certain Annuity Contracts," Internal Revenue Code (IRC) Sections 163(e) and 1271 to 1275. Any profits in foreign currency appreciation are also taxed. Since the policy is not tax-deferred, the policyholder may take early withdrawals, prior to turning 59½ years old, without paying the usual 10 percent penalty.

Tax-Deferred Earnings

A Swiss bond, annuity, or policy has the potential to earn profits and income, all tax-deferred, with no negative tax consequences, with the exception of the *fixed* insurance policy. Your Swiss insurance company can draft the insurance contract to comply with IRS rules in order to ensure the favorable tax-deferred treatment as variable policies, including the portfolio bond, receive under U.S. tax law. A correctly structured policy is important, but your Swiss insurance company has the knowledge of U.S. tax laws and expertise when it comes to "U.S. persons" and can tailor the insurance contract to meet your requirements. Under another U.S. tax feature, foreign insurance annuities receive much more favorable treatment than trusts, as only a small portion of life income comes from the annuity.

1035 Tax-Free Exchange

Although a fixed annuity can, for asset protection reasons, be placed in a U.S. tax-sheltered pension, including an Individual Retirement Account (IRA) or corporate plans, it would be wise to roll it over into a Swiss annuity so the policy can be physically held in a Swiss bank or by a Swiss fiduciary. You can transfer your existing insurance policy or annuity (Swiss or American) and swap it out for a new one. Just obtain an Absolute Assignment form to make a 1035 tax-free exchange. Your investment safety will also be greater in Switzerland and show better returns.

Swiss Taxes

The earnings on Swiss bond, annuity, and life insurance products are free from Swiss tax, including the 35 percent Swiss withholding tax on interest and dividends.

Compound Earnings and Interest

The money grows in the insurance structure, tax-free, giving the principal the maximum ability to compound and increase. Remember my discourse on compound interest in *Tax Havens Today?* Herbert Lee (H. L.) Barber, Benjamin Franklin, and Albert Einstein knew the power of compounding money and compounded interest. In summary, Einstein once said, "The greatest principle in the universe is the power of compound interest." There you have it! Here, through tax-free compound interest, is one of the rare opportunities for a U.S. taxpayer today to benefit from this law of financial physics and to maximize it to the fullest through use of a tax-free environment. It is a simple lesson often overlooked today, but it is still available thanks to our ability to invest through one of these Swiss insurance products.

Swiss Portfolio Bond

The Swiss portfolio bond, or "insurance wrapper," is a customized variable endowment policy combining the benefits of offshore banking and investing to create a unique holding structure. The best jurisdictions for this type of structure are Switzerland and Liechtenstein. This device affords the best asset protection with Swiss bank secrecy and is the perfect umbrella under which to safely keep your banking and investments from the prying eyes of your government or anyone else while you *quietly* build your fortune. Liechtenstein has a similar strong secrecy in banking and financial matters. And your investments will outpace U.S. counterparts. This is the Rolls-Royce of investment vehicles, providing maximum flexibility for an investor's portfolio, and it works much like a trust but provides *rock-solid* asset protection. Fortunately, it does not have any of the drawbacks of a trust, such as the possibility of forced repatriation and the expense to maintain it.

The customer establishes a relationship by buying a portfolio bond with a Swiss insurance company, essentially like an annuity, and in turn, the insurance company issues the bond or policy, a contract between the customer and the insurance company. Then the company invests the money at the client's direction, after which it is managed by an asset and investment manager. You the customer are always in control of your investments and assets. You may direct the insurance company to purchase shares of stock, bonds, unit trusts, cash deposits, mutual funds, money market funds—in fact, any investment where value can be established, as can be accomplished in a liquid market (i.e., where the security or asset can readily be traded on an exchange). Other assets can be valued through an appraisal by a reputable, certified appraiser or certified public accountant. Real estate, art, and stock in a closely held company are a few examples. By the way, Zurich is becoming the new hub of the international art world. Of course, a basket of currencies along with gold and silver would balance your investment portfolio, providing an excellent hedge and possibly excellent appreciation as described in Chapter 4, "Your Own Private Monetary Policy." Real estate and commodity funds are also worth looking into.

To facilitate these financial transactions, and to further insulate the client, the insurance company sets up a bank account with a bank or banks chosen by the customer. Switzerland and Liechtenstein are usually the first choices for these accounts. You can also establish a securities trading account through your insurance company. Switzerland and Liechtenstein are very similar as far as banking services, investment philosophy, and secrecy are concerned. Swiss financial professionals will often engage Liechtenstein's banking and insurance services in concert with its own, giving the client greater geopolitical diversity and asset protection. Liechtenstein also shares the Swiss franc. Imagine assets in Liechtenstein, double wrapped by Switzerland, as a vault within a vault. Once the account is established, the Swiss insurance company arranges for funds to be deposited with the bank on behalf of the client. And because the bank account is held by the insurance company and you are not a controlling signer on the account, there's no legal requirement to file the annual TD F 90.22-1 no matter how much money is in the account.

You also can purchase life insurance coverage through this structure. A nice feature of the portfolio bond is the ability to separate distributions from the estate and designate a beneficiary directly. Upon your death, the money would be quickly dispersed by the insurance company to the named beneficiaries, usually within a few days of proof of death. The insured person must be a natural person. Family members and nonfamily can be named as beneficiaries, as can a legal entity, such as a corporation, trust, pension plan, foundation, or establishment. In some cases, depending on the insurance company and the type of policy, the policyholder can be a legal entity. The policy owner is the party with control over the policy, and that can be a natural person or a legal entity. The biggest drawback to the portfolio bond may be the initial investment to set it up, which you can discuss with one of the Swiss investment counselors listed in Appendix B under "Swiss Investment Counselors/Insurance Brokers." Once the first premium is paid in, you are set up and ready to begin building your fortune, at whatever pace you like, or can manage. You can also add additional funds during the term of the policy in specified increments. All the while, your estate is secure from scrutiny or confiscation by anyone.

Swiss Annuity

The Swiss annuity offers many benefits, and it is a great way to create retirement income and receive tax-free withdrawals at any time. Unlike the life insurance policy, designed to cover you in the event you should die early, the annuity anticipates that you might live longer and that you will need to preserve your assets and have income for the duration. The annuity can either be single or joint. The word "annuity" actually means "annual payment." Annuities can be for an individual (*single*) or for a couple (*joint*). There are different types of annuities. The *immediate* annuity starts as soon as it has been created or up to anytime in the first year, and begins paying you a guaranteed income on a schedule to meet your needs. This time frame could be over your lifetime or for a specific number of years. It also may be based on someone else's lifetime. Based on the amount you purchase, the insurance company will compute the amount you will receive over that period. The annuity is an investment that provides for an established series of payments in the future. The *deferred* or *flexible* annuity provides for guaranteed payments of income starting later but at any time the investor decides that he or she needs them, and the amounts can be in installments or in a single sum. The advantage of the deferred annuity over the immediate annuity is the time available to invest and to build up savings, compounding the earnings, tax-deferred, until the plan is converted into the income phase, when annuity payments are received.

Taking it a step further, the fixed annuity clearly defines the return on investment, and the insurance company guarantees the principal. However, the variable annuity is more likely the preferred choice, as these are tax-advantaged. The value of the annuity is entirely based on the investments it holds, which can be selected by the policyholder or managed by the insurance company or your own asset and investment manager. Some Swiss investment counselors who are also insurance brokers are highly qualified to manage investment portfolios. As discussed, the portfolio typically contains stocks, bonds, funds, precious metals, and a basket of currencies. The currency basket is a liquid hedge of stable value and appreciation. Naturally, gold and silver serve this purpose well and provide an opportunity for fantastic future profits.

In the case of fixed annuities, insurance companies are required to maintain a *security fund* not only to match their obligations but to provide a safety margin that guarantees they cannot become insolvent. This fund is segregated so that in the event of bankruptcy, the insureds' assets are protected. A *variable* policy is protected by the financial strength of the insurer, and strength varies among companies. Many factors play into a company's capacities to meet its obligations. Your Swiss investment counselor works with and knows the insurance companies and can share with you their different strengths.

The Swiss policy provides guaranteed instant liquidity for all capital, including accumulated interest and dividends. Partial funds may be withdrawn as needed without any penalties, or the policy can be surrendered by paying a surrender fee and the monies can be repatriated. Annuities can be borrowed against, and life insurance can be used as collateral. Your funds are always freely accessible.

Like Swiss bank accounts, Swiss annuities are perfectly legal for U.S. citizens to have. There is always the possibility that this situation could change, but there is nothing foreseeable at this time. Actually, the U.S. government has treated Americans who purchase Swiss financial-related insurance products favorably for many years. In some ways, they are treated more favorably than are those who purchase similar U.S. products. It's surprising since the American insurance industry is so powerful in Washington. Imposing U.S. taxes on a taxpayer's initial purchase of an insurance product would be another way to control demand for these Swiss products and the outflow of capital investment from the United States. At the moment, this is nothing to worry about.

The Swiss annuity is benefited by several factors. Your Swiss insurance company will guarantee a competitive interest rate and dividend income that is generally higher than found in other fixed annuities. Your policy will share in a surplus, but to benefit, your policy needs to be with a top insurance company. Your Swiss investment counselor can advise you which companies have a history for surplus shares paid out. There are also several methods of dividend distribution to consider, such as declining dividends, "new money" dividends, and equal dividend payments, which the counselor also will be happy to explain.

The Swiss annuity also benefits from appreciation of the Swiss franc or other strong currency. Combined, over the past 30 years, these factors have contributed to money held in Swiss annuities having multiplied by a factor of more than 15 times. The Swiss annuity is a simple way to ensure a retirement income and be safely invested. Swiss law guarantees owners and beneficiaries armadillo-tough protection for assets and investments from outside creditors or government confiscation. Flexibility gives you the advantage to change policy options, including named beneficiaries, the payout schedule, and the deferment period while in the accumulation phase.

The Swiss annuity also can be placed in an offshore trust, such as an asset protection trust, and gain another layer of asset protection. The trust can be the policyholder and/or the beneficiary. The annuity can be for any length of time. Typically, they are for periods of 5 or 10 years and they are renewable, but longer periods of up to 50 years can be arranged. A beneficiary can and should be named, so if the purchaser of the annuity dies before the annuity distributes, it will bypass probate. Naming beneficiaries, although they can be changed at any time, assures full asset protection under the law. The full value of the annuity will go directly to your heirs and loved ones. A beneficiary also can be someone other than family. Ownership of the annuity works the same as in the case of the bond. In either case, if the policyholder dies, in the case of an individual and not an entity, a new owner can go on to replace the old policyholder, and no will, probate, or power of attorney is necessary to effect the change. The policyholder would give written notice, possibly in advance and without cumbersome formalities or expense.

The best way to purchase a Swiss annuity is to consult with a Swiss investment counselor and/or insurance broker. They are one in the same. Several excellent recommendations are given in Appendix B. I recommend contacting Swiss Insurance Partners AG, a specialist firm that will gladly provide you with in-depth information and advice to fit your requirements and will assist with the arrangements to purchase an annuity. The minimum investment changes occasionally. Today, anticipate that you will need the equivalent of US$50,000 to begin, which can be the initial single premium, but the more the better. The counselor may recommend Liechtenstein insurance and financial-related products and investments as an alternative or in concert with their fine Swiss products. In either jurisdiction, you are in good hands.

Your counselor will advise you on the best way to make your annuity payments. He or she may offer to establish a "premium deposit account," which is similar to a bank account, but its principal purpose is to provide a facility for making deposits until the insurance premiums become due. The account is denominated in Swiss francs, and it is interest-bearing and *not* subject to U.S. reporting requirements. Naturally, it provides a high degree of confidentiality under the Swiss secrecy act.

The deposits are considered premium deposits,—meaning they exist for making the eventual payments of insurance premiums as they come due—and you may deposit as much money as you like at any given time, and the money can sit in the account, tax-free. Your insurance premiums are deducted automatically from the account. Your policy number is used as reference instead of a bank account number. Interest payments that you receive from the account are tax-free. The insurance company will issue an annual statement.

Swiss annuities are no-load investments, meaning you will not pay additional costs or charges. The annuity can be canceled at any time, and there are no cancellation fees to reduce your principal and accumulated earnings.

There are a number of types of annuities and life insurance policies to discuss with your Swiss investment counselor. They include:

- Immediate annuity
- Deferred annuity
- Pure endowment
- Portfolio bond
- Endowment protection
- Whole life protection
- Level term protection
- Decreasing term protection

Swiss Life Insurance

We're all pretty familiar with life insurance, at least what is offered to the public in the United States and Canada. Other countries have similar types of insurance. But, in Switzerland, their idea of life insurance is a little different. The strength and stability of the country's insurance industry is uniquely financially sound, but the fact that you can combine life insurance with an investment portfolio is another feature that is not commonly known.

Like the annuity, a life insurance policy should be incorporated into any long-term financial plan. The insurance policy covers you in case you die unexpectedly or too soon; as mentioned, the annuity anticipates you living long or longer than expected. A life policy with an investment component (i.e., endowment policy) can be for a *fixed* term or *variable* period. The meanings are the same as for a fixed or variable annuity. A life insurance investment portfolio typically would include stocks, bonds, and fund shares. The life policy can be tailor-made, such as a portfolio bond. These policies may be denominated in any of the strong currencies, and the longer the term, the more important it is that the currency be stable. That means it has to be more than just strong today; it has to be strong for years or decades from now, for the duration of the investment. However, it is also possible to have a *currency-switch* option.

Beneficiaries of a Swiss insurance policy are not taxed on receipt of the death benefit when the policyholder dies, avoiding estate taxes known as generation-skipping taxes. With income taxes and estate taxes often gobbling up as much as 50 percent and more of the value of an estate, Swiss insurance is very attractive. It is also possible to borrow nearly the full value of the policy with no requirement to service the loan. Any Swiss bank will accept a Swiss life policy as collateral for a loan, including accumulated interest and dividends. Policy loans are tax-free.

As with other financial-related insurance products, excellent asset protection is afforded in Switzerland as legislation protects the death benefit and underlying investments, making it more challenging for an estate to be contested. In Switzerland, the secrecy act insures maximum privacy in today's world of transparency. Purchase of a Swiss life insurance policy is nonreportable, and if it is a variable policy, tax-deferred income and profits are allowed to accumulate and are nonreportable. Your investments and earnings will compound and grow at a faster rate. There are no Swiss taxes to impact your investment either. Your Swiss investment counselor can give you more information. Life insurance and annual maintenance fees to administer the policy are reasonable.

Appendix B provides several excellent contacts for Swiss investment counselors with whom you can consult about your investment and estate planning needs. The firm of Swiss Insurance Partners AG is highly recommended and is a good place to begin. You will get answers about Swiss annuities, portfolio bonds, or insurance policies that address your specific circumstances. Mr. Mario Gantenbein, managing director of Swiss Insurance Partners AG, is also author of *Swiss Annuities and Life*

Insurance: Secure Returns, Asset Protection, Safety & Privacy, scheduled for release by John Wiley & Sons, Inc., (available April 2008).

Blacked-Out, Forbidden, and Little-Known Investment Opportunities

Here is another wonderful feature of your new Swiss insurance product, an offshore investment vehicle extraordinaire, and baby boomer retirement exotica for the ages: investments that you never knew existed or were too afraid to ask about. That's right, investments that were blacked out to you, forbidden for you to acquire. These secret ways of getting rich faster are things your government doesn't want you to know about. But now, with your exotic new Swiss investment vehicle parked in the driveway, you're ready to rock. Each of the Swiss financial-related insurance products, whether bonds, annuities, or policies, are now entirely, and legally, at your disposal. You can now invest in foreign markets and in securities previously off limits to you.

The U.S. government restricted sale of these investments in this country, and they were not offered through U.S. brokers or on U.S. exchanges. Some foreign firms just do not want to deal with the red tape, expense, and U.S. bureaucracy associated with offering securities in the over regulated American markets. Just *don't* invest back into the U.S. markets, and you will avoid the Qualified Intermediary (QI) problem discussed in Chapter 5. It's true that many foreign investments have been off limits to U.S. investors, but by investing through the Ultimate Investment Plan, you are able to enter these lucrative markets. A world of investment opportunities will open up to you. Your Swiss banker and Swiss investment/insurance counselor can make investment recommendations in a wide array of choices, some of which would normally be unavailable to you from the United States.

My forthcoming book on offshore investments covers many of these areas and other lucrative investments that are ideal for investing in from offshore, and *they can make you rich,* in good times or bad.

Chapter 7

Alpine Retreat for Business and Pleasure

"I see in the future a crisis approaching that unnerves me and causes me to tremble for the safety of my country. As a result of war, corporations have been enthroned and an era of corruption in high places will follow, and the money power of the country will endeavor to prolong its reign until all wealth is concentrated in a few hands and the republic is destroyed."

—ABRAHAM LINCOLN, NOVEMBER 21, 1864

You may benefit in many ways with banking and investment relationships in Switzerland without ever having to visit. In fact, usually you won't have to leave your home to do business with your Swiss bank or invest anywhere in the world through your Swiss investment structure. The only scenario in which you may need to visit

Switzerland personally is if you want to establish a discretionary account and have your portfolio of investments managed by a Swiss bank. In this case, your prospective banker will most likely want to meet you face to face and discuss your investment plans. From there on he or she will be your personal contact to handle all of your business with the bank.

But should you wish to visit—and who wouldn't?—the country has many other attractions that may interest you. A personal visit would give you a firsthand feel for this unique little country and all it has to offer. You may want to stroll the broad, clean, and orderly streets and visit some banks before you settle on your final choice. With this book in hand, you will have what you need to do comparative shopping and have a good understanding of your options. If you are considering banking and investing through a Swiss financial-related insurance product, such as annuity, portfolio bond, or life insurance investments, a visit to meet your Swiss investment counselor would be a good plan, as he or she may be involved with managing your investments and it would be desirable, if not actually required, to establish a personal relationship.

In your offshore plans, Switzerland could play an important role in providing greater investment returns, protecting assets and planning your estate, and it could possibly include tax-advantaged residency, immigration, real estate investment, or setting up a Swiss company for business and/or investment purposes and likely even tax savings. Prior to any trip, it would be smart to prepare yourself so you are not wasting your time once you land. You can make advance plans and set appointments to meet those with whom you would like to discuss business. As you may not be familiar with the country, although it is relatively small, it's best to allow yourself plenty of time between appointments for travel time and dining and the magnificent, impossible-to-ignore scenery that will surround you constantly.

Business Practices

The Swiss have their particular practices just like every culture, and particularly in business, there are established norms that you should follow. Here are some Swiss-style etiquette guidelines and other basics that will help you as you proceed through your day.

- The Swiss are punctual and prompt in business and social settings. Strive to reciprocate.
- Always make an appointment to meet with a professional. Never drop in.
- Europeans express the date with the day first, month second, followed by the year, and it may be shown as: 16.07.08 or 16 July 2008. In the United States, it would typically be expressed as 7/16/08 or July 16, 2008.
- The work week is generally Monday through Friday starting at 7:30 AM until 5:30 PM.
- Lunch is usually one or two hours, the most common is noon to 1:00 or 1:30 PM.
- Retail stores are open Monday through Saturday from at 8:00 AM until noon and then reopen at 1:30 or 2:00 PM. They typically close at 6:00 or 7:00 PM. Large stores do not close for lunch. Some stores may not be open on Sunday or Monday. The red-light district is open all the time.
- Europeans frequently take the entire month of August off, although this is beginning to change in favor of a more western approach. Some may take the month of July off instead. September and October would be better months to visit Switzerland, and the weather is still nice; a visit in the springtime or early summer would also be desirable. Of course, if you plan to go skiing, the dead of winter may be perfect for you. But avoid the skiing holiday, a two-week period in February, and avoid Christmas time, especially between Christmas and New Year's Day.
- The Swiss take business and banking seriously, as they do money in general. Let the professionals you are meeting take the lead. They will likely get right down to business, but typically they are not adverse to warming up with a little small talk.
- Trust your banking, investment, and professional contacts to know their business, but feel free to establish a comfort level by asking important questions in the interest of satisfying yourself. Always exhibit due respect even if you disagree on an issue.
- Expect that your meeting will be businesslike, so act accordingly and avoid any stereotypes that may project the brash American (or North American).
- As mentioned, there are a number of cultures in Switzerland, and your sensibilities and values are likely to be different from those of some

people you will meet; be patient as they will be trying their best to be of service to you. And, after all, that's the whole point of being there.

- If you have a business card, present it at the time of your appointment. If you don't have a business card, you might want to have one printed before you leave. A calling card is an expected protocol, and will also give a professional first impression. Your calling card should be clean and to the point, giving your name along with basic contact information. Your card should be understated. Black on white still works in business.

- Most bankers, investment types, and professionals in the major cities speak English. If you find yourself in a remote canton, the bank will likely have someone who can translate to English.

- In conversation, you may chat a bit about sports, travel, current events, and Switzerland; but leave private and personal matters to a minimum. Stick to business. Your future banker will want to focus on your business and financial matters, in order to achieve the financial results you desire.

- Give extra respect to older people at all times.

- In general, behave in a civil, polite, and reserved manner. Never be loud in public.

- Your banker, investment counselor, or attorney may invite you to lunch or dinner. Leave it to him or her to ask. If you are invited to lunch expect informality; for dinner, anticipate a formal evening.

- It is normal to greet or make a new introduction with a handshake.

- Dress neatly and conservatively, and keep expensive jewelry to a minimum. The Swiss do not advertise their wealth.

- Address adults by their title followed by their surname.

- The Swiss are orderly, precise, and exacting, as if they were all born under the sign of Virgo.

Travel

Let's run through a few things that you'll need to know when traveling to or within Switzerland. We'll also touch on a few facts you may not need but which are good to know about this country that you, or at least your money, may be visiting one day.

Form of Government: Federal republic
Administration: Divided into 26 cantons
Legal System: Civil law (in contrast to the United States and Canada, which are common law countries)
Capital City: Bern
Largest City: Zurich
Land Area: Approximately 15,950 square miles
National Languages: German; French; Italian; Romansh, and others, including English in banking and business
Population: Approximately 7.5 million
Country Abbreviation: CH (also used as Internet address suffix .ch)
Country Code: 41
Time Zone: Central European Time (CET)=GMT+1 hour
Currency: Swiss franc
Exchange Controls: None. There are no restrictions on the import or export of local or foreign currencies.
Weather and Climate: July and August average 66° F to 86° F (18° C to 28° C); January and February between 32° F and 44° F (−2° C and +7° C). Southern Switzerland is usually mild year-round. Switzerland has the highest mountains in Europe, and altitude will have a bearing on the temperature.
Measurements: Metric system
Electricity: 220 volts AC, 50 Hz
National Public Holidays: New Year's Day: 1 January; Berthold's Day: 2 January; Good Friday: the Friday before Easter each year; Easter Monday: the Monday after Easter each year; Labor Day: 1 May; Ascension Day: 25 May; Pentecost Monday/Whit Monday: 5 June; National Day: 1 August; All Saints: 1 November; Christmas Day: 25 December; Boxing Day: 26 December
Travel Distance: Three to four hours across the country. Visit www .finaroute.ch to calculate time and distances.
Acceptable Payment Methods: Swiss francs. U.S. dollars, euros, and the British pound are accepted in airports, railway stations, and banks, with the merchant or bank calculating the conversion. Major credit cards, including American Express, MasterCard, and Visa, are widely accepted. ATM machines are a convenient way to obtain francs.

Local Tax: Swiss Value Added Tax (VAT) is added to all purchases of goods and services. As a non-Swiss citizen, you can get reimbursed on this tax. Visit www.globalrefund.com for more information.

Tips: Gratuity is generally included in all services by law.

Health Care: Switzerland is one of the cleanest and healthiest countries in the world. No immunizations are required to enter the country. Excellent, very expensive medical facilities are available. Private travel insurance is recommended.

U.S. and Canadian Embassies:

In the United States:

  Embassy of Switzerland

  2900 Cathedral Avenue, NW

  Washington D.C. 20008.

  Telephone (202) 745-7900

  Fax: (202) 387-2564

  Web site: www.swissemb.org/

  E-mail:was.vertretung@eda.admin.ch

  Office hours: Monday–Thursday 8:00 AM to 5:00 PM; Friday 8:00 AM to 4:00 PM.

In Canada:

  Embassy of Switzerland

  5 Marlborough Avenue

  Ottawa, Ontario K1N 8E6 Canada

  Telephone (613) 235-1837

  Fax (613) 563-1394

  Web site: www.eda.admin.ch/canada

  E-mail:ott.vertretung@eda.admin.ch.

  Office hours: Monday–Friday 9:00 AM to noon.

For Swiss embassies in other countries, visit

www.embassiesabroad.com/embassies-of/switzerland

Maps of Switzerland: www.swissinfogeo.org/www.map.search.ch/ www.map24.ch/

www.swisstopo.ch

Train Tables: Public transportation and train timetables, visit www.sbb.ch

Current Information: Visit www.swissnetwork.com
Statistical Data: Visit www. www.bfs.admin.ch
Crime Rate: Low. The country is very safe for travel.

Tax-Advantaged Residency

Like Monaco, Switzerland has been attracting the rich and famous who have chosen this little alpine setting as their new residence and haven from excessive income tax at home, leaving neighboring countries like France, Germany, and the United Kingdom up in arms. Other European countries with similar high to very high tax rates are not pleased either, and it doesn't help that Switzerland also has so many other enticing qualities, leading at times to a rather petty and jealous view of the beautiful little country.

Fortunately, so long as Switzerland does not join the European Union (EU), it will maintain its autonomy. Furthermore, for any of those who expect Switzerland to compromise its stature, the country has sovereign national rights. If its citizens are smart, they will continue to defy the will of the EU and their neighbors for as long as they can, as well as negative influences within their own government. I imagine there are a few regretful countries in the EU pot, stewing in their juices for having given up their rights to national sovereignty and compromising their individual and unique histories, traditions, and cultures.

The good news is that Switzerland hasn't joined the EU yet. What has led to increased pressure from the EU, France, Germany, and others is that the 26 Swiss cantons have been competing with each other to lower their tax rates to attract rich foreign business. Why not? The bankers have made it their job to attract money for decades. And, having their best depositors living nearby certainly couldn't hurt Switzerland; it may actually further stimulate the economy. Next, who knows? Perhaps those same people will choose next to relocate their corporate headquarters in Switzerland.

It appears that Switzerland has no intentions of compromising its tax-advantaged residency to suit foreign tax collectors. Three cheers for the Swiss! Regardless, there has been discussion of a twofold increase on the flat tax rate on foreigners. So far, it's only being discussed. President Micheline

Dalmy-Rey has sharply denounced the idea of any tax hike, saying that there is "absolutely no room for negotiation." We must appreciate the Swiss spirit of independence.

Tax competition among nations is healthy and keeps countries from the temptation of taxing more than they already do, which, in my humble opinion, is already more than they likely should. Few nations are accountable for their spending, so why should they be empowered further at the expense of the people who keep them in business?

In recent years, approximately 3,600 foreigners have discovered Switzerland and found it to be inviting, not just for tax reasons but also for the country's desirable living conditions and high standards. Sixteen of the cantons *cut* tax rates in the last year, and others are considering a similar move. The canton of Obwalden has cut the tax rate by 1 percent to 2.35 percent for individuals earning in excess of 300,000 Swiss francs (CHF300,000) annually, and it has also reduced property taxes. Obwalden also dropped corporate taxes to 6.6 percent.

Currently, foreigners pay less than local residents. Personal taxes for locals who are high-income earners run about 30 percent, when federal taxes are combined with cantonal and communal taxes. As the Swiss tax system is complex, no simple or exact figure can be quoted. Foreigners pay a property tax based on the value of their rental or owned property within Switzerland, less any mortgages or debt encumbrances. The rate is between 0.05 percent and 0.2 percent, in addition to the general wealth tax that varies by canton. As with other Swiss taxes, it is progressive and based on the taxpayer's net worth. Foreigners can benefit from tax-advantaged residency in Switzerland without the need to officially immigrate.

Prospective foreign residents can negotiate a lump-sum tax based on their standard of living as determined by their living expenses. Basically, you can calculate your annual rent times five to get the amount you can anticipate paying in taxes, plus the usual cantonal and communal taxes, which are generally low. This sum is not based on a person's worldwide income or assets so no financial disclosures are required. The cantonal tax, in particular, is generally very reasonable. Realistically, a person would need a high annual income to qualify for the lump-sum tax, say in the vicinity of CHF250,000 and over.

In order to stay in Switzerland for more than three months or to work in Switzerland, you would need to obtain a residence permit or a work permit that would allow you to work for a specified employer. If you seek local employment, of course, the benefits of tax-advantaged residency would not apply as in this case you must have a foreign income source and cannot have a Swiss one. The residence permits are granted by the Cantonal Migration Office of the canton in which you plan to live. The short-term residence permit is for less than a year, annual residence permits are for up to 10 years, and permanent residence permits are unlimited.

Only well-integrated foreigners, that is, those who can show a significant history of having already lived in Switzerland and thus are integrated in the Swiss life and culture, may take up Swiss nationality. Also, it is easier to obtain a residence permit if you are a foreigner seeking to invest in Switzerland or possibly to start a new company or relocate your existing company to Switzerland. This same holds true for rich and famous foreigners seeking relocation.

An interesting item is the option foreign residents have with regard to inheritance, estate, and gift taxes. There are no federal inheritance, estate, or gift taxes in Switzerland, but some cantons assess taxes—for example, of around 10 percent—in these areas. But some do not; the Canton of Schwyz for example has no inheritance or gift taxes. Under Swiss international private law, foreign residents can choose to be subject to Swiss inheritance law or that of their own country.

Foreigners desiring to relocate to Switzerland should consult with a professional in Switzerland who is knowledgeable in the field. This individual or firm can assist with international tax planning; asset protection; real estate; residency, immigration, and relocation requirements; and other legal aspects, facilitating an entire relocation program to save time, energy, and money. The law firm of Henley & Partners AG, located in Zurich and other Swiss cities, is highly recommended. Its Web site address is www.henleyglobal.com. Further contact information is in Appendix B.

Immigration

Switzerland has a two-tiered system for immigration by foreign nationals. Permits are more readily granted to European Union and the European Free Trade Association (EFTA) member nationals and more restrictive for everyone else. This last category is subject to the Foreign Nationals' Residence and Settlement Act, with emphasis on the limitation on the number of foreign nationals. Immigration decisions of non-EU or non-EFTA nationals are at the sole discretion of the authorities. Proof of potential employment is required. Application is made to the future cantonal authorities. The residence permit must be issued before entering Switzerland. The federal government establishes the criteria for immigrating, but the individual cantons are responsible for administering naturalization procedures. Further, people cannot even begin to apply for naturalization until they have lived in Switzerland for at least 12 years.

In 2006, a majority of Swiss voters ratified tougher asylum and immigration laws in hopes of preventing unskilled workers from outside of Europe, many of whom would happily stay indefinitely, from taking employment in Switzerland. This recent measure has proved unfavorable with the United Nations, which Switzerland joined in 2002. Human rights groups criticized the bill, which was favored and supported by the right wing's Swiss People's Party headed by billionaire Christoph Blocher. Using their powers of direct democracy, the Swiss people had spoken.

It would be unrealistic for non-EU or non-EFTA nationals to think of pursuing Swiss immigration, and it is unlikely that all the effort would result in Swiss citizenship. However, foreigners who can obtain residence permits to live in Switzerland can receive some excellent tax benefits, and for certain qualified individuals residency would be worth researching further.

Swiss Real Estate

Swiss real estate is guarded and much like immigration, is strictly controlled, and it is quite expensive. As demand for Swiss real estate outstrips supply, bureaucratic measures are in place to hinder foreigners from purchasing or developing properties. In some cantons, it is actually illegal for foreigners to buy property. Advance permission is required to make any purchases, and receiving such permission is very unlikely. However, if you do obtain a residency permit, you are able to buy a residence, such as a home or an apartment, with no prior approval necessary.

You may be able to get permission to buy real estate in the recreational areas, such as in the vicinity of a ski resort; however, that option may be limited to a condominium for vacation purposes or a holiday home. This type of real estate investment cannot be held by a corporation or other entity, but only by an individual. You will need to do your homework to determine which cantons allow foreigners to purchase real estate, and what types of properties and areas are most likely allowed to be acquired by a foreigner. A Swiss law firm such as Henley & Partners AG can assist, as it also has a real estate division, called Henley Estates Ltd., that specializes in Swiss properties. These folks know their business. Visit their Web site at www.henleyestates.com.

Swiss Real Estate Investment Companies

There are ways to get the benefit of investment in the Swiss real estate market without purchasing Swiss real estate itself. Such an investment could be a nice addition to a conservative investment portfolio, serving as a hedge against inflation and to diversify your investments. The fact that the real estate market is not wide open to just any purchaser makes this real estate more exclusive. Since Switzerland is small and demand is high, real estate values are strong. Therefore, if you invest in a well-managed company that specializes in the Swiss real estate market, you are likely to have a nice solid investment in a security that is easily held by a foreign individual or a foreign entity, such as an offshore corporation or trust. Use a non-Swiss entity to avoid Swiss taxes. Do not invest in Swiss securities through a Swiss bank or Swiss insurance company. Your Swiss banker can make recommendations, but here are some real estate companies that trade their stock on the SWX Swiss Exchange:

- Allread Holding AG
- BFW Liegenschaften AG
- Intershop Holding AG
- LO Holding Lausanne-Ouchy SA
- Mobimo Holding AG; Pax-Anlage AG
- PSP Swiss Property AG
- Swiss Prime Site AG; USI Group Holdings AG
- Warteck Invest AG
- Zublin Immobilien Holding AG

The Swiss Company

The Swiss company has appeal, as it can be established by a foreigner. To do so, it is wise to utilize the services of a top-flight law firm in Switzerland. Aside from the lawyer's help in the initial incorporation process, having a good Swiss lawyer is almost necessary to handle certain company affairs and to call on when questions arise. Switzerland is not a tax haven, but it *is* an asset haven and money-management center. Also, it is one of the lower taxing countries in Europe, and it attracts business for this reason. But it is not a tax haven in the true sense like the notorious havens of the Bahamas and the Cayman Islands.

There are several legal forms available to choose from including sole proprietorships, general partnerships, limited partnerships, companies limited by shares (AG or SA), and limited liability companies (GmbH or Sarl). The AG is the most common Swiss entity organized under the Laws of Obligation. It is a stock corporation that can issue registered shares and even bearer shares if the company's share capital is fully paid up. The AG would be the best vehicle for an international business person or for foreign investment purposes.

Having a Swiss company lends an air of prestige to your operations, automatically giving you the appearance of sophistication and worldliness. The initial cost of setting up the company and the annual maintenance expenses are typically much higher than in most tax haven jurisdictions. The Swiss company also is subject to Swiss corporate taxes.

The tax rate varies between 3.9 percent and 25 percent on worldwide income. The exact figure depends on the canton in which the business is located. There are tax exemptions for certain types of activities, but these would have to be negotiated. Further, withholding taxes on interest and dividends are figured at 35 percent. Switzerland has negotiated numerous double taxation agreements that help to avoid paying tax twice to two countries, including with the United States and Canada.

The AG Swiss company must have a minimum of three shareholders and one local director. No corporate directors are permitted; all must be individuals. Meetings must be held locally. No secretary is required. The minimum authorized capital stock is CHF100,000. The incorporation period is approximately two to three weeks. Redomiciliation of the company to another jurisdiction is allowed, so if circumstances in Switzerland become less favorable, the company could easily be relocated. This ability could also be important for various legal reasons.

Reporting requirements are attractive in Switzerland, as there is no requirement to disclose the identities of the beneficial owners (i.e., the stockholders). The local director would be on public record, and he or she would be responsible for filing the annual return, submission of accounts, and annual audit. Your Swiss attorney can be hired as the director of the company and maintain the corporate formalities when required and also hold meetings as necessary to conduct business.

Here are some costs associated with incorporating and maintaining a Swiss AG company. Expect to pay approximately:

- CHF4,500 to incorporate the company
- A domicile fee of CHF1,500
- An annual administration fee of CHF2,500
- An annual tax return of CHF2,500
- Varying government fees

The first-year expenses to start and maintain the company will run approximately CHF11,000.

The nominee shareholder can cost CHF300, and if a director is required, expect an additional annual director fee of CHF5,000. Adding these last two services to the list, your grand total would be CHF16,300. There may also be some miscellaneous fees, such as registry of commerce fees and notarization of documents. If all of these services were required annually to maintain the company, the minimum annual expenses would be approximately CHF12,000. When these figures are converted into the U.S. or Canadian dollar, the cost would be around US $10,275 at this writing.

Doing Business in Switzerland

Your Swiss company could be operated like an offshore company, but you can also establish an operating business in Switzerland or relocate an existing one. Switzerland is an excellent location, central in Europe, and has an exceptional business environment. Small, medium, and large companies, both domestic and foreign, have made Switzerland their home.

Improved tax reforms have made Switzerland one of the most ideal jurisdictions for establishing a holding company.

Switzerland has attracted e-commerce enterprise, and according to *IMD: The World Competitiveness Yearbook 2002,* Switzerland ranked first among 49 countries as being in the most favorable position to facilitate e-commerce activity—based on the number of computers, Internet users, and secure servers—and the country ranked third in data security.

Entrepreneurs have found Switzerland to be favorable with a wide range of opportunities. It has strong appeal to those firms with heavy financial activities or for financial departments of those firms, and also for research and development. Employees are motivated to relocate from foreign countries, knowing that Switzerland is quite safe and secure in comparison to most nations, and there are excellent educational and medical facilities and a pleasant environment for families. Newly organized Swiss companies know that the modern infrastructure will support their business activities and personal needs. There are also possible financial incentives for substantial investments.

According to the *Switzerland Business & Investment Handbook* of 2006, a few of the more notable foreign firms with branches in Switzerland include:

Alcoa European Headquarters
Alstom (Switzerland) Ltd.
Amgen (Europe) AG
Bulgari
Cemex
eBay Europe
Estee Lauder
Gillette Group International
Hamilton Bonaduz AG
Medtronic International
Michelin Finance Company
Wurth International AG-Grisons
Zimmer Holdings
ZLB Behring AG

Some Swiss companies that are traded on the SWX Swiss Exchange include:

ABB Ltd.
Credit Suisse Group
Compagnie Financiere Richemont SA
Holcim Ltd.
Julius Bar Holding AG
Novartis AG
Nestle AG
Roche Holding AG
Swiss Life Holding
Schweizerische Ruckversicherungs-Gesellschaft
UBS AG
Zurich Financial Services

They may be worth investigating for equity investment purposes from offshore or from outside Switzerland to avoid Swiss taxes.

Back Door to Switzerland

Campione d'Italia is an interesting enclave to know about. With just 3,000 residents, it is a possible alternative to living in Switzerland; although located within Switzerland geographically and is similarly clean, safe, and stable, it is actually Italian. This little-known venue comprises just under one square mile (1.6 square kilometers), and though a part of Italy, it is located on Lake Lugano in the southern Swiss canton of Ticino. Furthermore, although part of Italy's territory, Campione is completely self-governing. The official language is Italian, and it uses both the Swiss franc and the euro as its official currency. Along with Switzerland's currency, Campione also uses the Swiss license plate, postal system, telephone system, country code, traffic laws, visa regulations and more.

Furthermore, this tiny haven has a similar aesthetic wonder as Switzerland. It's been called the "back door to Switzerland," as residents have unlimited access to Switzerland and Liechtenstein. There is no border crossing into Switzerland. In Lake Lugano, only a 10-minute drive, you will find access to 40 Swiss banks. There are no restrictions on purchasing real estate, although it is very expensive, as it is in Switzerland. However, there are a variety of residential properties for rent. A foreign tax-free corporation can legally acquire real estate.

Campione has been supported from the revenues of Casino di Campione, the only casino and the largest employer to date. A new casino is currently under construction. Many potential tax benefits can be had by living and even doing business in Campione, including income tax concessions and the absence of inheritance and gift taxes. The law firm of Henley & Partners AG in Zurich has representatives in Lugano and Campione. They can provide expertise in tax matters, real estate purchases, Italian immigration, and other business related to Campione.

Chapter 8

The Best Alternatives
to Switzerland

*"The worth of a state, in the long run, is the worth of the individuals
composing it."*

—JOHN STUART MILL,
DISSERTATIONS AND DISCUSSIONS, 1859

Three European countries compete prominently with Switzerland, and all share many of Switzerland's attributes in the areas of
banking, investment philosophy, and privacy. And all three are
geographically close; Austria borders Switzerland, as does Liechtenstein,
and Andorra is landlocked between Spain and France in the eastern Pyrenees. All three countries have a long history of private banking and providing financial and investment alternatives to Switzerland, much to the
satisfaction of foreign investors around the world. In fact, Swiss bankers
and investment counselors themselves frequently employ Liechtenstein's

banking and financial-related insurance products in conjunction with or to enhance services provided in Switzerland, or as a combined strategy for the client's benefit. All three countries also have strict bank secrecy laws. They are often overlooked but are worth serious consideration.

You may be wondering why I point out three European alternatives to Switzerland, since I've written a book written a book specifically on Switzerland and argued why I believe Switzerland still has superior benefits. Should pressures from the European Union, the Organization of Economic Cooperation and Development, the United Nations, or the United States government, or other developments, such as a serious compromise or abolishment of the Swiss Bank Secrecy Act of 1934, occur, you may want to review your options. As changes occur in the universe faster than authors can revise their books and publishers can get them to market, I have included this section so that you can spend some time learning more about these options for future reference. Furthermore, in some cases and specific scenarios, the alternatives may prove to be superior and worthy of your consideration.

To begin, let's look at what I call the T-7, a list of my estimation of the current top tax havens in the world (which, incidentally, includes Andorra, Austria, and Liechtenstein).

T-7 Tax Havens

The collective countries known as the G-7—the industrialized nations of Canada, France, Germany, Italy, Japan, the United Kingdom, and the United States—are also some of the highest-taxing nations in the world. Of course, these seven giants are not the only tax-happy zealots. Australia and other nations, and organizations such as the European Union (EU), the Organization for Economic Cooperation and Development (OECD), the Financial Action Task Force (FATF), and the United Nations (UN), are all working to thwart or even crush the offshore opportunities of tax-haven nations. The UN also wants to be the new Global Internal Revenue Service. If that's not enough, it also wants to infringe on the U.S. Bill of Rights and the Second Amendment of the Constitution and take your gun away.

In response to this avalanche of bureaucracy, it seems appropriate to have provided a convenient reference for readers and others about the most advantageous havens to bank, invest from, and put your money for profit, privacy, and protection. If only we could take away the *taxman's* guns.

The OECD has its blacklist, so here's my "Green List" of the world's best offshore tax havens. This exclusive list of seven excellent countries includes tax havens, money havens, asset havens, and offshore banking centers. I have evaluated them using the 12 most important criteria for selecting a tax haven for use as described in my previous book, *Tax Havens Today: The Benefits and Pitfalls of Banking and Investing Offshore.* These factors are:

1. Tax structure
2. Political and economic stability
3. Exchange controls
4. Treaties
5. Government attitude
6. Modern corporation laws
7. Communications and transportation
8. Banking, professional, and support services
9. Legal system
10. Secrecy and confidentiality
11. Investment incentives and opportunities
12. Location

I will revise the T-7 list annually. The list will be distributed via a press release to the media and published at www.barberfinancialadvisors .com. In order of preference, here are my favorite offshore havens in 2007–2008:

1. Switzerland
2. Liechtenstein
3. Andorra
4. Austria
5. Panama
6. Belize
7. Saint Kitts and Nevis

The list has changed some since the 2006–2007 list was released in the fall of 2006. Andorra, a favorite of mine, now is number three on the list, replacing Austria, which has not signed a TIEA with the United States but *has* signed a Mutual Legal Assistance Treaty (MLAT). Andorra has signed neither. Hong Kong was bumped off the list, and Saint Kitts and Nevis were placed in seventh place. The reasoning behind my decisions has partly to do with my audience, most of whom are readers from the United States and Canada. These havens would have particular appeal to them in part because they have not signed a Tax Information Exchange Agreement (TIEA) or an MLAT, among other benefits. (The TIEA and MLAT are discussed in their own sections later in the chapter.) Of course, I have readers in other countries, and they should evaluate factors in selecting a tax haven or banking center with consideration for their own citizenship and residency as well as treaties between the countries, if any. Other tax havens may be beneficial to these people.

Because Andorra, tucked between Spain and France, would have more appeal to North Americans than Hong Kong, Andorra bumped the Asian capital off my list. This change in status is not really a reflection on Hong Kong, as it still is a superior tax haven and offshore banking center for Americans, Canadians, and others. I expect it will remain excellent for some time. The key factor is the attitude of Mainland China toward this former British financial enclave. Unless you have activities in Asia or very specific reasons for investing there, most North Americans would be more comfortable having their money and assets in Europe. Saint Kitts and Nevis are about neck and neck with Belize as far as secrecy laws, both are staunch no-tax havens, and neither has signed a TIEA or an MLAT. But from personal experience, the offshore trade in Belize is probably superior, with very professional and efficient banking and business support services and excellent services to support e-commerce offshore trade.

On the current 2007–2008 T-7 list, the top five are my favorite offshore banking centers and the bottom three are my favorite tax havens and jurisdictions from which to conduct offshore business. Panama overlaps and is excellent in both areas. All seven are considered money and asset havens, and none of the T-7 has signed a TIEA with the United States.

That's my reasoning and how I see it for the forthcoming year or so, at least until the fall of 2008, when I will update the list and again release my opinion on the best tax havens and offshore banking centers for Americans and Canadians. More changes may be ahead.

The offshore world *could* change, in part with the attitude of the U.S. Congress and that of certain Democrats who are vowing to eliminate tax havens. But abolishing tax havens is more of a fantasy than a likelihood. That doesn't mean they won't try hard to at least limit your access, and this is all the more reason people should work to establish themselves offshore financially as soon as possible. For example, exchange controls may be on the horizon, and getting money out of your country then would be very difficult.

If you would like to get offshore the fastest and safest way and based on your individual circumstances, you might want to consider having an offshore evaluation completed. Refer to Appendix C for further information.

The next three sections discuss my list of top alternatives to Switzerland, where benefits exist today and may be worth remembering for the future. The other real possibilities for North Americans, outside of Europe, include the T-7 tax havens of Panama, Belize, Saint Kitts, and Nevis, so I will cover them briefly later in the chapter. They are excellent tax havens for Americans and Canadians for getting offshore, for asset protection reasons, for securing strong privacy, and also for conducting offshore business. The time zones are favorable to North Americans, and the offshore banking and services sectors are easy to work with and efficient, especially in Belize. Also, in the last three examples, English is spoken, and in Panama typically you can get by in English for business and banking.

Liechtenstein

This principality is in good company, lying between the two other T-7 offshore havens of Switzerland and Austria, and it is politically and economically stable. Liechtenstein is the world's oldest tax haven; it passed asset protection legislation as early as the 1920s. Liechtenstein has strict bank secrecy, which it allows to be penetrated only in the case of criminal prosecution. The Swiss franc is the national currency. Although the country boasts only 16 banks, they are among the top in the world, and they are located in an important international financial center and tax haven. Further, companies domiciled in Liechtenstein are not subject to income tax on foreign-source income. This little nation is a popular venue for holding and domiciliary companies and is home to some unique corporate and trust structures. One is the *Anstalt,* commonly known as the "Establishment," which has the option to be a stock company, and the *Stiftungs,* a private foundation. Blacklisted by the OECD for refusal to cooperate, Liechtenstein adamantly refuses to succumb to outside pressures. As 38-year-old Crown Prince Alois said with a smile, "Bank secrecy is very firmly anchored in the population." I tip my hat to the crown prince for staying true to himself and his people and not cooperating with the OECD.

Affiliations: United Nations
Location: This postage-stamp–size enclave is situated in Western Europe and bordered by Switzerland to the west and Austria to the east.
Capital and Largest City: Vaduz
Government: Hereditary constitutional monarchy
Legal System: The prince of the state and the legislature pass law. Civil and criminal procedures have an Austrian influence; contract and property law has a Swiss orientation; and commercial law has a German base.
Official Language: German
Stability: One of the most stable countries in the world
Currency: Swiss franc
International Time: +1 hr. GMT
Country Code: 41 75
Embassy: No embassy in the United States
Exchange Controls: None
Treaties with the United States: No income tax treaty; no TIEA; signed an MLAT in 2003

Andorra

This parliamentary coprincipality of France and Spain remains autonomous and is very stable. The currency is the euro. The country has strict bank secrecy and numbered accounts, and also has the attributes of an excellent haven for expats. Of course, you would probably want to brush up on your French or Spanish and maybe learn Catalan or Portuguese, as these are Andorra's frequently spoken languages. Andorra has no diplomatic relations or extradition treaties with the United States. It is another tax haven that is quite willing to suffer being blacklisted by the OECD. There are no direct taxes, no income tax treaties with the United States, no TIEA or MLAT. It's nearly perfect! There is a limit on your stay for visiting, but if you rent or purchase property, you can stay indefinitely. And a new international airport is under construction. An ideal expat haven! The first step is to secure a "passive" residence permit, good for four years, which will grant you certain protections under the law. Unfortunately, it takes 25 years to become a citizen. Even though Andorra is not an EU member state, it has officially used the euro since 2002.

Affiliations: United Nations
Location: Tucked between France and Spain high in the Pyrenees Mountains in Western Europe
Capital and Largest City: Andorra la Vella
Government: The principality of Andorra achieved international recognition as an independent state in 1993.
Legal System: Civil law
Official Language: Catalan; Andorrans also speak French, Castillian, and Portuguese.
Stability: Extremely stable
Currency: Euro
International Time: +1 hr. GMT
Country Code: 376
Embassy:
  Embassy of Andorra/Permanent Mission to the UN
  2 United Nations Plaza, 25th Floor
  New York, NY 10017
  Telephone (212) 750-8064
Office of Immigration: Andorra la Vella. Telephone 376-826222.
Exchange Controls: None
Treaties with the United States: No income tax treaties; no TIEA or MLAT

Austria

This is another attractive European haven with a long tradition of bank secrecy. In recent years, due to EU pressures, Austria has eliminated two unique accounts: the anonymous *Sparbuch,* a bearer-type passbook account, and the anonymous *Wertpapierbuch,* a bearer-type passbook account coupled with a securities and commodities and securities trading account. Regardless, Austria prevails as an important money haven with its strict bank secrecy still intact, even after joining the EU in 1995. You can enjoy Austria's many charms while you visit your gold Philharmonics. Unfortunately, it is difficult to say how long Austria will remain attractive. The EU and OECD have put plenty of pressure on the country in the past.

Affiliations: European Union; United Nations
Location: At the heart of Western Europe, bordered by Germany and Czech Republic, Italy, Slovania, Switzerland, and Hungary.
Capital and Largest City: Vienna
Government: Federal Republic
Legal System: Based on the Federal Constitutional Act of 1920 providing for separate judicial and administrative functions.
Official Language: German
Stability: Very stable
Currency: Euro
International Time: +1 hr. GMT
Country Code: 43
Embassy:
  Embassy of Austria
  3524 International Court NW
  Washington DC 20006-3027
  Telephone (202) 895-6700
Treaties with the United States: No income tax treaty. No TIEA. Signed an MLAT in 1998. Member FATF.

Panama

Panama is a stable democracy with Latin-style politics and a free economy. It is the Latin American version of Switzerland or Hong Kong. This narrow country, which connects South and Central America, is one of the oldest tax havens in the world, dating back to the 1920s, like Liechtenstein. Panama also has adapted similar corporate and asset protection legislation as Liechtenstein. Today Panama is a modern international financial center with bank secrecy legislation as strict as anywhere.

There is a tight fraternity among Panamanian bankers. The country is a superior tax haven with no corporate or personal tax on income from foreign sources, and it is growing in popularity with expatriates from North America who find the country friendly to newcomers, with a reasonable cost of living. Panama is home to the Panama Canal and is a favorable flag-of-convenience country for yachtsmen and shipping companies. And the famous Panama corporation has armadillo-caliber impermeability and is useful in any international business scenario in which strong insulation is desired.

Affiliations: United Nations
Location: Central America; Costa Rica to the north, Colombia to the South, between the North Pacific Ocean and the Caribbean Sea
Capital and Largest City: Panama City
Government: Constitutional democracy
Legal System: Civil law
Official Language: Spanish. English is common in banking and business.
Stability: Very stable
Currency: Balboa and United States dollar
International Time: −5 hrs. GMT
Country Code: 507
Embassy:
  Embassy of the Republic of Panama
  2862 McGill Terrace, NW
  Washington, DC 20008
  Telephone (202) 483-1407
Exchange Controls: None
Treaties with the United States: No income tax treaty; no TIEA. Signed an MLAT in 1995.

Belize

Belize is a no-tax haven with progressive corporate and trust legislation. Once a British colony, Belize gained independence in 1981. This tropical Central American country has been aggressively promoting itself as an international financial center, and its future looks promising. There is strict bank secrecy, and there are no treaties or agreements with the United States or international organizations. The OECD had blacklisted Belize for a while in 2000 until the country made a few concessions, but none was anything dramatic. However, now your international business company (IBC) will not be able to issue bearer shares unless they are held in trust on behalf of the beneficial owner(s) by a licensed fiduciary, which still serves the purpose of anonymity and security, and Belize no longer has an Economic Citizenship Program. The tax haven does have the QRP, the Qualified Retired Persons program, which has attractive benefits for permanent residency for those who wish to retire in this tropical paradise.

The Belizian Supreme Court staunchly defends the nation's laws and protects depositors against outside attacks. This business-friendly haven offers a wide variety of offshore financial services. Belize is an excellent offshore e-commerce base and has one of the strongest asset protection trust laws found anywhere as well as good offshore banking services for individuals and offshore corporations and trusts.

Affiliations: Commonwealth of Nations; United Nations

Location: Formerly British Honduras. Central America, on the Caribbean Sea between Mexico and Guatemala.

Capital and Largest City: Belize

Government: Parliamentary democracy

Legal System: English common law

Official Language: English

Stability: Very stable

Currency: Belize dollar; U.S. dollar (other major currencies are also used in offshore banking)

International Time: −6 hrs. GMT

Country Code: 501

Embassy:
  Embassy of Belize
  2535 Massachusetts Avenue, NW
  Washington, DC 20008
  Telephone: (202) 332-9636

Exchange Controls: None

Treaties with the United States: No income tax treaty; no TIEA; signed an MLAT in 2003

Saint Kitts and Nevis

Often just called Nevis in the offshore world, this is a pure no-tax haven in the spirit of what a tax haven was originally meant to be. A little two-island nation, known formerly as Saint Christopher-Nevis (Saint Kitts and Nevis), it is completely independent, having no ties with Britain or any other imperial nation, and makes its law according to its good conscience. Nevis is a proactive tax haven with modern corporate and trust legislation. It strongly supports its offshore industry and protects its offshore trade. The strict bank secrecy is close to impenetrable. There are no detracting treaties like the TIEA or MLAT with the United States or with any international organization. Nevis offers legal, financial, and business support services, including services for offshore e-commerce business. Nevis, Belize, and the Cook Islands are the three best jurisdictions for establishing an asset protection trust (APT). Nevis IBCs can issue bearer shares, and beneficial owners can enjoy complete anonymity. This haven is an excellent choice for the quick redomiciliation of a foreign company. For a swift second citizenship or alternative citizenship, Nevis is one of the best, and the very few, available today for a fee. If expatriating or acquiring new citizenship is of interest to you, I recommend contacting Mr. Christian Kälin at Henley & Partners in Zurich, Switzerland (listed in Appendix B). Although offshore banking services are limited in Nevis, the Ministry of Finance has been working to establish good relations with Swiss bankers for the benefit of Nevis companies, a relationship that could benefit you if you choose to incorporate in Nevis.

Affiliates: Commonwealth of Nations; United Nations
Location: West of Antigua in the Lesser Antilles of the Caribbean Sea
Capital and Largest City: Basseterre (capital—St. Kitts); Charlestown (largest—Nevis)
Government: Constitutional monarchy
Legal System: English common law
Official Language: English
Stability: Very stable
Currency: East Caribbean dollar; U.S. dollar
International Time: −4 hrs. GMT

Country Code: 809
Embassy:
  Embassy of Saint Kitts and Nevis
  3216 New Mexico Avenue, NW
  Washington DC 20016
  Telephone (202) 686-2636
Treaties with the United States: No income tax treaty; no TIEA.
Signed an MLAT in 2000

Tax Information Exchange Agreement

The Tax Information Exchange Agreement (TIEA) has had a profound negative impact on tax havens that have elected to sign one with the United States. The TIEA has no redeeming value to U.S. citizens doing business in these tax havens. I provide information on the TIEA, although it does not apply to the T-7 tax havens, because the agreement is important to understand, particularly if things should change in the venues of your choice or consideration.

The TIEA was drafted simply to exchange domestic tax information between the U.S. Internal Revenue Service (IRS) and other countries, including the tax havens that might choose to be a party to it. The TIEA has no benefit to a private third party like the offshore investor. In fact, the only beneficiary of such a treaty appears to be the IRS. Secrecy laws in financial matters are the linchpin of success for tax havens and are the single most important reason for their popularity over the decades. But a TIEA serves to undermine this purpose. Knowing which countries have a TIEA in place with the United States is important. If financial confidentiality is a concern, you should not do business with a TIEA tax haven. Forget "bank secrecy" or confidentiality if a tax haven or other country has signed a TIEA; this warning pertains to attorney-client relationships in these countries too. The TIEA has undermined once-prominent tax havens, including such past standouts as the Bahamas and the Cayman Islands.

The next 13 tax havens countries have signed TIEAs with the United States and will surely pay the price for bowing to outside pressure. (Note that other tax havens could concede in the future.)

1. Antigua and Barbuda
2. Aruba
3. Bahamas
4. Barbados
5. Bermuda
6. British Virgin Islands (BVI)
7. Cayman Islands
8. Channel Islands (includes Guernsey and Jersey)
9. Costa Rica
10. Dominica
11. Grenada
12. Isle of Man
13. Marshall Islands

Three cheers for these tax haven countries, which have *not* signed a TIEA and should be considered first:

1. Andorra
2. Anguilla
3. Austria★
4. Bahrain
5. Belize★
6. Brunei Daraussalam
7. Cook Islands
8. Cyprus
9. Dubai (UAE)
10. Gibraltar
11. Hong Kong★
12. Labuan (Malaysia)
13. Liechtenstein★
14. Luxembourg
15. Madeira
16. Malaysia
17. Malta

★Denotes a T-7 tax haven, one of my most favored money havens for North Americans.

18. Mauritius
19. Monaco
20. Netherlands
21. Netherlands Antilles
22. Panama★
23. Saint Kitts and Nevis
24. Saint Vincent
25. Seychelles
26. Switzerland★
27. Turks and Caicos Islands
28. Vanuatu
29. Western Samoa

Fortunately, more tax havens have turned down the invitation to sign away their lucrative offshore business than have succumbed. Maybe the remaining countries have realized the harm they will cause themselves if they *do* sign a TIEA.

Mutual Legal Assistance Treaty

Here's another treaty that has no tax ramifications but that, in some cases, allows assets to be seized even without a court order. The Mutual Legal Assistance Treaty (MLAT) was created to help law enforcement in criminal investigations, but it is not used in tax evasion cases. This treaty lacks regard for due process of law, which requires "probable cause" under the Fourth Amendment of the U.S. Constitution, and substitutes it with "reasonable suspicion." Since its creation in 1973, 49 countries have signed the agreement with the United States, and together they split the booty—billions of dollars to date.

The following is the U.S. government list of those countries that have signed an MLAT with the United States: (Note that the information in the following two lists can change in the future.)

★Denotes a T-7 tax haven, one of my most favored money havens for North Americans.

1. Antigua and Barbuda
2. Argentina
3. Australia
4. Austria★
5. Bahamas
6. Barbados
7. Belize
8. Belgium
9. Brazil
10. Canada
11. Cyprus
12. Czech Republic
13. Dominica
14. Egypt
15. Estonia
16. European Union
17. Finland
18. France
19. Greece
20. Grenada
21. Hong Kong★
22. Hungary
23. India
24. Ireland
25. Israel
26. Italy (includes Campione)
27. Jamaica
28. Japan
29. Latvia
30. Liechtenstein
31. Lithuania
32. Luxembourg
33. Mexico
34. Morocco

★Denotes a T-7 tax haven, one of my most favored money havens for North Americans.

35. Netherlands
36. Panama★
37. Philippines
38. Poland
39. Romania
40. Russian Federation
41. Spain
42. Saint Kitts and Nevis
43. Saint Lucia
44. Saint Vincent and the Grenadines
45. South Africa
46. Switzerland
47. Thailand
48. Turkey
49. Trinidad and Tobago
50. United Kingdom, including Cayman Islands, Anguilla, British Virgin Islands, Montserrat, and the Turks and Caicos,
51. Uruguay
52. Venezuela

These tax havens have *not* signed an MLAT with the United States:

1. Andorra
2. Aruba
3. Bahrain
4. Bermuda
5. Brunei
6. Cook Islands
7. Costa Rica
8. Dubai (UAE)
9. Labuan (Malaysia)
10. Madeira
11. Malta
12. Monaco
13. Mauritius

★Denotes a T-7 tax haven, one of my most favored money havens for North Americans.

14. Seychelles
15. Vanuatu
16. Western Samoa

For non-U.S. citizens who are reading this book, these tax havens may offer more advantages as the treaties in place with your country of citizenship are likely to be different, and there is a good possibility that you are not subject to taxation on your worldwide income, as are U.S. citizens. These factors will have a great bearing on which tax haven will work best for you. If you are a British taxpayer, I suggest that you avoid former British crown colonies for your chosen tax haven. Quite likely British tax authorities will be applying more pressures on these countries in the future. Likewise, if you are in the European Union (EU), you will want to avoid Switzerland if financial privacy is desired due to the "EU savings tax directive" in Part 2.

Appendix A

Swiss Banks

This list of Swiss banks does not include all of them, but it does include most of the main branches in Switzerland with complete contact information, type of bank, and the year when it was established.

I invite readers to share with me their experiences with any of the banks, insurance companies, and other contacts I have provided here, so that I can better serve my clients and future readers. Please feel free to e-mail me at barberfinancial@hotmail.com or President@BarberFinancial Advisors.com.

ABN AMRO Bank (Switzerland) Ltd.
Commercial Bank/Investment Bank/Private Bank—Est. 1824
Address: Beethovenstrasse 33; PO Box 5239
CH-8022 Zurich, Switzerland
Tel: (41-44) 631 41 11
Fax: (41-44) 631 41 81
Web site: www.abnamro.ch
E-mail: info@abnamro.ch, contact@ch.abnamro.com

Adler & Co Privatbank AG
Private Bank—Est. 1923
Address: Claridentsrasse 22; PO Box 2055
CH-8022 Zurich, Switzerland
Tel: (41-44) 206 99 00
Fax: (41-44) 206 99 99
E-mail: info@adlerbank.ch

AIG Privat Bank AG
Private Bank—Est. 1965
Address: Pelikanstraqsse 37; PO Box 1376
CH-8021 Zurich, Switzerland
Tel: (41-44) 227 55 55
Fax: (41-44) 211 55 11
Internet: www.aigprivatebank.com
E-mail: info@aigpb.com

AKB Privatbank Zurich AG
Private Bank
Address: Bleicherweg 18
CH-8039 Zurich, Switzerland
Tel: (41-44) 283 83 83
Fax: (41-44) 283 84 83
Internet: www.akbprivatbank.ch
E-mail: info@akbprivatbank.ch

Alpha RHEINTAL Bank
Credit Bank/Private Bank/Retail Bank/Universal Bank—Est. 1868
Address: Auerstrasse 1
CH-9441 Berneck, Switzerland
Tel: (41-71) 747 95 95
Fax: (41-71) 747 95 90
Internet: www.alpharheintalbank.ch
E-mail: info@arb.rba.ch

Alternative Bank ABS
Commercial Bank
Address: Lebernsgasse 17
CH-4601 Olten, Switzerland
Tel: (41-62) 206 16 16
Fax: (41-62) 206 16 17
Internet: www.abs.ch
E-mail: contact@abs.ch

Amas Bank (Switzerland) Ltd
Investment Bank/Private Bank—Est. 1994
Address: Place de la Fusterie 3 bis; PO Box 1011
1211 Geneva, Switzerland
Tel: (41-22) 906 08 08; 906 08 26; 906 08 20
Fax: (41-22) 906 08 00; 738 59 97; 731 37 81
E-mail: info@amasbank.com, ehanna@amasbank.com, afarshori@amasbank.com

American Express Bank (Switzerland) SA
Private Bank—Est. 1990
Address: 50 Rue du Rhone; PO Box 3072
1211-3 Geneva, Switzerland
Tel: (41-22) 319 08 08
Fax: (41-22) 311 22 88

Anglo Irish Bank (Suisse) SA
Commercial Bank/Private Bank—Est. 1948
Address: 7 Rue des Alpes; Case Postale 1380
CH-1211 Geneva, Switzerland
Tel: (41-22) 716 36 36
Fax: (41-22) 716 36 76
Internet: www.angloirishbank.ch
E-mail: info@angloirishbank.ch

Anker Bank
Private Bank—Est. 1934
Address: Lintheschergasse 19
8023 Geneva, Switzerland
Tel: (41-22) 312 03 12
Fax: (41-22) 312 03 57
Internet: www.ankerbank.ch
E-mail: welcome@ankerbank.ch, zeier@ankerbank.ch

AP Anlage & Privatbank AG
Private Bank
Address: Kantonsstrasse 1
CH-8807 Freienbach, Switzerland
Tel: (41-44) 787 62 00
Fax: (41-44) 787 62 10
Internet: www.apbank.ch
E-mail: info@apbank.ch

Appenzeller Kantonalbank
Government Bank/Universal Bank—Est. 1899
Address: Bankgasse 2; PO Box 92
CH-9050 Appenzell, Switzerland
Tel: (41-71) 788 88 54
Fax: (41-71) 788 88 89
Internet: www.appkb.ch
E-mail: kantonalbank@appkb.ch

Arab Bank (Switzerland)
Commercial Bank/Corporate Bank/Investment Bank—Est. 1962
Address: Limmatquai 92; PO Box 2023
CH-8001 Zurich, Switzerland
Tel: (41-44) 265 71 11
Fax: (41-44) 265 73 30
Internet: www.arabbank.ch
E-mail: pbanking@arabbank.ch

Arvest Privatebank AG
Private Bank—Est. 1987
Address: Churerstrasse 82; Postfach
CH-8808 Pfaffikon, Switzerland
Tel: (41-55) 415 65 40
Fax: (41-55) 415 65 49
Internet: www.arvest.ch
E-mail: privatbank@arvest.ch

Arzi Bank AG Zurich
Investment Bank/Private Bank—Est. 1962
Address: Talacker 4; PO Box 1532
CH-8027 Zurich, Switzerland
Tel: (41-44) 227 10 70
Fax: (41-44) 227 10 71
Internet: www.arzibank.ch
E-mail: mail@arzibank.ch

Atlantic Forfaitierungs AG
Merchant Bank—Est. 1959
Address: 8 Othmarstrasse
CH-8008 Zurich, Switzerland
Tel: (41-44) 261 26 37
Fax: (41-44) 251 79 64
E-mail: info@atlanticforfaiting.com

Baloise Bank SoBa
Retail Bank/Universal Bank—Est. 1995
Address: Amthausplatz 4; PO Box 262
CH-4502 Solothurn, Switzerland
Tel: (41-32) 626 02 02
Fax: (41-32) 623 36 92
Internet: www.baloise.ch
E-mail: bank@baloise.ch

Banca Aletti & C. (Suisse) SA
Commercial Bank
Address: Via C Maraini 11; PO Box 263
CH-9600 Lugano, Switzerland
Tel: (41-91) 911 81 11
Fax: (41-91) 911 81 81
E-mail: info@alettibank.ch

Banca Arner SA
Private Investment and Merchant Bank—Est. 1984
Address: Piazza Manzoni 8.
CH-6901 Lugano, Switzerland
Tel: (41-91) 912 62 22
Fax: (41-91) 912 62 69
Internet: www.arnerbank.ch
E-mail: info@arnerbank.ch

Banca Commerciale Lugano (Handelsbank Lugano)
Commercial Bank/Foreign Exchange/Private Bank/
    Trade Finance—Est. 1963
Address: Viale Corlo Cattaneo 9; Casella Postale 5877
CH-6901 Lugano, Switzerland
Tel: (41-91) 910 43 43
Fax: (41-91) 923 55 73
Internet: www.bcl.ch
E-mail: info@bcl.ch

Banca del Ceresio
Private Bank—Est. 1958
Address: Via Pretorio, 13; PO Box 5895
CH-6901 Lugano, Switzerland
Tel: (41-91) 923 84 22
Fax: (41-91) 923 55 08
E-mail: mail@ceresiobank.com

Banca del Gottardo (Banque du Gothard)
Universal Bank—Est. 1957
Address:Viale S. Franscini 8; PO Box 2811
CH-6901 Lugano, Switzerland
Tel: (41-91) 808 11 11
Fax: (41-91) 923 94 87
Internet: www.gottardo.com
E-mail: info@gottardo.com

Banca del Sempione
Commercial Bank—Est. 1960
Address:Via Peri 5; PO Box 2825
CH-6901 Lugano, Switzerland
Tel: (41-91) 910 71 11
Fax: (41-91) 910 71 60
E-mail: banca@bancasempione.ch

Banca dello Stato del Cantone Ticino
Government Bank/Universal Bank—Est. 1915
Address:Viale H Guisan 5
CH-6501 Bellinzona, Switzerland
Tel: (41-91) 803 71 11
Fax: (41-91) 826 13 64
Internet: www.bsct.ch
E-mail: contatto@bsct.ch

Banca di Credito e Commercio SA
Credit Bank—Est. 1958
Address:Viale G Cattori 12; PO Box 563
CH-6902 Lugano, Switzerland
Tel: (41-91) 994 24 31
Fax: (41-91) 994 92 62
Internet: www.bankcredit.ch
E-mail: info@bankcredit.ch

Banca Eurmobillare (Suisse) SA
Commercial Bank/Private Bank
Address:Via Balestra 22; PO Box 2838
CH-6900 Lugano, Switzerland
Tel: (41-91) 912 55 55
Fax: (41-91) 912 55 22

Banca Gesfid
Private Bank—Est. 2004
Address:Via Adamini 10A
CH-6900 Lugano, Switzerland
Tel: (41-91) 985 74 00
Fax: (41-91) 993 09 70
Internet: www.bancagesfid.com
E-mail: info@bancagesfid.com

Banca Julius Baer (Lugano) SA
Private Bank—Est. 1947
Address: Piazetta San Carlo 1; Casella Postale 5847
CH-6901 Lugano, Switzerland
Tel: (41-58) 885 81 11
Fax: (41-58) 885 84 54
Internet: www.lugano.juliusbaer.com
E-mail: lugano@juliusbaer.com

Banca Popolare di Sondrio (Suisse) SA
Commercial Bank/Private Bank/Retail Bank/Universal Bank—Est. 1995
Address:Via Luvini 2a
CH-6900 Lugano, Switzerland
Tel: (41-58) 855 30 00
Fax: (41-58) 855 30 15
Internet: www.popso.ch
E-mail: contact@popso.ch

Banca Privata Edmond de Rothschild Lugano SA
Private Bank—Est. 1962
Address:Via Ginevra 2; PO Box 5882
CH-6901 Lugano, Switzerland
Tel: (41-91) 913 45 00
Fax: (41-91) 913 45 01
Internet: www.privata.ch
E-mail: info@privata.ch

Banca Unione de Credito
Universal Bank—Est. 1919
Address: Piazza Dante 7; PO Box 2861
CH-6901 Lugano, Switzerland
Tel: (41-91) 806 3111
Fax: (41-91) 22 70 09
E-mail: buc@buc.ch

Banco Mercantill (Schweiz) AG
Commercial Bank/Private Bank/Trade Finance—Est. 1988
Address: Stockerstrasse 38; PO Box 1052
CH-8039 Zurich, Switzerland
Tel: (41-43) 344 45 55; (433) 444 555
Fax: (41-43) 344 45 50; (433) 444 550
Internet: www.mercantilsuiza.com

Banco Santander (Suisse) S.A.
Commercial Bank—Est. 1988
Address: 5-7 Rue Ami-Levrier; Case Postale 1256
CH-1211/1 Geneva, Switzerland
Tel: (41-22) 909 22 22
Fax: (41-22) 738 67 28

Bancoa Commerciale Lugano (Handelsbank Lugano)
Commercial Bank/Foreign Exchange/Private Bank/Trade Finance—Est. 1963
Address:Viale Carlo Cattaneo 9; Casella Postale 5877
CH-6901 Lugano, Switzerland
Tel: (41-91) 910 43 43
Fax: (41-91) 923 55 73
Internet: www.bcl.ch
E-mail: info@bcl.ch

Bank am Bellevue
Investment Bank—Est. 1993
Address: Seestrasse 16
CH-8700 Kusnacht, Switzerland
Tel: (41-44) 267 67 67
Fax: (41-44) 261 61 60
Internet: www.bellevue.ch
E-mail: info@bellevue.ch

Bank CA St. Gallen
Commercial Bank/Cooperative Bank/Credit Bank/Development Bank/Foreign
    Exchange/International Bank/Investment Bank/Joint Stock Company/Loan
    and Investment Bank/Merchant Bank/Private Bank/Retail Bank/Trade
    Finance/Universal Bank/Wholesale Bank—Est. 1854
Marktplatz 1
CH-9004 Sankt Gallen, Switzerland
Tel: (41-71) 226 73 73
Fax: (41-71) 226 75 00
Internet: www.casg.ch
E-mail: info@casg.ch

Bank Cial (Switzerland)
Commercial Bank—Est. 1909
Marktplatz 11-13; PO Box 216
CH-4001 Basel, Switzerland
Tel: (41-61) 264 12 00
Fax: (41-61) 264 12 01
Internet: www.cial.ch

Bank Coop AG
Commercial Bank/Joint Stock Company/Retail Bank/ Universal Bank—Est.
  1927
Address: Aeschenplatz 3
4002 Basel, Switzerland
Tel: (41-61) 286 21 21
Fax: (41-61) 271 61 84
Internet: www.bankcoop.ch
E-mail: callcenter@bankcoop.ch

Bank EEK
Commercial Bank/Retail Bank/Universal Bank—Est. 1821
Address: Amthausgasse 14/Marktgasse 19; PO Box 309
CH-3000 Bern, Switzerland
Tel: (41-31) 310 52 52
Fax: (41-31) 310 52 99
Internet: www.eek.ch
E-mail: info@eek.ch

Bank Frey
Private Bank
Address: Stockerstrasse 23
CH-8039 Zurich, Switzerland
Tel: (41-44) 204 33 00
Fax: (41-44) 204 33 99
Internet: www.bank-frey.com
E-mail: info@bank-frey.com

Bank Hapoalim (Switzerland) LTD
Commercial Bank/Private Bank—Est. 1975
Address: Stockerstrasse 33; Postfach 870
CH-8039 Zurich, Switzerland
Tel: (41-44) 283 88 88
Fax: (41-44) 202 89 89
Internet: www.hapoalim.ch
E-mail: infodesk.zurich@hapoalim.ch

Bank Hofmann AG
Investment Bank/Private Bank—Est. 1897
Address: Talstrasse 27; PO Box
CH-8022 Zurich, Switzerland
Tel: (41-44) 217 51 11
Fax: (41-44) 217 51 99
Internet: www.hofmann.ch
E-mail: bank@hofmann.ch

Bank Hugo Kahn and Co. AG
Private Bank—Est. 1923
Address: Limmatquai/Torgrasse 2; PO Box 475
CH-6024 Zurich, Switzerland
Tel: (41-44) 265 34 34
Fax: (41-44) 265 34 45
Internet: www.hugokahn.ch
E-mail: bank@hugokahn.ch

Bank Huttwil
Commercial Bank—Est. 1876
Address: Stadthausstrasse 1
CH-4950 Huttwil, Switzerland
Tel: (41-62) 959 85 85
Fax: (41-62) 959 85 00
Internet: www.bankhuttwil.clientis.ch
E-mail: info@bankhuttwil.clientis.ch

Bank im Thai
Cooperative Bank
Address: Goldgasse 11
CH-4710 Balsthal, Switzerland
Tel: (41-62) 383 26 26
Fax: (41-62) 383 26 55
Internet: www.bankimthal.clientis.ch
E-mail: info@bankimthal.clientis.ch

Bank in Zuzwil
Commercial Bank—Est. 1904
Address: Mitteldorfstrasse 48
CH-9524 Zuzwil, Switzerland
Tel: (41-71) 944 15 51
Fax: (41-71) 944 27 52
Internet: www.bankbiz.ch
E-mail: info@bankbiz.ch

Bank Julius Bar & Co. LTD
Merchant and Investment Bank—Est. 1890
Address: Bahnhofstrasse 36; PO Box 8010
Zurich, Switzerland
Tel: (41-58) 888 11 11
Fax: (41-58) 888 11 22e

Bank Jungholz AG
Brokerage House
Address: Oberer Graben 3
CH-9001 Sankt Gallen, Switzerland
Tel: (41-71) 228 41 00
Fax: (41-71) 228 41 09
Internet: www.bank-jungholz.ch
E-mail: info@bank-jungholz.ch

Bank Leerau
Savings Bank—Est. 1836
Address: Dorfstrasse 162; Postfach 1
CH-5054 Kirchleerau, Switzerland
Tel: (41-62) 738 77 77
Fax: (41-62) 738 77 87
Internet: www.bankleerau.clientis.ch
E-mail: info@bankleerau.clientis.ch

Bank Leu Ltd
Private Bank—Est. 1755
Address: 32 Bahnhofstrasse
CH-8022 Zurich, Switzerland
Tel: (41-44) 219 11 11
Fax: (41-44) 219 31 97
Internet: www.leu.com

Bank Leumi le-Israel (Switzerland) AG
Private Bank—Est. 1953
Address: Claridenstrasse 24; PO Box 5131
CH-8022 Zurich, Switzerlad
Tel: (41-44) 207 91 11
Fax: (41-44) 207 91 00
Internet: www.leumi.ch
E-mail: infozh@leumi.ch

Bank Linth
Commercial Bank/Savings Bank
Address: Zurcherstrasse 3; PO Box 168
CH–8730 Uznach, Switzerland
Tel: (41-55) 285 71 11
Fax: (41-55) 285 72 57
Internet: www.banklinth.ch
E–mail: info@banklinth.ch

Bank Morgan Stanley AG
Investment Bank—Est. 1973
Address: Bahnhofstrasse 91
CH–8023 Zurich, Switzerland
Tel: (41-44) 220 91 11
Fax: (41-44) 220 98 00
Internet: www.morganstanley.com

Bank Sal Oppenheim Jr & Cie. (schweiz) AG
Private Bank—Est. 1899
Address: Uraniastrasse 28
CH–8022 Zurich, Switzerland
Tel: (41-44) 214 22 14
Fax: (41-44) 211 10 85
Internet: www.oppenheim.ch
E–mail: info@oppenheim.ch

Bank Sarasin & Co. LTD
Private Bank—Est. 1841
Address: Elisabethenstrasse 62; PO Box 4055
CH–4002 Basel, Switzerland
Tel: (41-61) 277 77 77
Fax: (41-61) 272 02 05
Internet: www.sarasin.ch
E–mail: marketing@sarasin.ch

Bank Sparhafen Zurich
Building Society/Cooperative Bank/Credit Bank/Savings Bank—Est. 1850
AddressL Fraumunsterstrasse 23; PO Box 2155
CH–8022 Zurich, Switzerland
Tel: (41-44) 225 40 50
Fax: (41-44) 225 40 69
Internet: www.bsz.clientis.ch
E–mail: info@bsz.clientis.ch

Bank Thur
Savings Bank—Est. 1889
Address: Kapplerstrasse 21; PO Box 131
CH-9642 Ebnat-Kappel, Switzerland
Tel: (41-71) 993 35 35
Fax: (41-71) 993 35 36
Internet: www.bankthur.clientis.ch
E-mail: info@bankthur.clientis.ch

Bank Vontobel AG
Investment Bank/Private Bank—Est. 1924
Address: Bahnhofstrasse 3
CH-8022 Zurich, Switzerland
Tel: (41-58) 283 71 11
Fax: (41-58) 283 76 50
Internet: www.vantobel.com
E-mail: info@vantobel.ch

BankMed (Suisse) S.A.
Private Bank
Address: 3 Rue du Mont-Blanc; Case Postale 1523
CH-1211/1 Geneva, Switzerland
Tel: (41-22) 906 06 06
Fax: (41-22) 906 06 07
E-mail: into@bames.ch

Banque Algerienne du Commerce Exterieur SA
Commercial Bank/Trade Finance—Est. 1981
Address: Talacker 41; PO Box 7484
CH-8023 Zurich, Switzerland
Tel: (41-44) 218 50 60
Fax: (41-44) 211 36 27
E-mail: info@bace.ch

Banque Audi (Suisse) S.A.
Private Bank—Est. 1936
Address: 2 Rue firmin-massot; PO Box 384
CH-1211 Geneva, Switzerland
Tel: (41-22) 704 11 11
Fax: (41-22) 704 11 00
E-mail: mail@bankaudi.ch

Banque Baring Brothers Sturdza S.A.
Commercial Bank—Est. 1989
Address: 112 Rue du Rone; PO Box 3024
CH-1211/3 Geneva, Switzerland
Tel: (41-22) 317 98 11
Fax: (41-22) 310 38 80
Internet: www.bbbsa.ch
E-mail: info@bbbsa.ch

Banque Bauer (Suisse) SA
Commercial Bank
Address: 7 Rue Jean-Petitot; Case Postale 5735
CH-1211/11 Geneva, Switzerland
Tel: (41-22) 819 15 70
Fax: (41-22) 819 15 99
Internet: www.banquebauer.ch
E-mail: info@banquebauer.ch

Banque Benedict Hentsch & Cie SA
Private Bank—Est. 2004
Address: 3, Rue du General-Dufour; PO Box 5110
CH-1211 Geneva, Switzerland
Tel: (41-22) 360 91 00
Fax: (41-22) 360 91 91
Internet: www.fidutec.com
E-mail: firstname.lastname@gem360.com

Banque Bonhote & Cie SA
Private Bank—Est. 1815
16, Rue du Basin
CH-2001 Neuenhof, Switzerland
Tel: (41-32) 722 10 00
Fax: (41-32) 721 43 42
E-mail: info@bonhote.ch

Banque Cantonale de Geneva
Commercial Bank/Savings Bank—Est. 1816
Address: 17, Quai de l'lle; PO Box 2251
CH-1211Geneva, Switzerland
Tel: (41-22) 317 27 27
Fax: (41-22) 317 27 37
Internet: www.bcge.ch
E-mail: actionnaires@bcge.ch

Banque Cantonale Neuchateloise
Government Bank—Est. 1883
Address: 4 Place Pury; PO Box 275
CH-2001 Neuenhof, Switzerland
Tel: (41-32) 723 61 11
Fax: (41-32) 723 62 36
Internet: www.bcn.ch
E-mail: bcn@bcn.ch

Banque Cantonale Vaudoise
Commercial Bank—Est. 1845
Address: Place Saint-Fancois 14; PO Box 300
CH-1001 Lausanne, Switzerland
Tel: (41-848) 808 880
Fax: (41-21) 212 12 22
E-mail: info@bcv.ch

Banque Contonale de Fribourg
Commercial Bank/Credit Bank/Private Bank/Retail Bank—Est. 1892
Address: 1 Boulevard de Perolles; Case Postale
CH-1701 Fribourg, Switzerland
Tel: (41-848) 223 223
Fax: (41-26) 350 77 09
Internet: www.bcf.ch
E-mail: info@bcf.ch

Banque Contonale du Jura
Commercial Bank/Credit Bank/Foreign Exchange/
    Private Bank/Retail Bank/Trade Finance/Universal Bank
Address: Rue de la Chaumont 10
CH-2900 Porrentury, Switzerland
Tel: (41-32) 465 13 01; 465 13 01
Fax: (41-32) 465 14 95
Internet: www.bcj.ch
E-mail: bcj@bcj.ch

Banque Cantonale du Valais (Walliser Kantonalbank)
Commercial Bank/Mortgage Bank/Savings Bank—Est. 1916
Address: 8 Place des Ceders; PO Box 222
CH-1951 Sion/Sitten, Switzerland
Tel: (41-27) 324 61 11
Fax: (41-27) 324 66 66
Internet: www.bcvs.ch
E-mail: info@bcvs.ch

Banque de Commerce et de Placements S.A.
Merchant Bank—Est. 1963
Address: Rue de Chantepulet 25; PO box 1221
CH-1211/1 Geneva, Switzerland
Tel: (41-22) 909 19 19
Fax: (41-22) 909 19 00
Internet: www.bcp-bank.com
E-mail: bcp.geneva@bcp-bank.com

Banque de Depots et de Gestion
Private Bank—Est. 1933
Address: 14 Avenue du Theatre; PO Box 54 15
CH-1002 Lauffen, Switzerland
Tel: (41-21) 341 85 11
Fax: (41-21) 341 85 07
Internet: www.bdg.ch

Banque de Gestion Financiere BAGEFI
Commercial Bank
Address: Muhlebachstrasse 23-25
CH-8032 Zurich, Switzerland
(41-44) 268 53 00
(41-44) 268 53 53

Banque des Lettres de Gage d'Etablissements Suisses de Credit
Authorized Institution
Address: Nansenstrasse 16; PO Box 6446
CH-8050 Zurich, Switzerland
Tel: (41-44) 315 44 55
Fax: (41-44) 315 44 66
Internet: www.pfandbriefbank.ch
E-mail: info@pfandbriefbank.ch

Banque de Patrimoiness Prives Feneve BPQ SA
Private Bank—Est. 1980
Address: 20-22 Ave de Miremont; PO Box 403
CH-1211/12 Geneva, Switzerland
Tel: (41-22) 830 16 16
Fax: (41-22) 839 16 78
E-mail: bpg@bpggeneva.ch

Banque Degroof (Suisse) S.A.
Private Bank—Est. 2001
5 Quai de I'lle
CH-1204 Geneva, Switzerland
Tel: (41-22) 817 35 00
Fax: (41-22) 817 35 01
E-mail: contact@degroof.ch

Banque Diamantaire (Suisse) S.A.
Commercial Bank/Credit Bank/Foreign Exchange/
    International Bank/Credit Bank/Trade Finance—Est. 1982
Address: 12 Rue Bellot; PO Box 3187
CH-1211/3 Geneva, Switzerland
Tel: (41-22) 839 96 66
Fax: (41-22) 789 18 61
Internet: www.banque-diamantaire.com
E-mail: operation@banque-diamantaire.ch

Banque Fiduciary Trust
Authorized Institution
Address: 29 Route de Pre-Bois; PO Box 156
CH-1215/15 Geneva, Switzlerand
Tel: (41-22) 710 60 70
Fax: (41-22) 710 60 80

Banque Franck, Galland & Cie S.A.
Private Bank/Retail Bank—Est. 1889
Address: 1 Rue Rodolphe Toepffer;
PO Box 3254
CH-1211 Geneva, Switzerland
Tel: (41-58) 310 40 00
Fax: (41-58) 310 40 50
Internet: www.franckgalland.com
E-mail: pamonnerat@bfranck.com

Banque Jacob Safra (Suisse) S.A.
Commercial Bank—Est. 1958
Address: 708 Rue du Rhone
CH-1211/11 Geneva, Switzerland
Tel: (41-58) 317 55 55
Fax: (41-58) 317 55 00
Internet: www.bankjacobsafra.ch

Banque Jenni & Cie S.A.
Commercial Bank—Est. 1924
Address: 20 Aeschengraben; PO Box 156
CH-4010 Basel, Switzerland
Tel: (41-61) 206 95 85
Fax: (41-61) 271 48 76
Internet: www.Banquejenni.ch
E-mail: info@jennicie.ch

Banque Jura Laufon
Savings Bank—Est. 1865
Address: Rue de l'Abbe-Monnin 30
CH-2800 Bassecourt, Switzerland
Tel: (41-32) 426 74 22
Fax: (41-32) 426 50 40
Internet: www.bjl.clientis.ch
E-mail: info@bjl.clientis.ch

Banque Pasche S.A.
Investment Bank—Est. 1885
Address: 10 Rue de Hollande; PO Box 5760
CH-1211/11 Geneva, Switzerland
Tel: (41-22) 818 82 22
Fax: (41-22) 818 82 25
Internet: www.pasche.ch
E-mail: pasche@pasche.ch

Banque Piguet & Cie SA
Private Bank—Est. 1856
14, Rue de la Plaine; PO Box 223
CH-1401 Yverdon-les-Bains, Switzerland
Tel: (41-24) 423 43 00
Fax: (41-24) 423 43 08
Internet: www.banque-piguet.com
E-mail: yverdon@banquepiguet.com

Banque Privee BCP (Suisse) S.A.
Private Bank
Address: 4, Place du Molard
CH-1204 Geneva, Switzerland
Tel: (41-22) 318 92 92
Fax: (41-22) 318 92 99

Banque Privee Edmond de Rothschild S.A.
Private Bank—Est. 1924
Address: 18, Rue de hesse
CH-1204 Geneva, Switzerland
Tel: (41-22) 818 91 11
Fax: (41-22) 818 91 21
Internet: www.lcf-rothschild.ch
E-mail: bankingrelations@bper.ch

Banque Safdie SA
Private Bank—Est. 1965
Address: 1, Rue de la Tour de I'lle; PO Box 5415
CH-1211/11 Geneva, Switzerland
Tel: (41-22) 817 88 33
Fax: (41-22) 817 88 13
Internet: www.safdie.com

Banque SCS Alliance SA
Private Bank—Est. 1991
Address: 6B, Route de Chancy; Case Postale 64
CH-1211 Geneva, Sawitzerland
Tel: (41-22) 839 01 00
Fax: (41-22) 346 15 30
Internet: www.scsalliancegroup.com
E-mail: info@scsallianec.com

Banque Syz & Co SA
Commercial Bank
Address: 30 Rue du Rhone; B.P. 5015
CH-1211/11 Geneva, Switzerland
Tel: (41-22) 819 09 09
Fax: (41-22) 819 09 00
Internet: www.syzbank.ch
E-mail: info@syzbank.ch

Banque Thaler SA
Investment Bank—Est. 1982
Rue Pierre Fatio 3
CH-1211 Geneva, Switzerland
Tel: (41-22) 707 09 09
Fax: (41-22) 707 09 10
Internet: www.banqwuethaler.ch
E-mail: info@banquethaler.ch

Banque Vontobel Geneve SA
Commercial Bank/Private Bank—Est. 1904
Address: 6, Place de l'Universite; PO Box 268
CH-1211/4 Geneva, Switzerland
Tel: (41-22) 809 90 90
Fax: (41-22) 809 90 91
Internet: www.banquethaler.ch
E-mail: info@banquethaler.ch

Bantleon Bank AG
Investment Bank—Est. 1994
Address: Bahnhofstrasse 2
CH-6300 Zug, Switzerland
Tel: (41-41) 728 77 30
Fax: (41-41) 728 77 50
Internet: www.bantleonbank.com
E-mail: secretariat@bantleonbank.com

Barclays Bank (Suisse) SA
Private Bank—Est. 1986
Address: 8-10 Rue d'Italie; PO Box 3941
CH-1211/3 Geneva, Switzerland
Tel: (41-22) 819 51 11
Fax: (41-22) 310 64 60

Basellandschaftliche Kantonalbank (Banque Contonale de Bale-Compagne)
Government Bank/Universal Bank—Est. 1864
Address: Rheinstrasse 7; PO Box H613
CH-4410 Liestal, Switzerland
Tel: (41-61) 925 94 94
Fax: (41-61) 925 95 94; 925 92 08
Internet: www.blkb.ch
E-mail: info@blkb.ch

Basler Kantonalbank
Commercial Bank—Est. 1899
Address: Spiegelgasse 2
4002 Basel, Switzerland
Tel: (41-61) 266 21 21
Fax: (41-61) 261 84 34
Internet: www.bkb.ch
E-mail: welcome@bkb.ch

Baumann & Cie
Private Bank—Est. 1920
Address: St. Jakobs-Strasse 46; Postfach 2282
CH-4002 Basel, Switzerland
Tel: (41-61) 279 41 41
Fax: (41-61) 279 41 14
Internet: www.baumann-banqueiers.ch
E-mail: info@baumannbb.ch

BBO Bank Brienz Oberhasli
Savings Bank—Est. 1851
Address: Hauptstrasse 115; Postfach 771
CH-3885 Brienz, Switzerland
Tel: (41-33) 952 10 50
Fax: (41-33) 952 10 69
Internet: www.bbobank.ch
E-mail: info@bbobank.ch

BBVA (Suiza) SA
Commercial Bank/Investment Bank—Est. 1982
Address: Zeltweg 63; Pstfach 3930
CH-8021 Zurich, Switzerland
Tel: (41-44) 265 95 11
Fax: (41-44) 265 98 91

Berenberg Bank (Schweiz) AG
Private Bank—Est. 1988
Address: Stocherstrasse 57
CH-8002 Zurich, Switzerland
Tel: (41-44) 284 20 20
Fax: (41-44) 284 20 22
Internet: www.berenberg.ch
E-mail: info@berenbergbank.ch

Berner Kantonalbank (Banque Cantonale Bernoise)
Universal Bank—Est. 1834
Address: 8 Place Federale
3001 Berne, Switzerland
Tel: (41-31) 666 11 11
Fax: (41-31) 666 60 40
Internet: www.bekb.ch
E-mail: bekb@bekb.ch

Bernerland Bank
Savings Bank—Est. 1859
Address: Kirchgasse 2; Postfach 34
CH-3454 Sumiswalk, Switzerland
Tel: (41-34) 432 37 37
Fax: (41-34) 431 13 74
Internet: www.bernerlandbank.clientis.ch
E-mail: info@bernerlandbank.clientis.ch

Bezirkssparkasse Uster
Commercial Bank—Est. 1836
Address: Bankstrasse 21; PO Box 47
CH-8610 Uster, Switzerland
Tel: (41-44) 905 75 55
Fax: (41-44) 905 75 56
Internet: www.bsu.clientis.ch
E-mail: info@bsu.clientis.ch

BGG, Banque Genevoise de Gestion
Investment Bank/Private Bank—Est. 1988
Address: Rue Roldolfe-Toepffer 15; Case Postale
CH-1211/3 Geneva, Switzerland
Tel: (41-22) 347 90 40
Fax: (41-22) 347 93 27

BGP Banca di Gestione Patrimoniale SA
Investment Bank—Est. 1999
Address:Via S. Balestra 10
CH-6901 Lugano, Switzerland
Tel: (41-91) 911 16 16
Fax: (41-91) 911 17 17
Internet: www.bancabgp.com
E-mail: bgp@bancabgp.com

BHF–BANK (Switzerland) Ltd.
Merchant Bank—Est. 1984
Address: SchulhausstraBe 6; PO Box 25
CH-8027 Zurich, Switzerland
Tel: (41-44) 209 75 11
Fax: (41-44) 202 56 06
Internet: www.bhf-bank.ch
E-mail: onfo@bhf.ch

Biene Bank im Rheintal
Savings Bank—Est. 1879
Address: Rorschacherstrasse 9; PO Box 63
CH-9450 Altstatten, Switzerland
Tel: (41-71) 757 82 82
Fax: (41-71) 757 82 83
Internet: www.bienebank.clientis.ch
E-mail: info@bienebank.clientis.ch

BIM—Banca Intermobiliare di Investmentie Gestioni Patrimoniali (Suisse) SA
Investment Bank
Address: Contrada di Sassello 10; Casella Postale 5838
CH-6901 Lugano, Switzerland
Tel: (41-91) 913 66 66
Fax: (41-91) 913 66 67

BIPIELLE Bank (Suisse)
Private Bank—Est. 1962
Via Nassa 11
CH-6900 Lugano, Switzerland
Tel: (41-91) 911 01 11
Fax: (41-91) 911 91 71
Internet: www.bipielle.ch
E-mail: info@bipielle.ch

Blom Bank (Switzerland) SA
Commercial Bank—Est. 1979
Address: 1, Rue de la Rotisserie;
PO Box 3040
CH-1211 Geneva 3, Switzerland
Tel: (41-22) 817 71 00
Fax: (41-22) 817 71 90
E-mail: dir.administr@blombank.ch

BNP Paribas (Suisse) SA
Universal Bank—Est. 1872
Address: 2, Place de Hollande; PO Box 5060
1211 Geneva 11, Switzerland
Tel: (41-22) 212 21 11
Fax: (41-22) 212 22 22
Internet: www.bnpparibas.ch

Bordier & Cie
Private Bank—Est. 1844
Address: 16 Rue de Hollande; PO Box 5515
CH-1211 Geneva 11, Switzerland
Tel: (41-22) 317 12 12
Fax: (41-22) 311 29 73
Internet: www.bordier.com
E-mail: publication@bordier.com

BS Bank Schaffhausen
Commercial Bank
Address: Heerengarten 16
CH-8215 Hallau, Switzerland
Tel: (41-844) 840 850
Fax: (41-52) 681 41 31
Internet: www.bsb.clientis.ch
E-mail: info@bsb.clientis.ch

BSI SA
Commercial Bank/Private Bank—Est. 1873
Address: Via Magatti 2; PO Box 5886
CH-6901 Lugano, Switzerland
Tel: (41-91) 809 31 11
Fax: (41-91) 809 36 78
Internet: www.bsi.ch; www.bsibank.com
E-mail: info@bsi.ch

BZ Bank Aktiengesellschaft
Investment Bank—Est. 1985
Address: Egglirain 15
CH-8832 Wilen, Switzerland
Tel: (41-44) 786 61 11
Fax: (41-44) 786 61 15
Internet: www.bzbank.ch

C.I.M. Banque
Private Bank—Est. 1990
16, Rue Merle d'Aubigne; PO Box 6297
Ch-1211/6 Geneva 6, Switzerland
Tel: (41-22) 818 53 15
Fax: (41-22) 818 53 45
Internet: www.cimbanque.ch
E-mail: info@cimbanque.ch

Caisse d'Epargne d'Aubonne
Savings Bank—Est. 1837
Address: 21 Rue Hotel de Ville
CH-1170 Aubonne, Switzerland
Tel: (41-21) 821 12 60
Fax: (41-21) 808 79 42

Caisse d'Epargne de District de Vevey
Savings Bank—Est. 1814
Address: 3, Avenuse Paul-Ceresole; PO Box 300
CH-1800 Vevey, Switzerland
Tel: (41-21) 925 80 25
Fax: (41-21) 925 80 20
Internet: www.cedv.ch
E-mail: info@cev.rba.ch

Caisse d'Epargne de Nyon
Savings Bank—Est. 1828
Address: 11 rue St. Jean; PO Box 128
CH-1260 Neuenhof, Switzerland
Tel: (41-22) 994 77 77
Fax: (41-22) 994 77 75

Caisse d'Epargne de Prez Corseret et Noreaz
Savings Bank
Address 9 Rte de Corserey
CH-1746 Prez-Vers-Noreaz, Switzerland
Tel: (41-26) 470 47 00
Fax: (41-26) 470 47 09
Internet: www.cep.clientis.ch
E-mail: info@cep.clientis.ch

Caisse d'Epargne de Siviriez
Savings Bank—Est. 1891
Address: Case Postale
CH-1678 Siviriez, Switzerland
Tel: (41-26) 656 13 40
Fax: (41-26) 656 17 40
Internet: www.cesiviriez.ch
E-mail: info@ces.rba.ch

Caisse d'Epargne de Vuisternens devant Romont
Savings Bank—Est. 1887
Address: Aux Chaussies; Case Postale 63
CH-1687 Vuisternens-Dt-Romont, Switzerland
Tel: (41-26) 655 12 28
Fax: (41-26) 655 12 68
Internet: www.cevuisternens-dt-rt.ch
E-mail: info@vui.rba.ch

Caisse d'Epargne du District de Courtelary
Savings Bank—Est. 1829
Address: 45 Grande Rue
CH-2608 Courtelary, Switzerland
Tel: (41-32) 945 10 50
Fax: (41-32) 945 10 69
Internet: www.cec.clientis.ch
E-mail: info@cec.clientis.ch

Caisse d'Epargne et de Credit Mutuel
Commercial Bank
Address: Case Postal
3671 Chermignon, Switzerland
Tel: (41-27) 483 44 51
Fax: (41-27) 483 43 51

Cassie d'Epargne de la Ville de Fribourg
Savings Bank—Est. 1829
Address: 1 Rue du Criblet
CH-1701 Fribourg, Switzerland
Tel: (41-26) 323 14 01
Fax: (41-26) 322 77 94
Internet: www.cef.clientis.ch
E-mail: info@cef.clientis.ch

Causse d'Epargne du District de Cossonay
Savings Bank
Address: Rue du Temple 2
Ch-1304 Cossonay, Switzerland
Tel: (41-21) 863 13 13
Fax: (41-21) 863 13 10
Internet: www.cedc.ch
E-mail: info@cedc.ch

Citibank (Switzerland)
Private Bank—Est. 1983
Address: Seestrasse 25; PO Box 3760
CH-8022 Zurich, Switzerland
Tel: (41-44) 205 71 71
Fax: (41-44) 202 15 32
Internet: www.citigroup.com
E-mail: surname@citigroup.com

City Bank AG
Commercial Bank—Est. 1954
Address: Talstrasse 58
CH-8021 Zurich, Switzerland
Tel: (41-44) 226 36 36
Fax: (41-44) 226 36 66

Clariden Bank
Investment Bank/Private Bank—Est. 1955
Address: Claridenstrasse 26
CH-8002 Zurich, Switzerland
Tel: (41-58) 205 62 62
Fax: (41-58) 205 63 03
Internet: www.clariden.com
E-mail: info@clariden.com

Commerzbank (Schweiz) AG
Private Bank—Est. 1985
Address: Lintheschergasse 7; PO Box 7383
CH-8023 Zurich, Switzerland
Tel: (41-44) 219 71 11
Fax: (41-44) 219 72 40
E-mail: commerzbank@commerzbank.ch

Compagnie Bancaire Espirito Santo SA
Private Bank
Address: 15, Avenue de Montchoisi
CH-1006 Lauffen, Switzerland
Tel: (41-21) 619 55 55
Fax: (41-21) 619 55 56
Internet: www.espiritosanto.ch
E-mail: mail@espiritosanto.ch

Corner Banca S.A.
Commercial Bank/Investment Bank/Private Bank/Retail Bank—Est. 1952
Address:Via Canova 16; PO Box 2835
CH-6901 Lugano, Switzerland
Tel: (41-91) 800 51 11
Fax: (41-91) 800 53 49
Internet: www.cornerbanca.com
E-mail: info@cornerbanca.com

Cosba Private Banking AG
Offshore Bank/Private Bank—Est. 1975
Address: Munsterhof 12; Postfach 2221
CH-8022 Zurich, Switzerland
Tel: (41-44) 214 91 11
Fax: (41-44) 214 92 85
Internet: www.cosba.ch
E-mail: info@cosba.ch; firstname.lastname@cosba.ch

Coutts Bank von Ernst Ltd
Joint Stock Company/Private Bank—Est. 1930
Address: Stauggacherstrasse 1; Postfach
CH-8022 Zurich, Switzerland
Tel: (41-43) 245 51 11
Fax: (41-43) 245 53 96
Internet: www.cbve.com
E-mail: info@cbve.com

Credit Agricole (Suisse) SA
Commercial Bank/Foreign Exchange/International Bank/Loan and Investment
    Bank/Private Bank/Trade Finance—Est. 1876
Address: 4 Quai General Guisan; PO Box 5260
CH-1211 Geneva 11, Switzerland
Tel: (41-58) 321 90 00
Fax: (41-58) 321 91 00
Internet: www.ca-suisse.ch
E-mail: name.surname@ca-suisse.com

Credit Agricole Financements (Suisse) SA
Loan and Investment Bank
Address: 67 Rue du Rhone
CH-1207 Geneva, Switzerland
Tel: (41-22) 737 65 00
Fax: (41-22) 737 65 90
Internet: www.ca-financements.ch

Credit Industriel SA
Industrial Bank
Address: Talacker 21
CH-8021 Zurich, Switzerland
Tel: (41-44) 234 31 53
Fax: (41-44) 234 42 46

Credit Mutuel de La Vallee SA
Credit Bank—Est. 1865
Address: La Tranchee 1; Case Postale 64
CH-1347 Le Sentier, Switzerland
Tel: (41-21) 845 56 06
Fax: (41-21) 845 43 22
Internet: www.cmv.clientis.ch
E-mail: info@cmv.clientis.ch

DekaSwiss Privatbank AG
Commercial Bank
Address: Thurgauerstrasse 54; Postfach 8310
CH-8050 Zurich, Switzerland
Tel: (41-44) 308 88 88
Fax: (41-44) 308 89 00
Internet: www.deka.ch
E-mail: customerservices@dekabank.ch

Deposito-Cassa der Stadt Bern (DC Bank)
Government Bank—Est. 1825
Address: Kochergasse 6; PO Box 3000
CH-3000 Berne, Switzerland
Tel: (41-31) 328 85 85
Fax: (41-31) 328 85 56
Internet: www.dcbank.ch
E-mail: info@dcb.rba.ch

Deutsche Bank (Suisse) SA
Private Bank—Est. 1980
Address: Place des Bergues 3; PO Box 1416
CH-1211/1 Geneva, Switzerland
Tel: (41-22) 739 01 11
Fax: (41-22) 739 07 00
Internet: www.db.com/pwm/ch

Dexia Private Bank (Switzerland)
Private Bank
Address: Beethovenstrasse 48; PO Box 970
CH-8039 Zurich, Switzerland
Tel: (41-44) 286 92 92
Fax: (41-44) 201 14 71
Internet: www.dexia-privatebank.ch
E-mail: Zurich@dexia-privatebank.ch

Dominick Company AG
Private Bank—Est. 1997
Address: Mittelstrasse 14
CH-8034 Zurich, Switzerland
Tel: (41-44) 388 73 88
Fax: (41-44) 388 73 00
Internet: www.dominickco.ch
E-mail: info@dominickco.ch

Dresdner Bank (Schweiz) AG
Private Bank—Est. 1972
Address: Utoquai 55; PO Box 264
CH-8034 Zurich, Switzerland
Tel: (41-44) 258 51 11
Fax: (41-44) 258 52 52
Internet: www.dresdner-bank.ch
E-mail: contact@dresdner-bank.ch

E Gutzwiller & Cie Banquiers
Private Bank—Est. 1886
Address: Kaufhausgasse 7
CH-4051 Basel, Switzerland
Tel: (41-61) 205 21 00
Fax: (41-61) 205 21 01
Internet: www.gutzwiller.ch
E-mail: info@gutzwiller.ch

EB Entlebucher Bank
Commercial Bank—Est. 1926
Address: Hauptstrasse 32
CH-6170 Schupfheim, Switzerland
Tel: (41-41) 208 08 08; 484 23 24
Fax: (41-41) 208 08 88
Internet: www.eb.clientis.ch
E-mail: info@eb.clientis.ch

EFG Bank European Financeial Group
Private Bank—Est. 1952
Address: Quai du Seujet 24
CH-1211 Geneva, Switzerland
Tel: (41-22) 918 72 72
Fax: (41-22) 918 72 73
Internet: www.efggroup.com
E-mail: office@efggroup.com

EFG Private Bank SA
Commercial Bank—Est. 1983
Address: Bahnofstrasse 16; PO Box 2255
CH-8001 Zurich, Switzerland
Tel: (41-44) 226 17 17
Fax: (41-44) 226 17 26
Internet: www.efgprivatebank.com
E-mail: enquiries_ch@efgbank.com

Edgobank SA
Private Bank
Address:Via Soave 1
6900 Lugano, Switzerland
Tel: (41-91) 910 30 10

Ersparnisanstlat der Stadt St. Gallen
Government Bank—Est. 1811
Address:Webergasse8/Oberer Graben; PO Box 561
CH-9001 Sankt Gallen, Switzerland
Tel: (41-71) 228 84 84
Fax: (41-71) 228 84 85
Internet: www.easg.ch
E-mail: info@esg.rba.ch

Ersparniskasse Affoltern I.E.
Savings Bank—Est. 1873
Address: Postfash
CH-3462 Affoltern Im Emmental, Switzerland
Tel: (41-34) 435 15 45
Fax: (41-34) 435 15 24
Internet: www.ekaffoltern.ch
E-mail: ingo@eka.rba.ch

Ersparniskasse des Amtsbezirks Interlaken
Retail Bank/Savings Bank—Est. 1852
Address: Rosenstrasse 1; PO Box 81
CH-3800 Interlaken, Switzerland
Tel: (41-33) 826 17 71
Fax: (41-33) 826 17 79
Internet: www.eki.ch
E-mail: info@eki.rba.ch

Ersparniskasse Erlinsbach
Commercial Bank/Universal Bank—Est. 1837
Address: Ochsenweg 1; Postfach 186
CH-5018 Erlinsbach, Switzerland
Tel: (41-62) 857 44 44
Fax: (41-62) 857 44 45
Internet: www.eke.clientis.ch
E-mail: info@eke.clientis.ch

Ersparniskasse Rueggisberg
Commercial Bank
Address: Dorf 22f Postfach
CH-3088 Rueggisberg, Switzerland
Tel: (41-31) 808 17 77
Fax: (41-31) 808 17 65
Internet: www.ekr.ch
E-mail: info@ekr.rba.ch

Ersparniskasse Speicher
Savings Bank—Est. 1819
Address: Haupstrasse 21; PO Box 145
CH- 9042 Speicher, Switzerland
Tel: (41-71) 344 10 66
Fax: (41-71) 344 41 22
Internet: www.ersparniskassespeicher.ch
E-mail: info@ersparniskassespeicher.ch

Esparnisanstalt Oberuzwil
Savings Bank—Est. 1874
Address: Wiesentalstrasse 11
CH-9242 Oberuzwil, Switzerland
Tel: (41-71) 951 52 75
Fax: (41-71) 951 80 11
E-mail: info@eao.clientis.ch

F. van Lanschot Bankiers (Schweiz) AG
Commercial Bank
Address: Mittelstrasse 19
CH-8008 Zurich, Switzerland
Tel: (41-43) 377 11 11
Fax: (41-43) 377 11 44
Internet: www.vanlanschot.ch
E-mail: vanlanschot@vanlanschot.ch

FIBI Bank (Schweiz) AG
Private Bank—Est. 2001
Address: Stockerstrasse 14
CH-8022 Zurich, Switzerland
Tel: (41-44) 206 69 69
Fax: (41-44) 201 14 41
Internet: www.fibi.ch
E-mail: fibi@fibi.ch

Fideuram Bank (Suisse) SA
Private Bank—Est. 2001
Address:Via Canova 1
CH-6900 Lugano, Switzerland
Tel: (41-91) 910 29 00
Fax: (41-91) 910 29 90

Finansbank (Suisse) SA
Private Bank/Trade Finance—Est. 1987
Address: 12, Rue du Mont-Blanc; PO Box 1449
CH-1211 Geneva 1, Switzerland
Tel: (41-22) 839 19 19
Fax: (41-22) 839 19 00
Internet: www.finansbank.ch
E-mail: info@finansbank.ch

Finter Bank Zurich
Private Bank—Est. 1958
Address: Claridenstrasse 35; PO Box 2299
CH-8022 Zurich, Switzerland
Tel: (41-44) 289 55 00
Fax: (41-44) 289 56 00
Internet: www.finter.ch
E-mail: info@finter.ch; zh@finter.ch

Fortis Banque (Suisse) SA
Private Bank—Est. 1958
Address: 20 Boulevard des Philosophes; PO Box 188
CH-1211 Geneva, Switzerland
Tel: (41-22) 322 03 22
Fax: (41-22) 322 04 22
Internet: www.fortisbanque.ch
E-mail: info@fortisbanque.ch

Freie Gemeinschatfersbank BCL
Private Bank
Address: Gerberstrasse 30; Postfach 248
CH-4001 Basel, Switzerland
Tel: (41-61) 269 81 00
Fax: (41-61) 269 81 49
Internet: www.germeinschaftsbank.ch
E-mail: info@germeinschaftsbank.ch

GEFS (Suisse) AG
Commercial Bank—Est. 1999
Address: Badenestrasse 9
CH-5201 Brugg, Switzerland
Tel: (41-56) 461 81 11
Fax: (41-56) 461 83 80
Internet: www.gecapitalbank.ch
E-mail: info@gecapitalbank.ch

Glarner Kantonalbank (Banque Cantonale de Glaris)
Government Bank—Est. 1884
Address: Haupstrasse 21; PO Box 365
CH-8750 Glarus, Switzerland
Tel: (41-55) 646 71 11
Fax: (41-55) 646 76 01
Internet: www.glkb.ch
E-mail: glkb@glkb.ch

Goldman Sachs Bank AG
Private Bank—Est. 1992
Address: Munsterhof 4; Munsterhof 4 Postfach
CH-8022 Zurich, Switzerland
Tel: (41-44) 224 10 00
Fax: (41-44) 224 10 50

Gonet & Cie
Private Bank—Est. 1842
Address: 6 Blvd du Theatre; PO Box 5009
CH-1211/11 Geneva, Switzerland
Tel: (41-22) 311 72 66
Fax: (41-22) 311 09 42
Internet: www.banquegonet.ch
E-mail: info@banquegonet.ch

Graubundner Kantonalbank
Government Bank—Est. 1870
Address: Grabenstrasse, Poststrasse; PO Box 13414
CH-7002 Chur, Switzerland
Tel: (41-81) 256 91 11
Fax: (41-81) 256 67 29
Internet: www.gkb.ch
E-mail: info@gkb.ch

GRB Glarner Regionalbank
Cooperative Bank
Address: Bahnhofstrasse 25; Postfach 660
CH-8027 Schwanden, Switzerland
Tel: (41-55) 647 34 50
Fax: (41-55) 647 34 59
Internet: www.rba.ch/grb
E-mail: info@grb.rba.ch

Habib Bank AG Zurich
Commercial Bank/International Bank/Private Bank/Trade Finance—Est. 1967
Address: Weinbergstrasse 59; PO Box 303
CH-8035 Zurich, Switzerland
Tel: (41-44) 269 45 00
Fax: (41-44) 269 45 35; 269 45 25
Internet: www.habibbank.com
E-mail: info@habibbank.com; hbzweb@habibbank.com

Heritage Bank & Trust SA
Private Bank—Est. 1993
Address: 12 Cours des Bastions; PO Box 3341
CH-1211 Geneva 3, Swtizerland
Tel: (41-22) 817 31 11
Fax: (41-22) 817 31 00
Internet: www.heritage.ch
E-mail: heritage@heritage.ch

Hottinger & Cie, Banquiers
Private Bank—Est. 1968
Address: Dreikoenigstrasse 55; PO Box 267
CH-8027 Zurich, Switzerland
Tel: (41-44) 284 12 00
Fax: (41-44) 284 12 99
Internet: www.hottinger.com
E-mail: bank@hottinger.com; hottinger.zurich@hottinger.com

HSBC Private Bank (Suisse) SA
Private Bank—Est. 2001
Address: 2, Quai du General Guisan; PO Box 3580
CH-1211 Geneva 3, Switzerland
Tel: (41-58) 705 51 51
Fax: (41-58) 705 51 51
Internet: www.hsbcprivatebank.com

HYPOSWISS Private Bank Ltd
Investment Bank/Merchant Bank/Private Bank—Est. 1889
Address: Bahnihfstrasse/Schuetzengasse 4; PO Box 6990
CH-8023 Zurich, Switzerland
Tel: (41-44) 214 31 11
Fax: (41-44) 211 52 23
Internet: www.hyposwiss.ch
E-mail: info@hyposwiss.ch

Hypothekarbank Lenzburg
Universal Bank—Est. 1868
Address: Bahnhofstrasse 2; PO Box 192
CH-5600 Lensburg, Switzerland
Tel: (41-62) 885 11 11
Fax: (41-62) 885 15 95
Internet: www.hbl.ch
E-mail: info@hbl.ch

IBI Bank AG
Private Bank—Est. 1997
Talacker 50
CH-8022 Zurich, Switzerland
Tel: (41-44) 215 50 60
Fax: (41-44) 215 50 61
Internet: www.ibi.ch
E-mail: info@ibi.ch

ING Bank (Suisse) SA
Private Bank—Est. 1962
Address: 30 Avenue de Frontenex;
PO Box 6405
CH-1211 Geneva 6, Switzerland
Tel: (41-22) 787 11 11
Fax: (41-22) 736 66 02; 735 18 40
Internet: www.ing.ch
E-mail: marketing@ing.ch

Investec Bank (Switzerland) AG
Private Bank—Est. 1970
Address: Talacker 41; PO Box
CH-8039 Zurich, Switzerland
Tel: (41-44) 226 10 00
Fax: (41-44) 226 10 10
Internet: www.investec.com/switzerland
E-mail: info@investecbank.ch

Israel Discount Bank (Switzerland) SA
Commercial Bank
Address: 8-10 Rue du Marche;
PO Box 3385
CH-1211/3 Geneva, Switzerland
Tel: (41-22) 591 10 00; 591 10 55
Fax: (41-22) 591 10 01; 591 10 28

J.P Morgan (Suisse) SA
Commercial Bank—Est. 1980
Address: 8 Rue de la Confederation;
PO Box 5160
CH-1211 Geneva, Switzerland
Tel: (41-22) 744 11 11
Fax: (41-22) 744 14 44

JP Morgan Fleming Asset Management (Switzerland) Ltd
Investment Bank—Est. 1983
Address: Dreikonigstrasse 21; Postfach 2623
CH-8039 Zurich, Switzerland
Tel: (41-44) 206 86 20
Fax: (41-44) 206 86 30
Internet: www.jpmorganfleming.com
E-mail: info.zurich@jpmorganfleming.com

Jyske Bank (Schweiz)
Private Bank—Est. 1970
Address: Wasserwerkstrasse 12
CH-8035 Zurich, Switzerland
Tel: (41-44) 368 73 73
Fax: (41-44) 368 73 79
Internet: www.jbpb.com
E-mail: jyskebank@jyskebank.ch

Kredietbank (Suisse) SA
Commercial Bank—Est. 1970
Address: 7, Blvd Georges-Favon
CH-11211/11 Geneva, Switzerland
Tel: (41-22) 316 63 22
Fax: (41-22) 316 64 44

La Roche & Co Banquiers
Private Bank—Est. 1787
Address: Rittergasse 25
CH-4001 Basel, Switzerland
Tel: (41-61) 286 44 00
Fax: (41-61) 286 43 24
Internet: www.larochebanquiers.ch
E-mail: mail@larochebanquires.ch

Landolt & Cie Banquiers
Private Bank—Est. 1780
Address: 6, Rue du Lion-d'Or; PO Box 6739
CH-1002 Lauffen, Switzerland
Tel: (41-21) 320 33 11
Fax: (41-21) 323 94 25
Internet: www.landoltetcie.ch
E-mail: info@landoltbanquirers.ch

Lavoro Bank AG
Commercial Bank/Private Bank—Est. 1959
Address: Talacker 21
CH-8001 Zurich, Switzerland
Tel: (41-44) 217 95 95
Fax: (41-44) 221 12 41
E-mail: lavoro@lavoro.ch

LB (Swiss) Privatbank AG
Private Bank
Address: Borsenstrasse 16
CH-8001 Zurich, Switzerland
Tel: (41-44) 265 44 44
Fax: (41-44) 265 44 11
Internet: www.lbswiss.ch
E-mail: privatebanking@lbswiss.ch

Leihkasse Stammheim
Commercial Bank
Address: Hauptstrasse 6
8477 Obert-Stammheim
Tel: (41-52) 745 21 15
Fax: (41-52) 745 26 74
E-mail: info@lks.rba.ch

Les Fils Dreyfus & Cie S.A. Banquiers
Private Bank—Est. 1813
Address: Aeschenvorstadt 16
CH-4002 Basel, Switzerland
Tel: (41-61) 286 66 66
Fax: (41-61) 272 24 38
E-mail: contact@dreyfusbank.ch

LGT Bank (Schweiz) AG
Private Bank—Est. 2004
Address: Lange Gasse 15; Postfach
CH-4002 Basel, Switzerland
Tel: (41-61) 277 56 00
Fax: (41-61) 277 55 88
Internet: www.lgt.com
E-mail: lgt.ch@lgt.com

LGT Bank (Schweiz) AG
Universal Bank—Est. 1920
Address: Glarniscstrasse 36
CH-8022 Zurich, Switzerland
Tel: (41-44) 250 83 34
Fax: (41-44) 250 82 21
Internet: www.lgt.com
E-mail: lgt.ch@lgt.com

Liechtensteinsche Landesbank (Schweiz) AG
Commercial Bank
Address: Klausstr. 19
CH-8008 Zurich, Switzerland
Tel: (41-44) 421 46 11
Fax: (41-44) 421 46 22
Internet: www.llb.ch
E-mail: llb@llb.ch

Lienhardt & Partner Privatbank Zurich AG
Real Estate Services/Private Bank/Universal Bank/Wholesale Bank—Est. 1868
Address: Ramistrasse 23
CH-8024 Zurich, Switzerland
Tel: (41-44) 268 61 61
Fax: (41-44) 268 61 62
Internet: www.lienhardt.ch
E-mail: info@lienhardt.ch

Lombard Odier Darier Hantsch & Cie
Private Bank—Est. 1796
Address: Rue de la Corraterie 11; B.P. 5215
CH-1211 Geneva 11, Switzerland
Tel: (41-22) 709 21 11
Fax: (41-22) 709 29 11
Internet: www.lodh.com

Luzerner Kantonalbank
Government Bank/Universal Bank—Est. 1850
Address: Pilatusstrasse 12
CH-6002 Luzern, Switzerland
Tel: (41-844) 82 28 11
Fax: (41-41) 206 20 90
Internet: www.lukb.ch
E-mail: info@lukb.ch

M.M. Warburg Bank (Schweiz) AG
Commercial Bank/International Bank/Private Bank—Est. 1966
Address: Parkring 12; PO Box 1960
CH-8027 Zurich, Switzerland
Tel: (41-44) 206 23 23
Fax: (41-44) 206 23 01
Internet: www.mmwarburg.ch
E-mail: mmwarburg@mmwarburg.ch

MediBank
Private Bank—Est. 1979
Address: Bahnhofstrasse 8–10
CH-6301 Zug, Switzerland
Tel: (41-41) 726 25 25
Fax: (41-41) 726 25 26
Internet: www.medibank.ch
E-mail: info@medibank.ch

Merrill Lynch Bank (Suisse) SA
Private Bank—Est. 1984
Address: 13, Route de Florissant; PO Box 3070
Ch-1211/3 Geneva, Switzerland
Tel: (41-22) 703 17 17; 703 14 14
Fax: (41-22) 703 17 27
Internet: www.mlbs.ch
E-mail: information_mlbs@ml.com

Merrill Lynch Capital Markets AG
Investment Bank—Est. 1952
Address: Stockerhof, Stockerstrasse 23; PO Box 773
CH-8039 Zurich, Switzerland
Tel: (41-44) 297 74 00
Fax: (41-44) 291 44 60
Internet: www.ml.ch
E-mail: mlcmag_aurich@ml.com

MFC Merchant Bank SA
Investment Bank/Private Bank—Est. 1971
Address: Kasernenstrasse 1
CH-9100 Heitenried, Switzerland
Tel: (41-71) 353 08 80
Fax: (41-71) 353 08 88
E-mail: mfc.mfcbank.ch

MIGROSBANK
Retail Bank—Est. 1958
Address: Seidengasse 12
CH-8023 Zurich, Switzerland
Tel: (41-44) 229 81 11
Fax: (41-44) 229 87 15
Internet: www.migrosbank.ch
E-mail: info@migrosbank.ch

Mirabaud & Cie
Private Bank—Est. 1819
Address: 3 Boulevard du Theatre; PO Box 5818
CH-1211 Geneva 11, Switzerland
Tel: (41-22) 816 22 22
Fax: (41-22) 816 28 16
Internet: www.miraboud.com
E-mail: contact-us@miraboud.com

Mitsubushu Tokyo Wealth Management (Switzerland) Ltd
Universal Bank—Est. 2002
Address: 67, Rue du Rhone
CH-1207 Geneva, Switzerland
Tel: (41-22) 718 66 00
Fax: (41-22) 718 66 66

Mizuho Bank (Schweiz) AG
Commercial Bank—Est. 1976
Address: Lowenstrasse 32
CH-8023 Zurich, Switzerland
Tel: (41-44) 216 91 11
Fax: (41-44) 216 92 22
E-mail: mail@mizuho.ch

Morval & Cie SA Banque
Private Bank—Est. 1976
Address: 18 Rue Charles-Galland; PO Box 339
CH-1211 Geneva 12, Switzerland
Tel: (41-22) 839 92 00
Fax: (41-22) 347 42 31
Internet: www.morval.ch
E-mail: morval-ge@morval.ch

Mourgue d'Algue et Cie
Investment Bank/Private Bank—Est. 1869
5 Rue de la Fontaine; PO Box 3485
CH-1211/3 Geneva, Switzerland
Tel: (41-22) 319 76 76
Fax: (41-22) 319 76 77
E-mail: Mabank@mabank.ch

Neue Aargauer Bank
Retail Bank/Savings Bank—Est. 1812
Address: Bahnofstrasse 49
CH-5001 Aarau, Switzerland
Tel: (41-46) 462 71 00
Fax: (41-56) 462 75 42
Internet: www.nab.ch
E-mail: info@nab.ch

Nidwaldner Kantonalbank
Savings Bank—Est. 1879
Address: Stansstaderstrasse 54
CH-6371 Stans, Switzerland
Tel: (41-41) 619 22 22
Fax: (41-41) 619 22 25
Internet: www.nkb.ch
E-mail: info@nkb.ch

Nomura Bank (Switzerland) Ltd
Corporation Bank/Investment Bank/Private Bank—Est. 1988
Address: Kasernenstrasse 1; PO Box 8021
CH-8004 Zurich, Switzerland
Tel: (41-44) 295 71 11
Fax: (41-44) 242 21 41
Internet: www.nomura.com

Nordkap Bank AG
Commercial Bank/Credit Bank/Export Bank/
    Loan and Investment Bank—Est. 1963
Address: Thurgauerstrasse 54
CH-8050 Zurich, Switzerland
Tel: (41-44) 306 49 10
Fax: (41-44) 306 49 11
Internet: www.nordkapbank.com

NPB Neue Privat Bank AG
Private Bank—Est. 2001
Address: Limmatquai 122
CH-8022 Zurich, Switzerland
Tel: (41-44) 265 11 88
Fax: (41-44) 265 11 89
Internet: www.npb-bank.ch
E-mail: info@npb-bank.ch

NZB Neue Zurcher Bank
Private Bank—Est. 2000
Address: Brandschenkestrasse 10; Postfach
CH-8039 Zurich, Switzerland
Tel: (41-44) 288 82 00
Fax: (41-44) 288 82 01; 201 64 76
Internet: www.nzb.ch
E-mail: info@nzb.ch

Obwadner Kantonalbank
Government Bank—Est. 1886
Address: Bahnhofstrasse 2; PO Box 176
CH-6061 Sarnen, Switzerland
Tel: (41-41) 666 22 11
Fax: (41-41) 666 22 60
Internet: www.owkb.ch
E-mail: info@owkb.ch

OZ Bankers AG
Investment Bank—Est. 1997
Address: Churerstrasse 47
CH-8808 Pfaffikon, Switzerland
Tel: (41-44) 215 63 00
Fax: (41-44) 215 63 90
E-mail: info@ozbankers.ch

Petercam Private Bank (Switzerland) SA
Private Bank
Address: 31 Route de l'Aeroport Centre Swissair; CP 1119
CH-1211 Geneva, Switzerland
Tel: (41-22) 929 72 11
Fax: (41-22) 929 72 95
Internet: www.petercam.com
E-mail: bjs.petercam.com

Pictet & Cie
Private Bank—Est. 1805
Address: 29 Blvd Georges-Favon; PO Box 5130
CH-1211 Geneva, Switzerland
Tel: (41-58) 323 23 23
Fax: (41-58) 323 23 24
Internet: www.pictet.com
E-mail: info@pictet.com, mail@pictet.com

PKB Privatbank AG
Universal Bank—Est. 1958
Address:Via S. Balestra 1; PO Box 2851
6901 Lugano, Switzerland
Tel: (41-91) 913 35 35
Fax: (41-91) 923 35 22
Internet: www.pkb.ch
E-mail: admmgt@pkb.ch

Pricatbank von Graffenried AG
Investment Bank—Est. 1992
Address: Marktgass-Passage 3; Postfach
CH-3000/7 Berne, Switzerland
Tel: (41-31) 320 52 22
Fax: (41-31) 320 52 11
Internet: www.graffenried.ch
E-mail: bank@graffenried.com

Privatbank Bellerive AG
Private Bank—Est. 1989
Address: Mittelstrasse 6; Postfach
CH-8034 Zurich, Switzerland
Tel: (41-44) 382 17 00
Fax: (41-44) 382 15 13
Internet: www.pbbellerive.com
E-mail: info@pbbellerive.com

Privatbank IHAG Zurich
Private Bank—Est. 1949
Address: Bleicherweg 18
CH-8022 Zurich, Switzerland
Tel: (41-44) 205 11 11
Fax: (41-44) 205 12 85
Internet: www.pbihag.ch
E-mail: info@pbihag.ch

Private Client Bank
Private Bank
Address: Utoquai 55; Postfach 835
CH-8034 Zurich, Switzerland
Tel: (41-44) 253 73 00
Fax: (41-44) 253 73 20
Internet: www.privateclientbank.ch
E-mail: info@privateclientbank.ch

Rahn & Bodmer Banquiers
Private Bank—Est. 1750
Talstrasse 15; Postfach
CH-8022 Zurich, Switzerland
Tel: (41-44) 639 11 11
Fax: (41-44) 639 11 22
Internet: www.rahnbodmer.ch
E-mail: info@rahnbodmer.ch

RAS Private Bank (Suisse) SA
Private Bank—Est. 2000
Address:Via Pretorio 13
CH-6901 Lugano, Switzerland
Tel: (41-91) 910 08 50
Fax: (41-91) 922 66 36
Internet: www.rasbanksuisse.ch
E-mail: info@rasbanksuisse.ch

RBA-Zentralbank
Commercial Bank—Est. 1964
Lagerhausweg 10; PO Box 5365
CH-3001 Berne, Switzerland
Tel: (41-31) 660 33 33
Fax: (41-31) 660 33 13
Internet: www.rba-zentralbank.ch
E-mail: info@rzb.rba.ch

Regiobank Mannedorf
Commercial Bank—Est. 1903
Address: Bahnhofstrasse 14
CH-8708 Mannedorf, Switzerland
Tel: (41-44) 922 13 00
Fax: (41-44) 922 13 09
Internet: www.rbm.clientis.ch
E-mail: info@rbm.clientis.ch

Regionbank Solothurn
Savings Bank—Est. 1819
Address:Westbahnhofstrasse 11
CH-4502 Solothurn, Switzerland
Tel: (41-32) 624 15 15
Fax: (41-32) 624 16 16
Internet: www.regiobank.ch
E-mail: RegioBox@regiobank.ch

Reichmuth & Co
Commercial Bank/Private Bank—Est. 1996
Address: Rutligasse 1
CH-6000/7 Luzern, Switzerland
Tel: (41-41) 249 49 29
Fax: (41-41) 249 49 39
Internet: www.reichmuthco.ch
E-mail: privatbankiers@reichmuthco.ch

Rosebank (Switzerland) SA
Commercial Bank/Joint Stock Company/Trade Finance/
    Universal Bank—Est. 1995
Address: 17, Rue du Rhone; PO Box 5734
CH-1211/11 Geneva, Switzerland
Tel: (41-22) 818 73 33
Fax: (41-22) 818 73 50
Internet: www.rosebank.ch
E-mail: rosebank@rosebank.ch

Rothschild Bank AG
Investment Bank/Private Bank—Est. 1968
Address: Zollikerstrasse 181; PO Box 300
CH-8034 Zurich, Switzerland
Tel: (41-44) 384 71 11
Fax: (41-44) 384 72 22
Internet: www.rothschildbank.com
E-mail: mail@rothschild-bank.ch

Royal Bank of Canada (Suisse)
Private Bank—Est. 1982
Address: 6, Rue Francois Diday; PO Box 5996
1211/11 Geneva, Switzerland
Tel: (41-22) 819 42 42
Fax: (41-22) 819 43 43
Internet: www.royalbank.com
E-mail: royal@royal.com

Rud, Blass & Cie AG
Private Bank—Est. 1925
Address: Selnaustrasse 32
CH-8039 Zurich, Switzerland
Tel: (41-44) 217 21 11
Fax: (41-44) 211 70 57
Internet: www.ruedblass.ch
E-mail: info@ruedblass.ch

Russian Commercial Bank Ltd (Russische KommerzialBank AG)
Commercial Bank—Est. 1992
Address: Hofackerstrasse 32; PO Box 1274
CH-8032 Zurich, Switzerland
Tel: (41-44) 386 86 86
Fax: (41-44) 386 86 87
Internet: www.rkb.ch
E–mail: info@rkb.ch

Sanpaolo Bank (Suisse) SA
Joint Stock Company—Est. 2001
Address:Via Frasca 5
CH-6900 Lugano, Switzerland
Tel: (41-91) 260 82 82
Fax: (41-91) 260 82 00
E–mail: ge@spprivatebanking.com

SB Saanen Bank
Commercial Bank
Address: Bahnhofstrasse
CH-3792 Saanen, Switzerland
Tel: (41-33) 748 46 46
Fax: (41-33) 748 46 56
Internet: www.saanenbank.ch
E–mail: info@saanenbank.ch

Schaffhauser Kantonalbank (Banque Contonale de Schaffhouse)
Government Bank—Est. 1883
Address:Vorstadt 53
CH-8201 Schaffhausen, Switzerland
Tel: (41-52) 635 22 22
Fax: (41-52) 625 38 48
Internet: www.shkb.ch
E–mail: info@shkb.ch

Schweizer Verband der Raiffeisenbanken
Cooperative Bank—Est. 1902
Address: Schreinerstrasse 6; PO Box 747
CH-9001 Sankt Gallen, Switzerland
Tel: (41-71) 225 88 88
Fax: (41-71) 225 88 87
Internet: www.raiffeisen.ch
E–mail: webmaster@raiffeisen.ch

Schwyzer Kantonalbank
Government Bank—Est. 1890
Address: Bahnhofstrasse 3; PO Box 263
CH-6431 Schwyz, Switzerland
Tel: (41-58) 800 20 20
Fax: (41-58) 800 20 21
Internet: www.szkb.ch
E-mail: kundenzentrum@szkb.ch

Scobag AG
Investment Bank—Est. 1968
Address: Henric Petric-Strasse 35
CH-4051 Basel, Switzerland
Tel: (41-61) 205 12 12
Fax: (41-61) 205 12 79

Sella Bank
Private Bank—Est. 1982
Address: Talstrasse 70; Postfach 624
CH-8039 Zurich, Switzerland
Tel: (41-43) 210 31 00
Fax: (41-43) 210 31 01
Internet: www.sella.ch
E-mail: info@sella.ch

SG Private Banking (Lugano-Svizzera) SA
Private Bank—Est. 1973
Address: Viale Canova 12; PO Box 2858
CH-6901 Lugano, Switzerland
Tel: (41-91) 923 76 42
Fax: (41-91) 922 08 08

SG Private Banking (Suisse) SA
Investment Bank/Private Bank—Est. 1986
Address: Rue de la Corraterie 6; PO Box 5022
CH-1211/11 Geneva, Switzerland
Tel: (41-22) 819 02 02
Fax: (41-22) 819 04 03
Internet: www.cbg.ch
E-mail: info@cbg.ch

SLB Commercial Bank
Commercial Bank—Est. 1998
Address: Freigutstrasse 16; PO Box 669
CH-8039 Zurich, Switzerland
Tel: (41-44) 250 56 56
Fax: (41-44) 250 56 05
E-mail: slb-bank@bluewin.ch

Societa Bancaria Ticinese
Commercial Bank—Est. 1903
Address: Piazza Collegiata 3; PO Box 2062
CH-6501 Bellinzona, Switzerland
Tel: (41-91) 821 51 21
Fax: (41-91) 825 66 18
Internet: www.bancaria.ch
E-mail: dir@bancaria.ch

Societe Bancaire Privee SA
Merchant Bank
Address: 11, Cours de Rive; Case Postale 3668
CH-1211 Geneva 3, Switzerland
Tel: (41-22) 818 31 31
Fax: (41-22) 818 31 00
Internet: www.sbp-banque.ch
E-mail: info@sbp-banque.ch

Spar-Leihkasse Steffisburg
Savings Bank—Est. 1863
Address: Glockentalstrasse 6; PO Box 177
CH-3612 Steffisburg, Switzerland
Tel: (41-33) 439 22 22
Fax: (41-33) 439 22 77
Internet: www.slsteffisburg.ch
E-mail: direction@ste.rba.ch

Spar-und Leihkasse Munsingen
Savings Bank—Est. 1870
Address: Dorfplatz 5; PO Box 1080
CH-3110 Munsingen, Switzerland
Tel: (41-31) 724 11 11
Fax: (41-31) 724 11 55
Internet: www.slm-online.ch
E-mail: info@slm.rba.ch

Spar-und Leihkasse Wynigen
Savings Bank—Est. 1929
Address: Dorfstrasse 3; PO Box 50
CH-3472 Wynigen, Switzerland
Tel: (41-34) 415 77 77
Fax: (41-34) 415 77 75

Spar & Leihkasse Bucheggberg
Commercial Bank
Address: Haupstrasse 69
CH-4584 Luterswil, Switzerland
Tel: (41-32) 352 10 60
Fax: (41-31) 352 10 70
E-mail: info@buc.rba.ch

Spar & Leihkasse Frutigen
Commercial Bank—Est. 1837
Address: Dorfstrasse 13; PO Box 80
CH-3714 Frutigen, Switzerland
Tel: (41-33) 672 18 18
Fax: (41-33) 672 18 88
Internet: www.slfrutigen.ch
E-mail: info@slf.rba.ch

Spare & Leihkasse Gurbetal
Commercial Bank
Address: Dorfstrasse 19
CH-3127 Muhlethurnen, Switzerland
Tel: (41-31) 808 19 19
Fax: (41-31) 809 22 16
Internet: www.slguerbetal.ch
E-mail: info@slg.rba.ch

Spar-und Leihkasse Kirchberg SG
Savings Bank—Est. 1911
Address: Gahwilerstrasse 7
CH-9533 Kirchberg, Switzerland
Tel: (41-71) 932 36 36; 931 41 81
Fax: (41-71) 932 36 37; 931 41 82

Spar-und Leihkasse Leuk und Umgebung
Commercial Bank
Address: Schulhausstrasse 12
CH-3953 Leuk Stadt, Switzerland
Tel: (41-27) 473 25 39
Fax: (41-27) 473 42 06

Spar-und Leihkasse Riggisberg
Commercial Bank
Address: Grabenstrasse 7
3132 Riggisberg, Switzerland
Tel: (41-31) 808 08 08
Fax: (41-31) 808 08 18
Internet: www.slr.ch
E-mail: info@slr.rba.ch

Sparkasse Bundespersonal
Savings Bank
Address: Christoffelgasse 5
CH-3000 Berne, Switzerland
Tel: (41-31) 322 61 34
Fax: (41-31) 322 61 13

Spargenossenschaft Mosnang
Commercial Bank
Address: Lindenplatz 2
9607 Mosnang, Switzerland
Tel: (41-71) 982 80 08
Fax: (41-71) 982 80 09
Internet: www.sgm.clientis.ch
E-mail: info@sgm.clientis.ch

Sparkasse Engelberg
Savings Bank—Est. 1879
Address: Dorfstrasse 34; PO Box 357
CH-6390 Engelberg, Switzerland
Tel: (41-41) 639 50 19; (941) 94 12 19
Fax: (41-41) 639 50 15
Internet: www.sparkasse-engelberg.ch
E-mail: info@sparkasse-engelberg.ch

Sparkasse Horgen AG
Savings Bank—Est. 1820
Address: Dorfplatz 1; PO Box 229
CH-8810 Horgen, Switzerland
Tel: (41-44) 727 41 41
Fax: (41-44) 727 41 47
Internet: www.skh.clientis.ch
E-mail: iofo@skh.clientis.ch

Sparkasse Kusnacht Zurich
Savings Bank—Est. 1838
Address: Untere Heslibachstrasse 9; PO Box 1508
CH-8700 Kunsnacht, Switzerland
Tel: (41-44) 913 39 00
Fax: (41-44) 913 39 15
Internet: www.skk.clientis.ch
E-mail: info@skk.clientis.ch

Sparkasse Schwyz
Savings Bank—Est. 1812
Address: Herrengasse 23; PO Box 564
CH-6431 Schwyz, Switzerland
Tel: (41-41) 819 02 50
Fax: (41-41) 819 02 51
Internet: www.sksnet.ch
E-mail: info@sks.rba.ch

Sparkasse Sense
Commercial Bank
Address: Mariahilfstrasse 4
CH-1712 Tafers, Switzerland
Tel: (41-26) 494 11 13
Fax: (41-26) 494 31 66
Internet: www.sks.clientis.ch
E-mail: info@sks.clientis.ch

Sparkasse Trogen
Savings Bank—Est. 1821
Address: Halden 129
CH-9043 Trogen, Switzerland
Tel: (41-71) 344 29 89
Fax: (41-71) 344 42 76
Internet: www.bank-trogen.ch
E-mail: info@sparkasse-trogen.ch

Sparkasse Wiesendangen
Retail Bank/Savings Bank—Est. 1903
Address: Schulstrasse 21; PO Box 133
CH-8542 Wiesendangen, Switzerland
Tel: (41-52) 320 99 66
Fax: (41-52) 320 99 69
Internet: www.skw.clientis.ch
E-mail: info@skw.clientis.ch

Sparkasse Zurcher Oberland
Cooperative Bank/Savings Bank
Address: Bahnofstrasse 3
CH-8620 Werzikon, Switzerland
Tel: (41-44) 933 54 00
Fax: (41-44) 933 54 09
Internet: www.szo.clientis.ch
E-mail: info@szo.clientis.ch

St. Galler Kantonalbank
Commercial Bank/Loan and Investment Bank/Private Bank/
    Retail Bank—Est. 1868
Address: St. Leonhardstrasse 25; PO Box 2063
CH-9001 Sankt Gallen, Switzerland
Tel: (41-71) 231 31 31
Fax: (41-71) 231 32 32
Internet: www.sgkb.ch
E-mail: info@sgkb.ch

SVRB, Niederl, Grabs/Werdenberg
Commercial Bank
Address: Vorderdorfstrasse 1
CH-9472 Grabs, Switzerland
Tel: (41-81) 758 00 00
Fax: (41-81) 758 00 05
E-mail: grabs@raiffeisen.ch

Swissfirst Bank AG
Investment Bank—Est. 1922
Address: Bellariastrasse 23; Postfach
CH 8027 Zurich, Switzerland
Tel: (41-44) 204 80 00
Fax: (41-44) 204 80 80
Internet: www.swissfirst.ch
E-mail: info@swissfirst.ch

Swissnetbank.com AG
Commercial Bank—Est. 1995
Address: Bahnhofstrasse 86
CH-8023 Zurich, Switzerland
Tel: (41-44) 560 10 80
Fax: (41-44) 212 11 88
Internet: www.swissnetbank.com
E-mail: help@swissnetbank.com

Swissquote Bank
Internet Bank
Address: 16 Route de Avouillons
CH-1196 Gland, Switzerland
Tel: (41-22) 999 94 11
Fax: (41-22) 999 94 12; 999 94 42
Internet: www.swissquote.ch
E-mail: info@swissquote.ch

Swissregiobank
Commercial Bank/Universal Bank—Est. 2002
Address: PostsraBe 4
CH-9201 Gossau, Switzerland
Tel: (41-71) 388 75 55
Fax: (41-71) 388 75 50
Internet: www.swissregiobank.ch
E-mail: info@swissregiobank.ch

Sydbank Schweiz AG
Private Bank—Est. 2003
Address: Postrasse 17
CH-9000 Sankt Gallen, Switzerland
Tel: (41-71) 227 81 00
Fax: (41-71) 227 81 01
Internet: www.sydbank.ch
E-mail: pbi@sydbank.ch

Syntheis Bank
E-trading/Online Investment Bank—Est. 1991
Address: 15, Rue des Aples; Case Postale 2164
CH-1211 Geneva 1, Switzerland
Tel: (41-22) 317 95 00
Fax: (14-22) 317 95 01
Internet: www.synthesisbank.com
E-mail: SynthesisBank@synthesisbank.com

The National Bank of Kuwait (Suisse) SA
Investment Bank
Address: 21 Quai du Mont Blanc; B.P. 1923
CH-1211/1 Geneva, Switzerland
Tel: (41-22) 906 43 43
Fax: (41-22) 906 43 99

Thurgauer Kantonalbank
Government Bank/Universal Bank—Est. 1871
Address: Bankplatz 1; Postfach 160
CH-8570 Weinfelden, Switzerland
Tel: (41-84) 811 14 44
Fax: (41-84) 811 14 45
Internet: www.tkb.ch
E-mail: info@tkb.ch; weinfelden@tkb.ch

Trafina Privatbank AG
Investment Bank/Private Bank—Est. 1991
Address: Rennweg 50
4020 Basel, Switzerland
Tel: (41-61) 317 17 17
Fax: (41-61) 317 12 80
Internet: www.trafina.ch
E-mail: info@trafina.ch

Triba Partner Bank AG
Commercial Bank—Est. 1901
Address: Kantonsstrasse 60; PO Box 24
CH-6234 Triengen, Switzerland
Tel: (41-41) 935 10 10
Fax: (41-41) 935 10 11
Internet: www.triba.clientis.ch
E-mail: info@triba.clientis.ch

UBS AG
Commercial Bank/International Bank/Investment Bank/Private Bank/
    Universal Bank—Est. 1872
Address: Bahnofstrasse 45
CH-8098 Zurich, Switzerland
Tel: (41-44) 234 11 11
Fax: (41-44) 239 91 11
Internet: www.ubs.com
E-mail: info@ubs.com

UBS Card Center AG
Consumer Credit Bank—Est. 1935
Address: Flughofstrasse 35; Postfach 1160
CH-8152 Glattbrugg, Switzerland
Tel: (41-44) 828 31 11
Fax: (41-44) 810 46 72
Internet: www.ubs.com

UEB (Switzerland)
Commercial Bank/International Bank/Investment Bank/Private Bank/
    Universal Bank—Est. 1872
Address: Aeschenvorstadt 1
CH-4051 Basel, Switzerland
Tel: (41-61) 288 50 50
Fax: (41-61) 288 45 76

UFJ Bank (Schweiz) AG
Universal Bank—Est. 1981
Address: Badenerstrasse 6; Postfach 2270
CH-8026 Zurich, Switzerland
Tel: (41-44) 296 14 00
Fax: (41-44) 296 14 96

UniCredit (Suisse) Bank SA
Commercial Bank—Est. 1998
Address: Via Bossi; B.P. 2809
CH-6901 Lugano, Switzerland
Tel: (41-91) 910 95 10
Fax: (41-91) 910 95 11
E-mail: unicredito@ticino.com

Union Bancaire Privee
Address: 96-98, Rue du Rhone; PO Box 1320
CH-1211 Geneva, Switzerland
Tel: (41-22) 819 21 11
Fax: (41-22) 819 22 00
Internet: www.ubp.ch

United Bank AG (Zurich)
Commercial Bank—Est. 1967
Address: Feldeggstrasse 55; PO Box 1176
CH-8034 Zurich, Switzerland
Tel: (41-43) 499 19 20
Fax: (41-43) 499 19 33
E-mail: info@ubag.ch

United Mizrahi Bank (Switzerland) Ltd
Merchant Bank—Est. 1980
Address: Nuschelerstrasse 31; PO Box 1330
CH-8021 Zurich, Switzerland
Tel: (41-44) 226 86 86
Fax: (41-44) 226 86 87

Urner Kantonalbank Staatsgarantie
Government Bank/Retail Bank/Universal Bank—Est. 1915
Address: Bahnhofstrasse 1; PO Box 1057
CH-6460 Altdorf, Switzerland
Tel: (41-41) 875 60 00
Fax: (41-41) 875 63 13
Internet: www.urkb.ch
E-mail: info@urkb.ch

Valiant Bank
Commercial Bank/Credit Bank/Foreign Exchange/Joint Stock Company/Loan
    and Investment Bank/Retail Bank/Savings Bank/Trade Finance/Wholesale
    Bank—Est. 2001
Address: Bundesplatz 4; PO Box 5333
CH-3001 Berne, Switzerland
Tel: (41-31) 320 91 11
Fax: (41-31) 320 91 12
Internet: www.valiant.ch
E-mail: info@valiant.ch

Valiant Privatbank AG
Commercial Bank/Private Bank—Est. 1997
Address: Bundesplatz 4
CH-3011 Berne, Switzerland
Tel: (41-31) 310 66 66
Fax: (41-31) 310 61 12
Internet: www.valiantprivatbank.ch
E-mail: valiantprivatbank@valiant.ch

Vontobel Holding AG
Investor Relations
Address: Todistrasse 27
CH-8022 Zurich, Switzerland
Tel: (41-58) 283 73 29
Fax: (41-58) 283 77 27
Internet: www.vontobel.com
E-mail: Susanne.borer@vontobel.ch

VP Bank (Schweiz) AG
Private Bank—Est. 1959
Address: Bleicherweg 50
CH-8039 Zurich, Switzerland
Tel: (41-44) 226 24 24
Fax: (41-44) 226 25 24
Internet: www.vpbank.ch
E-mail: info.ch@vpbank.com

Wegelin & Co. Private Bankers
Private Bank—Est. 1741
Address: Bohl 17; PO Box 164
CH-9004 Sankt Gallen, Switzerland
Tel: (41-71) 242 50 00
Fax: (41-71) 242 50 50
Internet: www.wegelin.ch
E-mail: wegelin@wegelin.ch

Wir Bank
Limited Purpose—Est. 1934
Address: Auberg 1
4002 Basel, Switzerland
Tel: (41-61) 277 91 11
Fax: (41-61) 277 92 39
Internet: www.wirbank.ch
E-mail: kontakt@wir.ch

ZLB Zurcher Landbank
Savings Bank—Est. 1851
Address: Am Lidenplatz
CH-8353 Elgg, Switzerland
Tel: (41-52) 368 58 58
Fax: (41-52) 368 58 59
Internet: www.zuercherlandbank.ch
E-mail: info@zlb.rba.ch

Zuger Kantonalbank
Government Bank—Est. 1892
Address: Baarerstrasse 37; PO Box 162
CH-6301 Zug, Switzerland
Tel: (41-41) 709 11 11
Fax: (41-41) 709 15 55
Internet: www.zugerkb.ch
E-mail: service@zugerkb.ch

Appendix B

Other Swiss Service Companies

Swiss Insurance Companies

AIG Life Insurance Company (Switzerland) Ltd. (AIG Life)
6932 Breganzona, Switzerland

Allianz Lebensversicherung (Schweiz) AG (Allianz Leben)
Lebensversicherungs-Gesellschaft
8022 Zurich, Switzerland

AXA Compagnie d'Assurances sur la Vie (AXA Vie)
1000 Lausanne, Switzerland

Basler Lebens-Versicherungs-Gesellschaft (Basler Leben)
4002 Basel, Switzerland

Berner Lebensversicherungs-Gesellschaft (Berner Leben)
8022 Zurich, Switzerland

Convia Lebensversicherungs-Gesellschaft (Convia)
6002 Luzern, Switzerland

Coop Leben AG (Coop Leben)
4103 Bottmingen BL, Switzerland

Elvia Leben (Elvia Leben)
8022 Zurich, Switzerland

Financial Assurance Company Limited (Financial Assurance Vie)
8050 Zurich, Switzerland

Forces Vives (Forces Vives)
1001 Lausanne, Switzerland

Generali Personenversicherungen (Generali Personenversicherungen)
8134 Adliswil 1, Switzerland

La Genevoise Compagnie d'Assurances sur la Vie (Genevoise Vie)
1211 Geneve 25, Switzerland

Groupe Mutuel Vie GMV SA (Groupe Mutuel Vie)
1920 Martigny, Switzerland

Imperio SA (Imperio)
1005 Lausanne, Switzerland

Schweizerische National Lebensversicherungs-Gesellschaft (National Leben)
4003 Basel, Switzerland

Patria Schweizerische Lebensversicherungs-Gesellschaft (Patria)
4002 Basel, Switzerland

Pax, Schweizerische Lebensversicherungs-Gesellschaft (Pax)
4002 Basel, Switzerland

Phenix Compagnie d'Assurances sur la Vie (Phenix Vie)
1001 Lausanne, Switzerland

Providentia Societe Suisse d'Assurances sur la Vie Humaine (Providentia)
1260 Nyon, Switzerland

Schweizerische Lebensversicherungs-und Rentenanstalt (Rentenanstalt)
8022 Zurich, Switzerland

SEV-Versicherungen (SEV Versicherungen)
4011 Basel, Switzerland

Skandia Leben AG (Skandia Leben)
8034 Zurich, Switzerland

La Suisse, Societe d'Assurances sur la Vie (Suisse Vie)
1001 Lausanne, Switzerland

UBS Life AG (UBS Life)
8098 Zurich, Switzerland

Vauddoise Vie, Compagnie d'Assurances sur la Vie (Vaudoise Vie)
1001 Lausanne, Switzerland

Versichenrung der Schweizer Arzte (Arzteversichenrung)
3000 Bern 9, Switzerland

Winterthur Leben (Winterthur Leben)
8401 Winterthur, Switzerland

Zenith Vie, Compagnie d'Assurances sur la Vie
1009 Pully, Switzerland

Zurich Lebensversicherungs-Gesellschaft (Zurich Leben)
8036 Zurich, Switzerland

Swiss Investment Counselors/Insurance Brokers

Contact these Swiss firms for information on Swiss and Liechtenstein
financial-related products and services, including Swiss annuities, Swiss
portfolio bonds, and Swiss life insurance.

Mr. Marco Gantenbein,
Managing Director
Swiss Insurance Partners AG
Neutadtgasse 12
8024 Zurich, Switzerland
Tel: (41-44) 266 22 66
Fax: (41-44) 266 22 67
E-mail: mg@sip.ch
www.sip.ch

Mr. Jurg M. Lattmann, Managing Director
JML Jurg M. Lattmann AG
Baaerstrasse 53
6304 Zug, Switzerland
Tel: (41-1) 726 55 55/00
Fax: (41-1) 726 55 90
E-mail: info@jml.ch
www.jml.ch

Mr. Darrell Aviss, Managing Director
SwissGuard International GmbH
Bahnhofstrasse 52
CH-8001 Zurich, Switzerland
Tel: (41-1) 214 62 47
Fax: (41-1) 214 65 19
E-mail: info@swiss-annuity.com
www.swiss-annuity.com
Toll-free from the USA 1-800-796-7496

Mr. Marc Sola, Managing Director
NMG International Financial Services Ltd.
Goethestrasse 22
8001 Zurich, Switzerland
Tel: (41-1) 266 21 41
Fax: (41-1) 266 21 49
E-mail: marcsola@nmg-ifs.com

Swiss Brokerage Firms

Synthesis Bank
15, Rue des Alpes
Case Postale 2164
CH-124 Geneva, Switzerland
Tel: (41-22) 317 95 77
Fax: (41-22) 317 95 40
www.synthesisbank.com
A Swiss bank that specializes in online trading.

ACM-Advanced Currency Markets SA
50, Rue du Rhone
1204 Geneva, Switzerland
Tel: (41-22) 319 22 09
Fax: (41-22) 319 22 01
E-mail: backoffice@ac-markets.com
www.ac-markets.com
A Swiss brokerage firm specializing in currency trading.

Swiss Investment Services

Mr. Adrian Hartmann / Mr. Robert Vrijhof
Weber, Hartmann, Vrijhof & Partners Ltd.
Zurichastrasse 110B
CH-8134 Adilswil, Switzerland
Tel: (41-1) 709 11 15
Fax: (41-1) 709 11 13
Web site: www.whvp.ch

Henley and Partners Group of Companies

Henley & Partners AG
Kirchgasse 22
8001 Zurich
Switzerland
Tel: (41-44) 266 22 22
Fax: (41-44) 266 22 23
Web site: www.henleyglobal.com/switzerland
Contact Person: Christian H. Kälin
E-mail: christian.kalin@henleyglobal.com
Private client and business advisors. Internationally recognized for its unique
    expertise in private residence solutions, the firm has also acquired a reputation
    in multijurisdictional real-estate advisory, tax planning, and fiduciary services.

H & P Trust Company (Switzerland) AG
Poststrasse 6
6300 Zug
Switzerland
Tel: (41-41) 729 63 63
Fax: (41-41) 729 63 64
Web site: www.henleyglobal.com/switzerland
Contact: Mr. Cees Jan Quirijns
E-mail: ceesjan.quirijns@henleyglobal.com

Trust and corporate services, including Swiss companies and structures involving Switzerland, as well as international corporate and trust structures.

H & P Structured Solutions GmbH
Poststrasse 6
6300 Zug
Switzerland
Tel: (41-41) 729 63 63
Fax: (41-41) 729 63 64
Web site: www.henleyglobal.com/switzerland
Contact: Mr. Hans Fraats
E-mail: hans.fraats@henleyglobal.com
Structured finance transactions, including the tax efficient structuring of cash-rich companies, mergers and acquisitions, etc.

Henley & Partners Ltd.
Kirchstrasse 79
9490 Vaduz
Liechtenstein
Tel: 423 235 5535
Fax: 423 235 5536
Web site: www.henleyglobal.com/liechtenstein
Contact: Mr. Walter Vogt
E-mail: walter.vogt@henleyglobal.com
Trust and corporate services including Liechtenstein foundations, trusts and companies.

Henley Estates Ltd.
Schifflände 26
8024 Zurich
Switzerland
Tel: (41-44) 266 22 33
Fax: (41-44) 266 22 34
Web site: www.henleyestates.com
Contact: Ms. Flavia Wetzel
E-mail: flavia.wetzel@henleyestates.com
Specialist advisers and brokers for exclusive residential real estate in Switzerland.

Swiss Insurance Partners AG
Neustadtgasse 12
8024 Zurich
Switzerland
Tel: (41-44) 266 22 66

Fax: (41-44) 266 22 67
Web site: www.sip.ch
Contact person: Mr. Marco Gantenbein TEP
E-mail: marco.gantenbein@sip.ch
A leading independent insurance consultancy with strong expertise in advising
international clients on Swiss and Liechtenstein annuities and life insurance,
including complex private-banking insurance wrapper solutions.

Swiss Physical Storage Facilities
(Non–Bank Related)

Safes Fidelity SA
6, place Chevelu
CH-1211 Geneva 1, Switzerland
Tel: 41 22 731 78 90

Via Mat Management AG
Obstgartenstrasse 27, PO Box 635
CH-8302 Kloten, Switzerland
Tel: (41-44) 804 92 92
Fax: (41-44) 804 92 93

Swiss and Other Organizations

Insurance Information Institute—Annuities Section
www.iii.org/individuals/annuities

International Financial and Legal Network (IFLN)
www.ifln.com

International Tax Planning Association
www.itpa.org

Society of Trust and Estate Practitioners (STEP)
www.step.org

Swiss Federation of Private Insurance
www.bpv.admin.ch/de

Swiss Insurance Association
www.svv.ch

Swiss National Bank
Borsenstrasse 15
PO Box 2800
8022 Zurich, Switzerland
Tel: (41-44) 631 31 11
Fax: (41-44) 631 39 11
www.snb.ch

Variable Annuities Knowledge Centre
www.variableannuityfacts.com

Appendix C

Resources

Tax Information

Tax-News
www.tax-news.com
News on international tax issues, offshore jurisdictions, more.

Expatriating/Overseas Retirement/Offshore Investing

AXA Retirement Scope
Global comparative information on attitudes towards retirement
www.retirement-scope.axa.com

Offshore Evaluation Service (OES)
www.barberfinancialadvisors.com
www.offshoreevaluationservice.com
Telephone (604) 608-6177
Fax (604) 608-2984
E-mail: OES@BarberFinancialAdvisors.com

Personalized evaluations to help you safely and successfully start your journey
offshore. Available exclusively through Barber Financial Advisors, Vancouver, B.C.,
Canada, and the Offshore Evaluation Service Review Board headed by the author.

International Living
www.internationalliving.com
Excellent source for information on expatriating, living abroad, and foreign real
estate investment. Subscribe to their free daily e-mail postcards. Membership is
recommended and reasonable.

The Sovereign Society
www.sovereignsociety.com
Stay on top of the fast-paced offshore world and preserve your wealth. Free daily
e-mail newsletter, "The Sovereign Society Offshore—A Letter." Membership is
recommended and reasonable.

World Bank Resources

Banks Web Sites Worldwide
www.qualisteam.com

Financial Standing of Banks Worldwide
www.fitchratings.com

Thomas Bank Directory, World Bank Directory
Accuity Solutions, 4709 W. Gold Road, Suite 600
Skokie, IL 60076-1253 USA
Telephone (847) 676-9600
Fax (847) 933-8101
E-mail: custserv@AccuitySolutions.com
www.accuitysolutions.com

Important Swiss Contacts

Swissnetwork Media AG
Schifflande 26, Suite 201
8024 Geneva, Switzerland
Telephone 41 44 266 60 30
Fax 41 44 266 60 31
www.swissnetwork.com
Information on Switzerland and the financial industry.

Swiss Annuities
Published by Swissnetwork Media AG
www.swissannuities.com
A leading Web site about Swiss annuities and life insurance, featuring general,
 easy-to-read information as well as specific articles, views, news, and opinions
 from leading professionals and companies active in this area.

Barber Financial Advisors

The author is president of Barber Financial Advisors (BFA), located at 355 Burrard Street, Suite 1000, Vancouver, B.C. V6C 2G8 Canada. Telephone (604) 608-6177. Fax (604) 608-2984. E-mail: info@Barber-FinancialAdvisors.com or BarberFinancial@hotmail.com. Web site: www .barberfinancialadvisors.com and www.barberfinancialadvisors.bz. The company is a subsidiary of Barber Financial Advisors Ltd., a Belize international business corporation.

BFA provides a host of efficient and economical offshore financial services, including offshore corporations, management and administrative services, asset protection, offshore bank accounts, prepaid travel money cards, offshore credit cards, offshore brokerage accounts, and the Offshore Evaluation Service (OES).

Offshore Evaluation Service

Barber Financial Advisors offers a popular and unique service, the Offshore Evaluation Service (OES), which takes the mystery out of going offshore and provides clients with customized evaluations based on their current situation. Clients complete a six-page OES questionnaire, which the company evaluates and then presents clients with reliable offshore information addressing their particular areas of interest and concern and making recommendations regarding offshore financial services, reputable professionals, and offshore financial institutions.

Further suggestions are offered in areas that may be of interest to clients or that are recommended for more thorough investigation. OES clients are given personal referrals to the experts they may require in their specialized fields. This service can save clients thousands of dollars and much time, and guide them quickly to the offshore solutions that would serve them best.

By using the services of OES, clients can avoid inaccurate and unreliable information and services often touted offshore.

The OES covers:

- Banks
- Banking services
- Investments
- Investment services
- Financial, tax, and estate planning
- Asset protection strategies
- Offshore citizenship programs
- Offshore business and e-commerce
- Tax havens
- Foreign real estate investment
- Expatriating
- Tax problems
- Professionals
- Economical influences
- And more

Many foreign financial institutions today require prospective customers to be referred by an advisor or professional. A portion of modest cost for the personalized evaluation is credited toward future business with Barber Financial Advisors should the client require other offshore services and/or structures through Barber Financial Advisors.

The Offshore Evaluation Service is conducted by The Offshore Evaluation Review Board and headed by the president of Barber Financial Advisors, author Hoyt Barber. For further information about this economical but valuable service, please call (604) 608-6177or e-mail OES@BarberFinancialAdvisors.com. Feel free to visit our Web site at www.barberfinancialadvisors.com. New Web sites are being developed at www.offshoreevaluationservice.com and www.offshoreevaluationservice.bz.

Appendix D

Suggested Reading

Books on Switzerland and Offshore

All titles were released in 2006/2007 by John Wiley & Sons, Inc., Hoboken, NJ. Visit www.wileyfinance.com or www.wiley.com.

Swiss Annuities and Life Insurance: Secure Returns, Asset Protection, Safety & Privacy by Marco Gantenbein and Mario A. Mata. This is an excellent source of information on Swiss annuities, portfolio bonds, and life insurance investments. A perfect companion to my book, *Secrets of Swiss Banking*.

Switzerland Business & Investment Handbook by Christian H. Kalin. The "bible" on the business of Switzerland, with contributions by leading Swiss authorities, provides a comprehensive review of Switzerland today as a leading international financial center.

Tax Havens Today: The Benefits and Pitfalls of Banking and Investing Offshore by Hoyt Barber. Tax havens, along with the all-important offshore topics are thoroughly covered in my 2007 book, including the areas of banking, investing, asset protection, and estate planning. Special emphasis is placed on individual sovereignty and personal freedom.

Books on Investment

Be Smart, Act Fast, Get Rich: Your Game Plan for Getting It Right in the Stock Market by Charles Payne

Crash-Proof: How to Profit from the Coming Economic Collapse by Peter D. Schiff and John Downes

Demon of Our Own Design: Markets, Hedge Funds, and the Risk of Financial Innovation by Richard Bookstaber

The Dhandho Investor: The Low Risk Value Method to High Returns by Mohnish Pabrai

Empire of Debt by Bill Bonner and Addison Wiggin

Equities: An Introduction to the Core Concepts by Mark Mobius

Financial Day of Reckoning: Surviving the Sift Depression of the 21st Century by Bill Bonner and Addison Wiggin

Free Cash Flow and Shareholder Yield: New Priorities for the Global Investor by William W. Priest and Lindsay H. McClelland

Future Energy: How the New Oil Industry Will Change People, Politics and Portfolios by Bill Paul

Get Rich with Options: Four Winning Strategies from the Exchange Floor by Lee Lowell

Getting Started in Exchange Traded Funds (ETFs) by Todd Lofton

Getting Started in Forex Trading Strategies by Michael Archer

Gold Trading Boot Camp: How to Master the Basics and Become a Successful Commodities Investor by Gregory T. Weldon

Income Investing Today: Safety and High Income through Diversification by R. Lehmann

An Introduction to Mutual Funds Worldwide by Ray Russell

Investment U's Profit from China by Investment U

Investment U's Profit from Uranium by Investment U

A Maniac Commodity Trader's Guide to Making a Fortune in the Market: A Not-So Crazy Roadmap to Riches by Kevin Kerr and Agora

Morningstar Stocks 500:2007/Morningstar ETF 150:2007/Morningstar Funds 500: 2007 by Morningstar, Inc.

The Only Three Questions That Count: Investing by Knowing What Others Don't by Kenneth L. Fisher

The Savage Number: How Much Money Do You Need to Retire? by Terry Savage

The 25% Cash Machine: Double Digit Income Investing by Bryan Perry

Unwarranted Intrusion: The Case against Government Intervention in the Marketplace by Martin Fridson

Books on Economics, Investments, and Others of Interest

The Coming Collapse of the Dollar and How to Profit From It; Make a Fortune by Investing in Gold and Other Hard Assets by James Turk and John Rubino. New York: Doubleday, 2004. www.dollarcollapse.com.

The Coming Generational Storm by Lawrence Kotlikoff and Scott Burns. Boston: First MIT Press, Massachusetts Institute of Technology, 2005.

Financial Armageddon: Protecting Your Future from Four Impending Catastrophes by Michael J. Panzer. New York: Kaplan Publishing, 2007. www.financialarmageddon.com.

Gold: The Once and Future Money by Nathan Lewis

International Real Estate Handbook by Christian H. Kalin. Hoboken, NJ: John Wiley & Sons, Inc.

Your House Is Under Arrest by Brenda Grantland, president of Forfeiture Endangers American Rights (FEAR). Visit www.fear.org.

About the Author

Hoyt Barber has a diverse international business background and has been a recognized authority on tax havens, offshore banking and investing, and asset protection for over 20 years. Barber was one of the early pioneers in the Nevada corporate services field, having started his own company to compete in 1978 with the Delaware self-incorporation explosion.

Barber has authored 10 books, both nonfiction and fiction, including his most recent titles, *Tax Havens Today: The Benefits and Pitfalls of Banking and Investing Offshore,* released in December 2006 by John Wiley & Sons., Inc., and an international thriller, *From Hell to Havana,* released in the spring of 2007 by Durban House Publishing, Inc.

Currently, Barber is writing two more nonfiction books, one on individual sovereignty and personal and financial freedom, and the other on offshore investments and strategies. Also, his second novel has been completed and is expected to be released in the near future.

Barber is president of Barber Financial Advisors in Vancouver, British Columbia, Canada, a subsidiary of his Belize international holding company. The company provides offshore financial services to investors and expatriates from North America and many other countries who seek refuge from excessive bureaucracy. For more information on his company, visit its Web site at www.barberfinancialadvisors.com.

Visit Hoyt Barber's author Web site to learn more about him and his books at www.hoytbarber.com.

Index

267